SPILLING THE BEANS

SPILLING THE BEANS

Clarissa Dickson Wright

HODDER &
STOUGHTON

Copyright © 2007 by Clarissa Dickson Wright

First published in Great Britain in 2007 by Hodder & Stoughton
A division of Hodder Headline

A Hodder & Stoughton Book

1

A CIP catalogue record for this title is available from the British Library

ISBN 978 0 340 93388 6

Typeset in Bembo by Hewer Text UK Ltd, Edinburgh
Printed and bound by Clays Ltd, St Ives plc

Hodder Headline's policy is to use papers that are natural, renewable
and recyclable products and made from wood grown in sustainable
forests. The logging and manufacturing processes are expected to
conform to the environmental regulations of the country of origin.

Hodder & Stoughton Ltd
A division of Hodder Headline
338 Euston Road
London NW1 3BH

Dedication

To survivors everywhere, and to their friends who keep them sane.

And with thanks to Rowena Webb, who listens to the radio; my friend and agent Heather Holden-Brown and her assistant Elly James, for making me laugh on the darkest days; John Humphrys, who caused this book; Morag Lyall, my copy editor, for her patience; Helen Coyle for her perseverance; Marianne More-Gordon for the title and all my friends who kept me sane while writing it.

Picture Acknowledgements

Most of the photographs are from the author's collection.

Additional sources: Courtesy of Asprey London, 10 bottom. © BBC Photo Library, 11 bottom, 14 bottom. © Christine Coleman, 6 bottom. © The Daily Telegraph, 15 top. © Express Syndication, 7 top. © PA Photos, 11 top, 15 bottom. Derick Pickering, 16. © Carin Simon, 9 bottom, 10 top, 12 top, 13, 14 top, 15 centre.

Every reasonable effort has been made to contact the copyright holders, but if there are any errors or omissions, Hodder & Stoughton will be pleased to insert the appropriate acknowledgement in any subsequent printing of this publication.

Contents

1

You can't choose your family

I was conceived in a bath in Norfolk in September 1946. How can I know? Well, my mother told me. As she put it they were all rather exhausted after the war and there weren't that many opportune occasions. I was born in the London Clinic on 24 June 1947 and my first journey in the world was in a London taxi. My mother had become bored waiting for my father to collect us, so she wrapped me in a blanket, went outside, hailed a taxi and took me home, leaving the luggage for my father to pick up later. The only really good advice my mother ever gave me was 'If in doubt take a taxi,' and I have followed it devotedly ever since.

I am very much the youngest of four: my eldest sister Heather is nineteen years older than me, my second sister June seventeen years older and my brother Anthony was thirteen years older so I had all the disadvantages of an only child and none of the advantages. My father was fifty when I was born and my mother thirty-nine so really I was a nasty shock to everyone, although as my mother kindly put it, 'I truly did need someone else to hand things round at cocktail parties, darling'!

My father Arthur Dickson Wright was a very famous and brilliant surgeon, a rebel in an establishment world who turned down repeated offers of a knighthood because, as he put it, he had worked very hard to become Mr and any industrialist could buy an honour. The relevance to those of you who haven't grasped it is that in the medical world only surgeons are strictly referred to in etiquette as Mr.

My mother was Australian and an heiress, which I rather expect is why my father married her, and a woman of extraordinary charm and elegance, but more of them later.

All of us are an accumulation of the traits, genetic tendencies, geographicals and peculiarities of our forebears. These are the ingredients that we and the adventures and misfortunes of our lives process into the finished dish that becomes ourselves. Looking at the contents of my personal larder I find a curious selection. Originally my father's family came from Richmond in Yorkshire, a county in which I have always felt very much at home. I knew this because in the hall at home hung a portrait of a powerful-looking man in a ruff, the label reading Sir Edmund Wright, 1646. My sister June and I tracked him down to a large house in Middlesex called Swakeleys, now owned by the Post Office, and discovered that he had been Lord Mayor. We also discovered what was probably the start of the alcoholic gene on this side of the family. Lady Wright's little black page-boy complained once too often of the cold and she, while flown with wine, put him in the bread oven to warm him up; sadly the oven had not cooled down sufficiently and the page-boy died. As this was before the abolition of slavery it was not of course any sort of crime. Sir Edmund was a member of the Muscovy Company and the Richmond Merchant Adventurers. I can just see him sitting in his counting house swearing, 'Eee, those boogers in London aren't looking after my money proper. I'd best go down south and sort them out.' He was a dedicated Cromwellian, married his daughter to the Regicide Sir James Harrington and sent his son with Cromwell. The son, Captain

James Wright, was thrown out of Cromwell's New Model Army for drunkenness but was taken back for the Irish Campaign and decided to stay over there. James built a house on the outskirts of Drogheda, a town still bleeding from the terrible massacre when Cromwell, having offered the citizens of the town their lives in exchange for surrender, then chopped off their hands and feet and left them to die. With consummate tact he named the house Golgotha (the place of the skull). Some years ago when speaking at the Yorkshire Guild of Butchers' Shrove Tuesday Feast I met the Warden of the Richmond Warden Adventurers Company and mentioned Sir Edmund. He knew all about him and added, 'Those are the Wrights that financed Guy Fawkes, the family of Jack and James Wright who died with him.' I remembered this some years later as I stood in Parliament Square in the rain cooking breakfast for 600 hunting women on a charcoal barbecue.

My father's parents, along with other Irish ascendancy gentry, became caught up in the Plymouth Brethren movement and moved to Scotland because, as they declared, they wouldn't walk on the same side of the road as a Catholic nun or priest. As they lived in Dublin then this must have entailed walking in the tramlines most of the time. The Brethren were a nonconformist sect which grew up in the nineteenth century and spread to Ireland around the 1870s. They are virulently opposed to all the bells and smells of the Catholic and High Anglican Churches, and do not go out or engage in any activity on the Sabbath other than reading the Bible. They practise adult baptism and believe that only Brethren hold an entrance ticket to heaven, although not all of them will get there as the places are limited. My grandparents moved to Helensburgh and my grandfather, who was a doctor (my family has a long tradition of younger sons going into medicine), ran a practice there and another in Govan which he hoped would enable him to convert the slum dwellers to the Brethren, a task in which I believe he failed dismally. I suspect my grandfather, who I never knew, had a well-hidden but deeply frivolous streak as he often ran off to sea to act as a locum ship's doctor, a trait that deeply irritated my grandmother. She would retaliate by burning his book collection or even the early shares in Shell that she discovered. Nevertheless they still found time to have nine children: all the boys went into some form of medicine and all the girls married doctors except for my Aunty Holly who, shock horror, ran off with a Belgian publican and produced a son who was the most brilliant medic of that generation of our family.

My grandmother, known generally as 'Muddy' was an in-domitable woman who once sacked a maid without a reference for picking a pear off a tree in her garden. She ruled her children with a rod of iron, sending my father to Latimer School despite the fact that he had won scholarships to Eton and Westminster because she thought the education the best in the country. My Uncle Douglas, a brilliant athlete, won the Yule Tennis Cup (the schools cup played at Wimbledon) with a battered old racquet. My grandmother was seated in the stands next to the father of his opponent who declared, 'If I had a son who played tennis like that I would see he had the finest racquet money could buy,' to which my grandmother replied, 'If you had a son who played like that you wouldn't have to.' The children were sent to do their homework in an unheated attic seated on really uncomfortable forms and woe betide any of them who didn't reach her standards of perfection.

My grandfather damaged his lungs with dust during the First World War when he went into a house hit by a bomb from a Zeppelin to treat trapped victims (a feat for which he was decorated). My grandmother sent him to Cromer to recuperate as that was such a bracing place; in February it was found to be a little too bracing and he died of pneumonia. Subsequently my grandmother moved to London to be near her children. Freed from such tethers of respectability she took to a tent in her own drawing room. This was not a defence against a leaking Irish roof but rather a nostalgia for safaris she had never taken. It was the type of tent one sees on the Camp coffee bottle label. The gardener was instructed to hammer the spikes into the parquet floor. In there she would sleep soundly on her camp bed or take her exquisite meals (no rough camping fare for her) at a collapsible table seated on her canvas chair, the food served in billycans or mess tins. The Anglo-Irish are noted for their eccentricities and I believe we are related to the lady who lived in a railway carriage in her drawing room in Ireland so everything's relative, but what made this all the more extraordinary is that my grandmother lived in a large house by the bridge in Little Venice (subsequently bought by Joan Collins). When Muddy went to stay with her children the grandchildren were mystified because she would arrive with only a small shoe bag; when she came down for tea they would rush upstairs and the cupboard in her room would be full of clothes. The truth was she used to wear everything one on top of the other to save luggage. As I find myself in middle age loving camping (something I never did as a child) and hating luggage with a passion I begin to worry for the future and so, I suspect, do my friends.

Muddy played the piano badly and sang worse, though she didn't recognise this fact and was delighted to find, on moving to Little Venice, that when she played with the French windows open there would be a queue of people whose heads she could just see over the garden wall; in her mind they were standing there listening to the music. It was a brave family member who told her there was a bus stop over the wall! My father, in a foreword to a celebrity cookery book compiled for the Imperial Cancer Research Fund, describes a scene where all the children are clustering round the kitchen table as my grandmother mashes baked potatoes with butter and milk then returns the mixture to the skins and breaks an egg into each to cook in the heat. It is a touching picture but I suspect untrue and more a product of wishful thinking as I don't believe my grandmother cooked. My grandparents numbered among their friends Sir Arthur Conan Doyle and apparently my grandfather used to prescribe his cocaine for him. Conan Doyle was a spiritualist and came to an agreement with my grandmother that whoever went first would come back and tell the other all about it, but my grand-mother complained years after his death that she was still waiting.

My father survived the whole of the First World War first as a gunner and then, tired of the mud, he went into the Royal Flying Corps as a navigator and subsequently as a pilot. I always wondered why he had so few male friends of his own generation but most of them had died. He went to war with the poems of Robert Burns in his pocket and apparently could lose himself in a book under the most frightful barrage conditions. The letters he sent home were largely involved with food, praise for a fruit cake or a request for some more tea from Fortnum's. It was a generation that didn't talk about the horrors it had seen and my father was no exception. The only thing he ever told me about the war was that when flying Sopwith aeroplanes, which were lubricated with castor oil, it wasn't just bombs you wanted to drop on the Germans because the laxative effects from the oil blowing back in your face were quite forceful. As souvenirs he kept the remains of a propeller from a plane he had pranged which was about the thickness of my arm and a gauntlet that had had the thumb shot away; happily my father had withdrawn his thumb in an effort to warm it. When I was young I spent a lot of time reading books like *All Quiet on the Western Front*, and *Her Privates We* or *Memoirs of a Fox-hunting Man* to try to understand how people including my father could have lived in such dreadful conditions but to no avail and when I asked him how they coped he would reply that they just did.

He was, however, fascinated by all things medical as he had decided to follow the family tradition and study medicine and would talk about the use of maggots by Country Regiments to avert gangrene. Apparently if you place maggots on a wound that is turning bad they will eat away the diseased flesh and drop off when they have cleared it and so of course gangrene is averted. He was also present and assisted at the famous case when a surgeon removed an appendix that was about to rupture; this happened under fire in the front line amid all the mud, rats and corpses, their only instruments a pocket knife and a soup spoon, but the operation was a success and the man lived. They do say that most surgical techniques come from wartime conditions and I suspect these experiences were what made my father always more open-minded on solutions than his contemporaries.

When he returned home to the house in Little Venice the rod of iron hadn't diminished. For instance if my father came downstairs wearing morning dress to go racing he would have to lie to Muddy that he was going to a funeral or she would have forbidden him to go. After the war my father went to St Mary's Paddington to study medicine. Although all admitted he was brilliant, when he qualified he failed to obtain a registrarship at St Mary's, which went to the Rhodes scholar Arthur Porritt. Porritt was an athlete and a great friend of the hurdler the Marquis of

Burghley, whose influence was generally acknowledged as the reason for the appointment. A rivalry was created which was to rankle with my father all his life. My father sought advice from his uncle Sir Almroth Wright, who was to become with his junior Alexander Fleming the Wright in the Wright-Fleming Institute of Virology at St Mary's. Uncle Almroth, later known as the Plato of Praed Street, was really rather a dreadful man. He was an arch anti-feminist and wrote articles in *The Times* abjuring equal rights for women on the basis that they had inferior brains to men; he was unsurprisingly frequently picketed by suffragettes. He did however discover the cures for both yellow and blackwater fevers, thus allowing large tracts of the world to become habitable and releasing New Orleans from centuries of misery. He was regarded as a great wit. I think his best quote was: 'A lady is a woman who does not object to being referred to as a woman.' Think about it. Almroth had a phenomenal memory and was able to recite the whole of *Paradise Lost* and *Paradise Regained*, and told the story of how during the Second World War he had gone into a bomb shelter in the East End of London and in order to regale and calm the nervous crowd he had recited Milton to them with, as always, his eyes tight shut. So carried away was he by his recitation, he told my siblings, that he must have failed to hear the all-clear for when he opened his eyes the shelter was empty. We all felt the cockney crowd must have preferred the German bombs to Milton. In any event, Almroth told my father to go east and study tropical diseases and so my father took a registrar-ship at the Tan-tok-sing Hospital in Singapore, without which decision I should not be here. So you will observe on my father's side some very odd ingredients and nothing but dysfunctionalism for 400 years.

So, what of my mother's side? I know much less about their

history. My mother's grandfather on her mother's side, Henry Richard Gordon, was an Aberdonian and an engineer. He had married a woman from Schleswig-Holstein, at that time still part of Denmark, when he was working on the Kiel Canal and had three children, Mildred (Millie), Elsie (my grandmother) and a boy, also Henry Richard. He set out for Australia when my grandmother was thirteen, taking the family with him, to work on some project in Victoria. My great-grandmother bolted with a sutler named Sutton who I believe she met on the boat out and is buried up country in Malaya and so Henry was left with three children under fifteen to raise in a strange land. They were a close-knit family and coped well with the difficulties of life.

My mother's father came of Cornish stock, tin miners and sea-captains, who ended up in Australia following tin and copper scams. My grandfather Tom Bath was, I believe, a superb horseman who recreated the Australian bushwhacker Ned Kelly's famous leap when, while escaping from pursuing law officers in the Blue Mountains, he had leapt a huge gorge and had to turn his horse in mid-air to land safely. Tom went to the Boer War with the Queensland Mounted Light Infantry. I always thought the family had got the name wrong until having a drink in the Artists Rifles' Mess in Chelsea Barracks one day I saw their badge on the wall. My grandfather was a mining engineer who spoke ten dialects of Chinese learned for the most part through what he referred to as a sleeping dictionary, in other words a Chinese mistress. He became an explorer for the tin mining companies and would sit down to dinner in the jungle in white tie and tails on his own. He was a ferocious drinker and a gambler; on one occasion he bet his employees' wages on his horse and when it was pipped at the post challenged the rival owner to a repeat race for double or quits which fortunately he won.

How my grandmother Elsie Gordon met Tom I don't know but I expect it was through engineering circles. He was a handsome man and as I have said a fine horseman as was my grandmother. Most of the pictures one sees of Elsie are taken of her in riding dress, usually surrounded by dogs and often minus the skirt of her side-saddle habit. She used to pig-stick side-saddle, a frightening thought as I assume you would have to lean over and spear your pig on the far side where there was of course no stirrup. Elsie was only eighteen when she married Tom and he was thirty-two. They went up country in Malaya and she would tell hair-raising stories of jungle bungalows with tigers roaring outside. One such was when my grandfather, who was six foot four, was thrown from his horse when it was spooked by a tiger and knocked unconscious. My grandmother had to dismount and haul him over his saddle, remount and lead him away with the tiger roaring in the undergrowth.

My grandfather bred ducks and once when he returned early from up country my grandmother instructed the cook to kill one and serve it up for dinner. Tom, replete and rather drunk, went out on the veranda after dinner and spotted that one of his ducks was missing. In a fury he grabbed his gun and threatened to shoot Elsie. She, with great presence of mind, remarked that he was so drunk he couldn't even hit a duck let alone her. In a rage, Tom killed all the ducks and then collapsed in fits of laughter, and my grandmother survived. Tom died at thirty-eight when alcohol did for his one kidney; he had lost the other playing Aussie rules football for Queensland as a young man. Knowing he was dying and not wanting to leave Elsie behind, he chased her down the hospital corridor with a revolver but fortunately the sarong he was wearing slipped and he fell over and so my grandmother escaped. He died leaving her a widow of only twenty-four with two young children, my uncle Vivien Cullinan (so called because Tom had struck up a friendship with one of the South African diamond family during the Boer War) and Molly, my mother, who was christened Aileen but whose only legacy from her father was that he called her his little Molly, a name she carried to her grave.

So there was my grandmother in Singapore with two children aged six and two, with very little money and a bit of ore-bearing land up country. She was the only one of my grandparents I knew and she was a formidable and resourceful woman until her death in her early eighties. She was a great believer that God would provide so she gave the children a great Christmas and on Boxing Day went to a party she had been invited to. A woman called May Campbell had brought a newcomer to the party, a short dark Sephardic Jew with the splendid name of Ezeckiel Manasseh and when he saw my grandmother he fell head over heels in love. He called on Elsie and offered to handle her business affairs, which really only amounted to the ore-bearing land up country. Eze was spectacularly rich and the scion of an old, respected and wealthy Jewish family from Calcutta. It was said of them that they had a better lawn than Government House. Eze had been sent out east to handle that side of the family affairs. After several visits to my grandmother Eze declared his love and proposed. My grandmother told him she couldn't possibly marry him because he was a Jew and she was a Catholic but rather bizarrely for 1911 agreed to live with him. This was, I suspect, bad news for May Campbell but she compromised by marrying my great-uncle Henry!

Uncle Eze built a house for him and Elsie called Eden Hall, which today is the Residency for the British High Commission in Singapore. It had an upper and a lower riding ring, spacious stables where each horse had its own sice, as grooms were called, and about sixty servants. He also built the synagogue. So rich and influential was he that the couple were invited everywhere even in the ultra-Victorian atmosphere of pre-war Singapore. Perhaps it was not so for the children. Nannies are a conventional breed and my mother vaguely remembered children being hustled away from her when she was playing in the Botanical Gardens. In any event my grandmother decided to send Vivien aged eight and my mother aged four and a half to boarding school in Australia. Elsie eventually married Eze and they lived very happily together until 1942 when she got out on the last boat before the Japanese invasion and he died in Changi prisoner-of-war camp, leaving his entire estate to Elsie. Eze spent the last months buying up properties from departing residents and realising he had to hide the deeds he put them in a meat safe at his offices, placed a board with a leg of lamb on top and left the door open. When the Japanese arrived they broke into the safes but turned away from the maggot-infested joint and the deeds were still there in 1945. I have always loved that story.

My mother's arrival at the Loreto Convent Ballarat in South Australia was a horrifying experience and one that changed her life for ever. My grandmother left the small child, promising to return later. Molly stood by the window all afternoon waiting for her mother, of whom there was no sign; my grandmother obviously couldn't face the scene that was bound to ensue. It began to grow dark but none of the nuns could lure her away for tea. Finally an old nun called Mother Aethelraeda came and sat in the room saying nothing; like all children my mother became curious and when she looked at the nun she was asked how old she was. Tearfully she replied, 'Four and a half.' The nun asked her if she knew who Jesus was and she nodded. 'Do you know how old Jesus is?' said the nun. My mother replied, 'Awfully old.'

'No,' said the nun. 'He's four and a half too and when you're five he'll be five and so on all your life; you will find that everyone will let you down sometimes but he'll always be your friend. So why don't you take his hand and you'll both come and have some tea.' So my mother went to tea and from that moment on she had her new friend who was with her all her life. She was surprisingly unreligious but all her life she had what the Bible describes as the 'faith of a child'.

During my mother's time at Loreto her brother would walk over and see her at weekends bringing a bag of oranges. Possibly it was the war that prevented my grandmother visiting much but my mother stayed at that school for the next six years. She remembered Marshal Foch coming to the school and that she presented him with a bunch of flowers because she was the youngest girl in the school, and she learned to play backgammon from an Irish nun but not much else so presumably she was quite happy.

In 1919 Molly and Vivien were transferred to school in England, a quite usual event in those times. Vivien went to Beaumont and Molly to St Mary's Ascot. Like all colonial children home was too far away to visit in the holidays, and there were no relatives in Britain for them to stay with so they stayed at school. Vivien was allowed to go and stay with friends. When Reverend Mother wrote to my grandmother asking for permission for Molly to do the same my grandmother wrote back that she would only give such permission if the convent could completely guarantee my mother's safety. Reverend Mother blinked and my mother spent all her holidays at school except when Elsie and Eze came over to visit, probably once every two years. It always amazes me that my mother didn't become institutionalised, and that believing firmly in God as her friend she never wanted to stay in the only world she really knew and become a nun. It is a great credit to the convents that raised her that she coped with the difficult life that was to follow far better than many from conventional homes did in similar circumstances. She also made good friends who stayed with her throughout her life. I shall name them now so that you will know them later in this narrative: Doris, known as Goldfish, whose parents lived in Chile; Antonia from Estremadura in Spain; and Bertja from Holland, who became my godmother.

In 1924 Molly was sixteen and my grandmother took her home to Singapore. There followed the only three years of home life my mother was to know, back at Eden Hall with its servants, its horses and dogs. My grandmother was very keen on her dogs, and at one time she had twelve salukis. My mother described how the postman once lost his nerve and turned and ran down the drive with the salukis bouncing after him and my grandmother shouting at him to stand still. The dogs grabbed the edge of his sarong, which came unwrapped revealing all to watching eyes and it needed a lot of Singapore dollars and consoling of hurt pride to persuade him ever to deliver the post again.

It was possibly the happiest time of my mother's life: she adored Uncle Eze, put her mother on an unwonted and probably unwanted pedestal, enjoyed the parties, the trips in the electric canoe on the property at Changi, the sea bathing at the Singapore swimming club, with the frisson of danger of shark and barracuda attack. There was an old Malay fisherman who had had his head seized in a shark's mouth and by dint of gouging its eye out had escaped. He had the marks of a complete set of shark's teeth round his head and for a Singapore dollar would take his hat off and frighten the young. Molly was good-looking, athletic, an excellent horsewoman with good prospects and she blossomed. But then into Eden came a snake, you might say.

My father was a hard-working young doctor, and Singapore gave him advantages he would not have had at home, but he had little money. He invented the operation of stripping out varicose veins while working on the rickshaw coolies, who were of course dreadfully afflicted with this condition. The bandage that he later developed for varicose veins with F.E. Smith of Smith and Nephew still bears his name. He was the first surgeon to remove a bullet from someone's spine so deftly that the man walked again. On my Uncle Vivien's twenty-first birthday Vivien lost control of his brand-new motorbike and drove into the gate pillar at Eden Hall. My father was sent up from the hospital to deal with it. My grandmother did not mix in expat society, preferring to socialise with the rich business community who included Jews, Chinese and Malays, and my father was certainly not part of their circle. My mother was impressed that my father picked up my six foot two uncle and carried him indoors but otherwise didn't really notice him. My father fell in love, but I have always wondered with what: the glitter and luxury of Eden Hall or my seventeen-year-old mother? My father was eleven years older and a veteran of the war, a brilliant cerebral man, while my mother had a limited education and was not really interested in acquiring any more.

In any event my father courted her, and persuaded Eze to let him stable a horse at Eden Hall. He didn't actually own a horse but having started his army career as a horse gunner he could ride and so he bought one cheaply. Then he would arrive first thing to join my mother for an early morning ride and exercise his not inconsiderable charm on her, although she still didn't much care for him. However one day her horse spooked at crossing a rickety bridge over a monsoon drain. There was no room to lead the horse so my father managed to mount and ride her back and my mother was impressed. My grandmother noticed this, and since my father was not what she wanted for Molly she made arrangements to accompany her back to England to be presented at court; out of sight was to be out of mind. But, not to be outdone, my father gave up his job at the hospital and arranged to escort a patient home on the same boat. By the time they reached Suez my mother was in love and my grandmother, knowing when she was beaten, agreed that they should be married in Paris.

They disembarked at Marseille and took the train to Paris. A raft of telegrams had been sent from the boat to invite friends to the wedding, but the main reason for the decision to be married in Paris was to disguise the fact that Muddy would not have come to the wedding even if they had married on her doorstep. My father had written to her that my mother was a Catholic and received a missive back which included the line: 'I would rather she were a black naked heathen whore than a papist.' My mother took great delight in framing this letter and hanging it in the downstairs loo at their first home. Molly may not have been overly religious but she was staunch, so if they were to marry it would be in a Catholic church with my father promising that the children were to be raised and educated as Catholics. My father agreed. They were married in the church of St Joseph in the 16th *arrondissement* on 2 February 1927. This is the day after the end of the shooting season and my Uncle Vivien, who hated my father whom he considered a fortune-hunter who didn't love my mother, said it was the only gentlemanly thing that he had ever done.

Vivien had one last try at sabotage: on the eve of the wedding all the men went out on a stag night in Montmartre. Rupert, Eze's youngest brother, lost his umbrella and convinced the barman had stolen it hauled him across the bar, shouting in execrable French, '*Où est mon parapluie?*' A fight ensued and all of them, including my father, ended up in the local police nick. My Uncle Douglas, my father's youngest brother who was in the navy, arrived from Scapa Flow at 3 a.m. to be greeted by my anxious grandmother who had smelled trouble. He was despatched to search and duly found the incarcerated party. After a substantial sum of money had changed hands they were sprung and at 10 a.m. the next morning my parents were married. As my father was unbaptised they were married off the high altar but not before my father had been pursued round the church by a deacon intoning, '*Seulement un peu d'eau, monsieur,*' only a little water.

The couple eventually arrived in England and Molly was taken to meet Muddy. She was greeted with the challenge, 'Your crowd believe in the power of the Virgin Mary. Give me one instance of this.' My mother replied, 'The marriage feast at Cana,' and my grandmother, always a respecter of the quick reply, decided she might make a suitable wife for her favourite son. After the honeymoon the couple returned to Singapore but in early 1928 went back to England to further my father's practice and in September 1928 my sister Heather was born. Molly and Dick had a mansion flat in Bickenhall Mansions on Baker Street. They hired a cook after my mother burned the sausages and mash and nearly the flat, and of course a nanny for Heather. My mother's horse Star was sent over by boat for her to ride in Rotten Row, and my father put up his plaque in Wimpole Street and was reunited with St Mary's Paddington. In 1930 my sister June was born, followed four years later to the day by my brother Anthony.

The family was complete or so it seemed. They moved to a larger house in Elsworthy Road. My father's career, aided by Uncle Eze's rich connections, prospered. They were as happy as they were ever going to be.

2

The deck I was dealt

In 1939 the war came. My mother refused to take the children to America and the family stayed in London. A bomb dropped in the garden but my mother remained resolute that she was not going to run away. The girls were boarding at St Mary's Ascot and Anthony at Worth Abbey but during the holidays they remember my mother saying they would all send up a barrage of prayers. Anthony used to ride round on his bike after a raid to view the new bomb sites. Finally the house received a direct hit but fortunately everyone had gone to the cinema taking Louise the cook with them. They moved temporarily to a large cottage just outside Billingshurst. When my mother would go to collect my father from the station he told her to uncover the headlights so that she might distract a bomb from London by showing a light which would attract a bomber's attention!

I don't know when my father's violent behaviour began but my sister June described how, towards the end of the war, one or other of the children would crawl along the parapet at 36 Circus Road to see if my father had killed my mother. He was also violent to the children, particularly Anthony, and on one occasion bashed my brother's head against the garage wall so hard he caused a hairline fracture. My mother was forever telling people she had tripped over the Hoover when she appeared with a black eye or a fractured cheekbone, which she tried to cover with make-up. On more than one occasion she attempted to go to the lawyers about a divorce but the medical profession closed ranks and told her they would have her certified if she tried. With her family so many miles and a war away and most of them either killed or imprisoned by the Japanese she was isolated and alone with no one to turn to and her allowance from my grandmother unpaid because of the hostilities.

The war ended and a couple of years later I was born. I have given you all this background so that you can understand what a complicated family I was born into. If this seems like a long road to you I expect it did to everyone else too.

First there was the problem of naming me. Having had two girls and a boy my mother assumed I would be another boy and was all set to call me Thomas after her father. Thomasina was however voted down as was Verbena and even Nigella when my brother pointed out that the other name for that plant was 'love in the mist'! Finally they blindfolded my mother and turned her loose in the library where she pulled out a copy of Richardson's *Clarissa*. I am grateful for this as it stood dangerously near to the volumes of the *Encyclopaedia Britannica* and Thomas Paine's *Birth of a Nation*. The mind boggles. Having chosen a first name I can only surmise that they got pissed to celebrate the fact, as I own to Clarissa Theresa (as in the Saint of Avila), Philomena (my mother's favourite saint), Aileen (for my mother), Mary (as a Catholic child), Josephine Agnes (two rich relatives who did not remember me in their wills), Elsie Trilby (for my grandmother), Louise (for the cook) and Esmerelda for my father's favourite pig as I was born in the Chinese year of that animal. I will give a bottle of champagne to anyone who successfully makes an anagram of my names.

How was I received? Well, my mother was delighted; here was proof that she and my father were still together. My father was quite pleased with the proof of virility my birth entailed. My sister Heather, I think, hated me on sight; a sweet little blonde baby who was of an age to have been her own daughter. My sister June raised her head from her books to smile and my brother was rather pleased not to be the youngest any more.

When I was three months old we all moved across the road into 39 Circus Road, St John's Wood, the place that was to be my home for the next twenty-eight years. The house was built in 1809 for a Miss Sinderby, Lord Leconfield's mistress, and stood on two floors surrounded by three-quarters of an acre of garden and a wall. Nine bedrooms, three bathrooms, a library, a drawing room and a gallery which had been built on for cricketing lunches due to the proximity to Lord's cricket ground, a dining room, four cellars for various purposes, a kitchen, a pantry, a large servants' sitting room and, best of all, along the whole of one side wall ran a covered loggia with Spanish-style brick arches. A perfect place for parties, for a ping-pong table, a table to eat meals at in fine weather and for me a place to play outside when it rained. Apart from the family there was Louise the cook who had been with us since before the war, and a parlour maid named Betsy Bundrop because her hair was always coming unpinned. Betsy played the tambour-ine in the Salvation Army Band and swore like a trooper much to our amusement and her undying shame. Nurse Ancliffe, my nursery nurse, came from Eye in Suffolk and looked like a witch with long hairs growing from a mole on her chin. My mother tried to persuade her to pluck them but she said they fascinated her babies and refused. There was also Mr Jordan the gardener and my father's chauffeur but they didn't live in. All the servants doted on me and I lived in the nursery wing with little to trouble or vex me.

I have two memories from these early days, both of which were to affect my later life. The first concerns food. When I was about three and a half we went on a picnic to the RHS gardens at Wisley. I remember a couple of things from this day very clearly: one was peeling a hard-boiled egg so that the shell came off cleanly – a wonderful sensation and one I still enjoy today – and the other was a cold sausage, which became the benchmark for all sausages and I carried it in my head for forty-five years and no sausage was ever as good.

In 1996 at a Food Lovers' Fair someone on a stall offered me a sausage. I took it and kept walking then screeched to a halt. 'This is my sausage!' I cried. They looked at me kindly and agreed they had just given it to me. I explained and they looked doubtful but when the company checked their books they found that at that date they had been supplying my mother. They are Musk's of Newmarket and this was the breakfast sausage they had made for Edward VII's breakfast and kept going at the request of the Queen Mother. Whether we had them because my grandmother had horses in training at Newmarket or on the recommendation of the QM I don't know but I love them still and recommend them to you.

The second event I remember was learning to read. June and Anthony used to take turns to read to me when I was ill in bed and obviously got fed up with it. I must have been about four when they marched into my bedroom and declared they weren't leaving until I had learned to read for myself. I remember the book, which was *Brock the Badger's Swimming Pool*, and I also remember the words sliding into place and making sense and since that day reading has been one of the greatest pleasures of my life.

My father was very keen to develop my memory and concentration. Apparently when I was a little baby he would spend ten minutes every day making me focus on his finger or some other object. Once I was old enough he started teaching me poetry, which I would recite to him in the car when I went about with him. I can still recite 'John Gilpin', 'The Rime of the Ancient Mariner', the Horatius part of the *Lays of Ancient Rome* and various others; happily for my friends I don't, no doubt deterred by stories of Uncle Almroth. When I was small my father was, I'm told, very fond of me. I was a pretty child and bright and merry. He would take me round the hospital to visit the staff and his patients; it was somewhat unnerving to be put into a room with a total stranger lying in bed, often with drips attached, and left to entertain them but I don't remember minding. Sometimes they died but I didn't really understand this as sooner or later they all left anyway. This hospital visiting came to an end when a splendid old lady called Mrs Richardson died and left me £100, a good sum then, in her will. She advised her solicitors to give the money to my mother for me, as she believed my father would fail to pass it on to me. She was spot on. As I grew older my father was always making me write thank you letters for gifts I never received because he would keep them and sell them in aid of Cancer Research. To this day I have an inability to write letters, especially of the bread and butter variety and I am sure it stems from this time.

I liked the hospital, because the nurses and patients all made a fuss of me and there was a swimming pool where I was sometimes taken. The other place my father used to take me to was the rugby. It was my father who turned St Mary's into a rugby hospital with a keen team. I'm told that when interviewing a prospective student he would throw them a rugby ball. If the student dropped it his chances of admission were limited, if he caught it well and good, and if he drop-kicked it into the wastepaper basket he was in however dim he was. Lou Cannal, the England International, was the longest serving student at St Mary's; it was suggested that he didn't pass his finals till his rugby days were over. Five Internationals played for the team during my youth including Tommy Kemp and J.P.R. Williams. My father persuaded Lord Beaverbrook to buy the pitch for the hospital by exerting a little pressure. On the day my father was due to operate on him he went into Beaverbrook's room with a shaking hand. 'Look,' he said, 'I'm in such a state. I don't know where my boys will play next year.' Beaverbrook said, 'If I survive the operation I'll buy you the land you want at Teddington.' My father whipped out the document of sale. 'Best you sign now,' he said, 'and if you survive you can pay for the grandstand.' Beaverbrook thought this really funny and signed, survived and built the stand and clubhouse.

I loved the rugby, all the players were kind to me and I sold them raffle tickets. Other surgeons' children came to the matches and we played together and tried to kick the heavy balls over the posts. As I got older I came to understand the game and I remain deeply passionate about it though I have never wanted to play it. It also inspired another of my passions, men's legs. When you are four years old all you could see were legs and in my mind rugby players' legs are the best!

In my early childhood mine was the life of a well-to-do privileged London child in the days when the map of the world was still coloured red and the sun never set on the British Empire. I went to children's parties with people from similar backgrounds, and my nanny took me to Regent's Park to feed the ducks. My father was a Fellow of the Zoological Society and on Sundays when the zoo was closed we were allowed to go on private visits behind the scenes. At one point we walked through the feeding corridor behind the cages and while I didn't mind the great cats who reached through the bars and swiped their claws towards you, I dreaded Guy the gorilla who, with his huge black hands, seemed most likely to grab you. We also walked in Queen Mary's Rose Garden and I can remember being addressed by this stately woman in a toque who asked me, 'Do you like my Rose Garden, little girl?' I thought how odd, if she were a Queen why wasn't she wearing a crown and ermine like in my story books, but being polite I told her I did and she asked my name. Then she offered me a chocolate, to which I responded that my mummy wouldn't let me take sweets from people I didn't know. She found this very funny and retrieving the cardboard box from a lady-in-waiting gave it to me. I expect Nanny nicked it and sent it home as a holy relic. I thought Queen Mary was great, and often saw her after that; when she died I cried for several days. King George VI died too and I went to Paddington Station to see his coffin being loaded on the train, which took a long time and I remember I ate an awful lot of smoked salmon sandwiches.

My world began to change in 1953, as I suppose did the nation's. My father took me to his club on Pall Mall to watch the coronation. I sat on the balcony in the drizzle and waved a chicken drumstick at the new Queen and cheered Queen Salote of Tonga, who alone of the procession had the roof of her carriage down. My mother was furious as we were supposed to have been at a party at home watching the new TV set but I am glad to have seen it for real. I started at primary school in Fitzjohn's Avenue and made new friends. A boy called Christopher Woodhouse walked along the garden walls and came to play often. He proposed to me with a ring from a Christmas cracker, having announced to all and sundry that he was going to marry me. He was five to my four and a half.

My father, mother and I went to Singapore to visit my grandmother, and although I had been flying from the age of three months this is the first flight I remember. It took an awfully long time and we disembarked into charabancs at Karachi and were taken to a hotel where we showered and had breakfast while they disinfected the plane. I loved Singapore: the smell, the rains that swept a marble table off the patio, the monkey in the baobab tree in the garden which I was not allowed to feed. My mother, grandmother and I would pile into the car and go to the Chinese quarter where a man in a grubby vest would cook us noodles in a huge iron wok. A portion cost a Singapore dollar, very little money, and you got an egg with that and whatever he had to add to it – maybe shellfish or poultry; it was all deeply unhygienic but delicious. They wrapped it in a banana leaf for us to take home and it was still hot when we ate it. There was the wonderful taste too of Gula Malacca, tapioca cooked with coconut milk and palm sugar, and the rotten smell and creamy taste of durian fruit, lychees and rambutans. You will notice how many of my memories are centred on food. Delicious too were the chips and tomato ketchup we ate at elevenses after swimming at the Tanglin Club, where I yearned to dig a knife into the big traveller's palm to see the water it contained spout out.

One incident has perhaps a particular relevance. While every-one had their afternoon nap my grandmother put me to work killing flies with a swat; I was paid a cent per fly and usually killed about fifty or so. On the dining room sideboard stood a decanter of bright green liquid which when I tried it had a delicious peppermint taste; it was of course crème de menthe and my first taste of alcohol. Every day I took just a little which made me feel happy and dreamy until one day I came back to discover Ah Poo, the cook, my friend, had been sacked for lying about taking the stuff. I owned up and he was reinstated; my grandmother rewarded me and my mother gave me a good spanking which was all very confusing.

We went on to Australia to see the stud farm that my grandfather had started in the Hunter Valley and which my Uncle Vivien had enlarged into a racing stud. I was sent briefly to the Loreto Convent at Ballarat where my mother had been. I know my mother had lost a lot of her relatives under the Japanese including her beloved stepfather and a lot more had suffered imprisonment, but I don't remember my father being with us in Australia. It was quite a lengthy visit so I often wonder if my mother had intended to leave my father and was dissuaded. I shall never know.

The following year my parents and I went to Brazil by ship and harmony had obviously been restored. It was a Blue Star Line boat, partly cargo and partly passenger. I loved the sea and when going through a very rough Bay of Biscay demanded to be taken down to breakfast, so my rather green father dumped me in the dining room and fled. I was the only person in there and had my porridge and kippers, at which point even the waiters went slightly pale. One event on this trip stuck in my mind: there was a steward who in exchange for comics lured me to a bathroom and got me to wank him off. I found this fascinating, the growth of the penis, the velvet feel of it and the subsequent detumescence. I persuaded a little friend to come and share the experience and she told her mother who I heard created stink. My mother made no fuss to me so I suffered no trauma, the man was taken off the ship and my mother gently explained that some things were only for grown-ups. I was therefore unharmed by the experience and the fascination remains with me to this day. Years later when I was in treatment a counsellor had the screaming abdabs at this story, appalled at such child abuse. No doubt it was but my mother's handling of it left me with no scars. Over the years I have met many people who suffered sexual abuse as children and one of the most consistent problems is the shame they feel, largely as a result of the reaction of discovering adults which makes the child think they were to blame in some way, so I have much cause to be grateful to my mother.

I loved Brazil, the brightness, the music, the humming birds, the Christ of the Andes, but when I returned to school and the nuns asked me what I liked most about Brazil I told them my best memory was of fejoiada, black beans with braised beef and rice. One day we went into the jungle to a snake serum farm. Ma and I were shown into a long wooden hut to wait for my father, who had arrived earlier, when suddenly I noticed a huge snake curled up at one end of the hut, quite uncaged. My mother and I tore out of the hut to be greeted by the staff in howls of laughter. It was a giant anaconda, which we were told couldn't cross the wet teak boards of the floor – a useful tip to remember.

Home and the world changed again. My sister June married an American concert pianist, Byron Janis, and I was allowed off school to hear him play at the Brussels Exhibition. I think I preferred the Atomium, the famous giant replica of the atom that towered over the exhibition and which I thought was wonderful, and Knorr chicken noodle soup, the first time I ever tasted artificial flavouring. June went to live in America and I seldom saw much of her again. My sister Heather left home too and I moved into their room in the main house. I missed June a bit but Heather was no loss as I had always felt that she had hated me from birth and seemed to me never to have any time for me. I cannot explain this; maybe it was that I was the only other blonde child of us four and nineteen years younger so she was afraid I might usurp her place in my father's affections, as she had been his favourite when the elder children were young. Or maybe she particularly resented the proof that my parents were still sexually active. Whatever the reason I can't have caused it by any action of mine other than by being born. But Anthony, the next in age to me who had always spent time playing with me or taking me out in his old car and so was much beloved, had gone for a short service commission instead of National Service and was still around from time to time. I was a solitary child but not I think lonely. I had my books and my toys; the garden was my plaything, turning from jungle to wild weald to forest with whatever game I was playing. I would spend hours stalking the gardener in the shrubbery; he must have heard me but like all the servants he was my friend.

The first time I saw my father hit my mother I was six. I can still see it clearly: he was standing at the hall table after breakfast reading a piece of paper and my mother in her housecoat leant over his shoulder to see what it was. He drew back his elbow and backswiped her in the chest, then as she reeled away he turned and punched her for no apparent reason. A huge rush of anger welled up in me and I darted in and kicked him on the shins, shouting, 'Pick on someone your own size, like me.' He glared at me, snorted with laughter and stalked off to kick the dog. From that moment on violence entered my life and I knew that it was up to me to guard and protect my mother. I was not afraid but it was the start of the hatred I felt for my father and which was to burden me for much of my life. I did not know then that this occasion was only one of a long history of violence; as is always the way once you become aware of something you notice it thereafter. Living in the nursery wing I had been protected from the rows and beatings that were part of my family life. It is possible that my father's alcoholism had now come to a point where he was unable to control himself even in front of a small child. Certainly from what I have heard, my father's alcoholism seems to have escalated in the period immediately before the war, which would place my father in his early forties which is quite consistent with alcoholic progression, and following this incident in his mid-fifties his violence became increasingly worse. I never saw my father drink at home but on one occasion I was poking through cupboards at his consulting rooms and came across a great stash of bottles, far more than one would need for offering drinks around. My father saw me and pushed me away, slamming the cupboard shut and locking it. Obviously that was where he did his private drinking.

I had my friends: Dippy Parker who I used to go and stay with some weekends, whose mother had been in the Greek Resistance and had rescued her father by dressing him up as a soldier in the short tutu skirt, tights and shoes with pompoms of the Evzones. He had a tattoo on his arm of a tiger's head; apparently George V had had one and a lot of smart young men had copied him, rather like a Princess Diana hairstyle, I suppose. The Marquess of Waterford had a tattoo of a hunt in full cry down his back with the fox's brush disappearing down his bottom cleft! The Parkers lived in Brent Pelham in the Puckeridge country and I was allowed to go to the hunt on a borrowed pony. Captain Barclay was the Master and was always cheery to children. Another friend was Francesca D'abreu who lived in one of the Nash Terraces off Regent's Park, where we were forbidden to slide down the hugely tall spiral staircases so of course we did. And there was Avril Stoneham, who had been one of my first friends at the age of four. Her grandfather was the man who had built Le Touquet and turned it into a 1920s society holiday venue, with a golf course and a casino to which the rich and sporting flocked.

During the war his son Vincent had escaped to fight with the Free French and had met his wife Jean who had been somehow connected with the Resistance, which I found very romantic and heroic. Vincent was a patient of my father's and we used to spend holidays with them in Le Touquet, where they ran a golf hotel. I loved our times there, where my father played golf with Vincent and Anthony or took us children to the beach in the boot of his R-type Bentley, while Heather and June would take my mother off shopping or to the casino, and we resembled a proper family. I remember Jacques Tati of *Monsieur Hulot's Holiday* fame stayed there too, and my grandmother, who sometimes came with us, sleeping in the room he vacated, swore she found a flea.

There was a tunnel under our house which dated back to Elizabethan times. Babington, a Catholic gentleman who had plotted against Elizabeth I, planning to put Mary Queen of Scots on the throne of England, had been captured at the bottom of the garden so it had obviously been a recusancy house (from the reign of Elizabeth I recusants were Catholics who refused to attend Anglican services or pay the fines levied, and clandestinely housed priests who took Mass in the house, often building secret passages to enable a swift escape). One day a friend, Candy, and I went down there and left lighted candles; fortunately somebody found us or I might have burned down the house. My mother smacked me with a Mason Pearson hairbrush, which hurt a lot, but the next day took me out and bought me a torch. When I read of all this legislation to stop parents smacking children I despair. I was smacked by my mother on several occasions, which taught me not to repeat the misdemeanours again, but I never confused it in my mind with the beatings of pure violence that I was to receive from my father in the years ahead: one was discipline, the other abuse.

31

I suppose I should introduce the other two people who inhabited our house, the ghosts. Before we moved my mother was at the house measuring up when she saw a figure walking across the lawn in Regency dress. The woman passed her into the house and my mother followed her; she went to a window and stood looking out, weeping, clearly in distress. This happened on subsequent occasions and my mother, following her look, found what looked like a dog's grave in the shrubbery. She had it dug up and there was the skeleton of a baby. After medical examination it was decided that the child had either been stillborn or died shortly after birth. My mother had the child buried with a blessing and the ghost ceased crying. We think she was the Miss Sinderby for whom the house was built. Many people saw her and she shared our space quite happily. The other ghost was a man, we believe a Captain Green who taught Edward VII drawing and had the loggia built on to the house.

My mother was very psychic, thanks to a strong Highland streak and her ghosts fell really into two categories: the first you might have explained away as some form of electric photograph left behind. On one occasion we were visiting Dippy's family in their new home, a mid-fifteenth-century house in the middle of the village of Hatfield Broad Oak. They had only just moved and it was our first visit. It was winter and we were all seated at dinner when my mother remarked what a strange time of day it was to hear a horse trotting up the village street; no one else heard anything but we all kept quiet. 'Odd,' said my mother, 'it's stopped outside. Are you expecting anyone?' At that point the candles flared and blew as if someone had opened a door. 'Who is it?' said Lilly Parker and my mother quite calmly described a man in chainmail with a tabard with an orange star on it. I got very cross, pointing out it was the wrong period of house for chainmail. My mother just turned her wide blue eyes on me and said nothing. The next day Dippy and I went to the church which none of us had visited before. There in front of the high altar was the tomb of Roger de Vere, Earl of Essex, and yes, you've guessed it, in chainmail. He had built a chapel on the site of the house at an earlier date for monks to pray for the soul of his first wife.

Another time we were driving down to lunch in the Cotswolds and my mother observed a wounded horseman, a knight again in mail, and turned off the road to follow, despite my scorn and acid remarks about the speed of a motor car as opposed to an ambling horse. Finally she pulled up in front of a flat grass field. 'There you are, darling, you know how you love castles, you can't be cross now.' Needless to say all I could see was an empty field. On the map there was no indication of a castle. I carefully marked the place and it took me several hours in the reference library to find, yes, there had been a castle there whose owner had been wounded at the Battle of Tewksbury and had returned safely home. Now if you feel this is bunkum, imagine how I felt. I was cynical, pragmatic and disbelieving, but time and again I used my skills only to discover my mother was right. She was not cerebral or well educated so I have no doubt she hadn't done any prior research.

The second type of ghosts were even more convincing, as these were attached to strangers and had some message to relay. Let me give you an example. Seated at a long Sunday lunch table at a friend's house, she turned to a woman halfway down the table who she had never met and announced that her husband was standing next to her and wanted to speak to her. The woman had the sense to ask, 'What does he want?' My mother calmly replied that he wanted to tell her on no account to give the shares to his brother or trust him on this issue. The woman thanked my mother and the lunch continued. The woman's husband had died a year earlier and her brother-in-law had been urging her to make over to him some shares in a defunct company which, as it later emerged, had a large and valuable building site as an asset. I could quote you many such incidents. I could also try to tell you how much I hated it all at the time. There are more things in heaven and earth etc.

I was about sixteen when I saw my first ghost away from Circus Road. Carrots, Christine and I were in Winchester walking in the cathedral close when I saw three men playing with some sort of ball against the cathedral buttresses and pointed them out, thinking it was some sort of student rag. Carrots said I was quite red in the face. They could see nothing and as we walked towards them the figures just dissolved before my eyes. I am not psychic as my mother was but I see the odd passing ghost from time to time. If you don't believe in ghosts that's your privilege but it's probably because you've never seen them. Most ghosts aren't frightening; that is just people scaring themselves with the unknown.

My father was by now a renowned surgeon and we entertained a lot of distinguished and well-known people; my mother took her duties as a hostess seriously and she and Louise worked hard on menus and food generally so we all, including the servants, ate very well. My mother's theory was that if you didn't feed your servants the same as you ate then how would they learn to appreciate the food. Strangely my father, who was notoriously mean, accepted this and never queried the household bills. Louise, who had trained at Chatsworth, had very set views, while my mother, who was a devotee of Elizabeth David's works and who in any event had travelled extensively, was more cosmopolitan in her choice of dishes. I remember once finding

Louise on one of the three little Georgian balconies that ran along one side of the house shouting, 'Madam, if you make me cook that I'll jump,' and my mother replying with great calm, 'If you won't cook it you might as well jump.' I was standing below, watching the balcony bend under her weight and was yelling, 'Weezy, go in or you won't have to jump.' It was an age when all the surgeons were running off with their theatre sisters and someone asked my mother if she objected to my father's close relationship with his. My mother replied quite seriously, 'No more than he does to mine with my cook,' meaning if you worked together you were no doubt on the same wavelength.

I didn't realise that the people who came to the house were often famous. There was the nice man who stood on his head to amuse me and who I called Udi who was Yehudi Menuhin. He once said to my mother, 'Molly, I love you because you never ask me to bring my violin.' Of course he sometimes did. There was the funny little man who once cooked a sponge cake in a frying pan to entertain me who was Philip Harben, the first TV cook. There was the sweet Welshman who sang to me with a wonderful voice who was Harry Secombe. There was the serious Scotsman Uncle Alex Fleming who did tricks of legerdemain to divert me; and so many others. One of my mother's great friends was Audrey Pleydell-Bouverie who would sweep in smelling wonderful and call me poppet. She was lady-in-waiting to the Queen Mother, and when the King was alive she used to collect risqué jokes from my father for the QM to tell the King who adored them. She was the woman who had introduced the Prince of Wales to Wallis Simpson, thereby doing the country a great favour, as she put it. The Prince of Wales, later Edward VIII, had a very unpleasant side; he was also born with one ball and a tiny penis so his obsession with Wallis was entirely sexual, and by using alum to

35

shrink her vagina and cold cream to lubricate it she enabled him to have 'normal' sex for the first time. As Audrey said, he wasn't a potential breeder so had the monarchy survived him we would have ended up with Queen Elizabeth in any event.

I was a sickly child, spending much of my winters in bed with ear infections. My mother was very stern and insisted I worked twice as hard as I would have done at school and had no special treats because I was ill. One year my ear really blew up, and the eardrum came out beyond the ear; it was horribly painful and wouldn't respond to penicillin or any other treatment. Sir John Simpson, the most senior ENT surgeon, was at a loss as was my father. I understood that if it burst I would die and if they operated I would possibly be totally deaf. The swelling just got larger and finally they decided to operate the next day. My mother had a relic of Blessed Martin de Porres, the black Brazilian Dominican monk, which she had been given when we were in Brazil, and that night she placed it on my ear when I was in the worst pain I have ever known. Ma said she saw a figure cross the room to my bedside and put a hand to my head; apparently I said, 'Thank you,' and fell asleep. All I can remember was a total cessation of pain like someone turning off a switch. The next morning I was sitting up eating a hearty breakfast when my father came in. He asked why I was eating as I was meant to be going to the operating theatre. My mother told him I was cured as indeed I was. Both he and 'Uncle John' were at a total loss to explain it. Eventually they reluctantly wrote a report of this for the Bishop and the Devil's Advocate and I was one of the miracles that contributed to the final canonisation of St Martin. Again, please don't believe it if you don't care to but the two witnesses were the most cynical atheist medics you could ever find! My mother and I went to Lima for the canonisation ceremony. I had no doubt it was a miracle and not the only one I have had in my life.

So that really was my childhood, learning about things, travelling, learning to ride, to play tennis, to swim, and over my shoulder always hung the dark cloud of violence that was to erupt increasingly often as the years went by. I was ten years old but realised something else was not well: my sister Heather had been barred from the house by my father and my mother was forbidden to see her because she was living with a man with the unfortunate name of Jack Free Taylor, ill chosen because he was a man who was to spend a lot of his life in jail. He was some years older than my sister and had already done time when she took up with him. He was a very clever chartered surveyor but had an unfortunate trait that led him always to look for the crooked path. My brother, who had captained the English Schoolboys at rugby and played for the army, was now at Cambridge, mainly on the strength of his rugby, when Jack inveigled him to join a scheme for selling ladies underwear by post. The scheme was bent and Anthony ended up with a large sum of money to pay or a prosecution pending. My father refused to pay and eventually after much begging by my mother my grandmother coughed up. Anthony left both university and home as a result and I wasn't to see much of him for a long time. I was heartbroken and wrote a sad poem to commemorate the event. Now I was alone with my parents. None of the others ever came back to Circus Road for many years. I can see why they didn't, in their shoes I probably wouldn't either but the fact left me very isolated.

June visited once or twice when Byron was playing a concert in London, bringing my nephew Stefan with her. When Stefan was a little boy he wouldn't finish his lunch and June was making a fuss so my ma said, 'If you eat it I will jump out of the dining room window.' The food vanished in a trice and out my mother leapt. Stefan was entranced and declared he wouldn't call her Grandma but was going to call her Mollypop, a name she carried ever after.

Christmases were the worst. My father hated the festival and every year read me the opening chapters of *A Christmas Carol*. I was fifteen before I read it for myself and discovered it had a happy ending. He would do everything to ruin things, for instance saving the budgerigar in formaldehyde to bury it on Christmas morning. He needn't have worried; for me it was a sad time anyway, as there were no young people let alone children. Christmas lunch was always attended by a couple older than my parents called Harrison. I was fond of William Harrison the rest of the year as he was a great cricket enthusiast and always took me to cricket matches but his wife was truly dreary. She always got drunk on one champagne cocktail and would start regaling us with the story of her cat who she was convinced was the reincarnation of her fiancé who had died. William was allegedly jealous of the cat, which slept on her bed, and was supposed to have kicked it off the fire-escape where it was found at the bottom with a broken neck. This tirade always ended in a row and they would stomp off home after the pudding.

The first time my father hit me was over Christmas. He had closed all the accounts just out of spite, knowing my mother had no money to buy presents for anyone. I realised he would not have closed his account at John Bell and Croyden, the surgical suppliers, and Ma and I went off and had a lovely time buying soaps, scent and such like. When my father discovered this he went berserk and when I stepped in and told him it was my idea, he turned on me and clouted me hard across the head. I fell to the floor and he kicked me in the ribs, but I managed to roll away and run into the downstairs loo where the door resisted his efforts to break it down.

It is not so much the actuality of violence that is dreadful, which has an energy of its own, an adrenalin surge that gets one through the moment, nor even the aftermath, the bruises or broken bones, but the tension, the anticipation of the next outbreak. It is like having a wild animal in the house: one never knows when it is going to roar. It is very tiring waiting for something to happen, and the only time my mother and I really felt safe was when my father was abroad.

3

With shining morning face

When I was eleven the decision was taken to send me to boarding school. I had assumed I would go to St Mary's Ascot as had my mother and both my sisters but my mother decided against it, saying it hadn't worked for my sisters. June thinks it was because of her shame at Heather's association with Jack Taylor but the scandal hadn't hit the fan then so I really don't know. Mollypop decided I was to go to the Sacred Heart at Woldingham but Mother Ignatius, the head of the IBVM school I was attending, was determined I should go to Ascot. My mother was a generous patron and Ig-pig, as we called her, wanted that money for her order. She talked to Mother Shanley, the head of Woldingham, and played, I suspect, the Jack card; in the event I was refused a place at Woldingham. My father in the meantime had determined that I should go to St Paul's Girls' School as a day girl. Into this mêlée stepped my new sister-in-law Angela, who'd married Anthony a year before, and persuaded my father to let me board, for which I shall be ever grateful; had I stayed at home I should probably have ended up in Broadmoor. My father's violence had if anything increased; he came home drunk more often and when he did he would hit my mother about; sometimes he would come into my room, haul me out of bed and throw me against the wall. I was constantly verbally abused and worn out by anticipating the blows, waiting for his return, trying not to fall asleep so that I could run and hide. I used to plot ways to kill him, reading books on herbal poisons and searching for the key to the gun cupboard.

In the event it was sorted and I set off to the Sacred Heart at Hove. My trunk was packed and Harrods provided the uniform, and because I was tall for my age the outfitter decided that I should wear stockings not socks. For some reason I arrived after supper and was sent straight to my dormitory. I woke early, to find the dormitory full of light and then there was a clatter, the door opened and in came a sister carrying jugs of steaming water which were set on mats along the floor. Another girl was awake and looking out of her cubicle; she smiled and I smiled back. I suddenly realised that I was in a safe place. From that moment on I loved boarding school if for no better reason than that I was safe. We were roused from our beds by a nun coming down the aisle with a bell chanting, 'Sacred Heart of Jesus, Immaculate Heart of Mary,' to which we were meant to reply, 'I give you my soul.' We then took our basins and filled them from the jugs and went back to our cubicles to wash and dress. I had never made a bed so in my first week I received a bad note, a form of weekly demerit, for bad bed-making!

All these years later I am still at a loss to explain why I emerged from my cubicle with an Australian accent. True, from my visits I adored Australia and things Australian, and I identified the country with my mother not my hated father, but Mollypop didn't have an accent, nor did her mother or indeed my Uncle Vivien. Perhaps I thought it would make me more interesting, perhaps I could use it to create a world in which I didn't have to explain the reality of my bitterly unhappy home. The nuns dealt with it pragmatically by giving me elocution lessons and Miss Sinclair was amazed at how quickly I learned to talk proper

English. Her method of teaching was to make her pupils read poems in all types of accents to avoid over Received Pronunciation. For instance one beginning, "Twas early in September nigh to Framlingham on sea' was recited in a Suffolk accent. As I had spent Sunday afternoons reading Dickens to my father so that he could fall asleep and had amused myself with personalising the different characters, and a lot of my time reading recipes to the cook who couldn't read, I loved these lessons. However soon I lost my fake accent I spent the next thirty years of my life weaving stories of a happy Australian childhood to the delight of my friends.

The thing we all remember about school was how beautiful it smelled, the scent of beeswax polish, flowers and incense, all provided with love to the glory of God. The Sacred Heart order had been founded by St Madeleine-Sophie Barat on the eve of the French Revolution to teach the daughters of the rich some much needed humility and recognition of the humanity of those less fortunate than themselves. Her rule, which was read to us at the beginning of each school year, was a comprehensive pattern for life including not only spiritual wisdom but also carving and advice not to carry open scissors in your pocket and, unusually for the day, education for women on a wide variety of academic subjects. The attempt came too late for France and the founder and her sisters embarked for England in the teeth of the guillotine. The nuns wore a full habit with a starched wimple framing the face, the dress of an eighteenth-century woman, which was, I have been told, terribly hindering and uncomfortable; it did, however, look very gracious and dignified and lent a huge air of authority. The order was enclosed, and the nuns only left the convent if they were being transferred to another house or to go to hospital. They did not eat with us and nor did we ever see them eat, all of which was a source of fascination to small girls and we were forever trying to peek into the dormitory nun's cubicle to see what she wore at night. Any entry to the enclosure was strictly forbidden, probably for the nuns' peace and quiet, and strangely even the naughtiest of us never did more than open the door, peep in and run away.

There was a lot of church-going: when I arrived we went to Mass every day and had prayers morning and evening; the following year this was changed to attendance at Mass three days a week, and towards the end of my time only Fridays and Sundays were obligatory though one could of course go every day from choice. Mass was in Latin which I still prefer. I have never been much inspired by organised religion and neither was Mollypop, who had had it all the days of her childhood. Mollypop liked going to Mass but not on Sunday when she said it was too crowded. Back then non-attendance on Sunday was a mortal sin punishable by hellfire but as ever money unlocks the doors of forgiveness in churches everywhere. I am the only Catholic I know who doesn't suffer from guilt. When I went to school Mollypop told me, 'Remember nuns wear calico underwear, and if the soap is improperly washed out the discomfort is unbearable, so if you hear something you find harsh or unpalatable just remember the soap!' It worked. In any event, having been told my Heavenly Father loved me I could not believe that the punishments of hell would be worse than home. There is a piece in the New Testament which says if you ask your Father for bread will he give you a stone, if you ask for an egg will he give you a snake; as in my case the answer was undoubtedly yes, there wasn't a lot left that could scare me!

So here I was in these beautiful surroundings, of above average intelligence and good at games; the only trouble was my lack of people skills. When I was three some children on the beach wouldn't play with me; I ran to my father who told me to go back and hit them with my bucket and spade. Of course they wouldn't play with me after that but it took me a long time to unlearn that lesson. True, I dealt with the school bully with ease; she was a large girl and tried to push me about. I picked her up and threw her against the radiator. The nuns asked me if I didn't think I had overreacted to which I replied, 'Well, she won't do it again,' and true enough she didn't. I had a hairline temper as I do to this day and it was very much of the red mist variety. The first group I joined were with one exception slightly afraid of me and I went to a girl called Christine asking if I couldn't be friends with her lot as I was too naughty for the original group. Christine laughed this away, but one day I lost my temper and kicked over a desk to get at a girl who was teasing me about the damn stockings. Christine frog-marched me out on to the lacrosse field and talked me down until I found myself laughing. Used to growing up with brothers, she was physically stronger than me and had no fear of anything in any event. She became my best and lifelong friend and is probably the other reason I managed to skip Broadmoor. My second great school friend was from my first group: Caroline, known as Carrots. I am very lucky to have two such good and loyal friends. Carrots loved baths, I have never known anyone so devoted to them, but it was not a devotion I shared; at school we were allowed three baths a week. Carrots' ma made the most fantastic flapjacks so I swapped two of my baths each week for a portion of her flapjack delivery. Ever the foodie, but before you have a picture of a fat child I was incredibly skinny and very athletic.

School food was quite horrid; when Mollypop had been told that we had cornflakes and fried eggs for breakfast no one had added, together! It's true: we were served a dish of cornflakes with the fried eggs sitting on top. I never have found out the rationale behind this. On feast days the Maltese sisters in the kitchen were allowed a free hand with the menu and then the food was quite yummy including a particular sweet dish of fried sugared bread dough. Mollypop used to sympathise and sent me food parcels quite regularly, whose contents ranged from the usual chocolate biscuits and tins of sardines to whole corner gammons and once a chicken that wasn't properly cooked so I cut it up and boiled it with a packet of onion soup in a kettle. The smell was amazing but, perhaps fortunately, we were discovered before we could eat it! On my first birthday at school Jack Taylor sent me a lavish Fortnum's hamper, which fed the whole class for a party. On another birthday Mollypop sent me strawberries which were meant for my party but the headmistress made me share them with the whole school, and sadly there weren't really enough for that.

What I particularly loved about school was the fact that the rules stayed the same; if you chose to break them you were punished but you knew what they were and what choice you were making. In an alcoholic home the goalposts move on a daily basis so that what you are laughed at for one day you are thumped for the next.

Once I had made friends I really enjoyed myself. Christine's parents lived to the east of Lewes in the village of Selmeston and I was invited home for weekends. It was a large Edwardian house called charmingly Little Bells and was always full of people; Christine was one of eight children and there were usually other additions so supper time was a noisy, jolly meal overseen with a light hand by her father, an ex-army colonel with a great sense of humour. Her mother was a beautiful woman who seemed to float above her family and Christine's parents were and remained very much in love, a totally new concept to me. Selmeston lies below the South Downs at Firle Beacon and I thought it was heaven. As I write now my screen-saver all these years and after all my travelling is still of the road to those downs. I think Christine and Little Bells gave me whatever sanity I have, in a world so far removed from my own where the only threats were being locked in the coal hole by her brothers or being chased in the spinney by the geese which tried to peck your legs as you raced past them to climb up to the tree house. We slid down the long ladder in the barn on hay bales and made houses in the hay, or laid planks atop the dense frieze of macracapa trees and bounced round above the world. We would walk to the top of the downs and run, blown by the wind and arms outstretched, to the Beacon. In spring there was the bluebell wood and in summer if there was no one to take us to the beach at Seaford we walked along the top of the downs to the sea. The mundane chores were new to me so that collecting eggs or picking frozen Brussels sprouts was a delight.

One day, early in my visits, Christine and I walked to the Beacon to see the sun come up; we travelled through a chill mist but when we reached the top it was clear. We sat and watched the sun rise and the mist broke up the land below into little cameo pictures, a barn here, some cows there, a cockerel crowing to greet the dawn, and I realised that these surroundings were quite new to me, totally different from my urban environment and I was determined to learn more about them. If I have been of help to the countryside in recent years I owe it to that moment.

The Colemans had a Welsh Mountain Pony called Misty, who was a real brute; one muddy day I tried to give her a rub down and I still have the bruise where she cow-kicked me just to the side of my right knee. Riding in the country was quite different to London where I got all dressed up in my jodhpurs and tweed jacket and was driven to Berkshire for a lesson or hacked out in the Great Park at Windsor. I had one of those ponies straight out of Thelwell; she was called Aster and was very round, and you could kick and kick to no avail then suddenly she would bolt off and if I wasn't careful I would shoot over her rear and sit watching the others gallop off with Aster in hot pursuit, stirrups flapping. She was, as is so often the case, a great training machine but I can't say I loved her very much. At the Colemans', dressed in any old thing, we would grab a bridle and some sort of saddle and off we would go. Misty would probably drop a shoulder and fling you in the nettle patch or stop dead and hurtle you over her head but she was much easier to love.

It was during these visits that I first met Johnny Scott with whom I was to make *Clarissa and the Countryman* for TV so many years later. His father Sir Walter was the local squire, chairman of the Southdown Hunt and of the Hailsham Magistrates Bench and District Chief Inspector of the Pony Club. He was a huge man of great wit and charm and a fantastic cook. A lot of parties were held in one or other of his barns and he was held in great affection by the neighbourhood. Johnny and I met at a children's party, where I was the strange girl from London who probably behaved as badly as he did. Johnny is a natural horseman who rode anything beautifully but oh, so wild. He loved his ferrets and his terriers more than anything and always had a ferret in his jersey, and consequently he smelled rather strange. For years I always thought that smell was Johnny, as I had never met anyone who kept ferrets before. He was the leader of a group of local boys who got into all sorts of scrapes and teased the girls unmercifully. Bruce Shand was hunting with the Southdown then and the only girl who could silence the boys was his daughter Camilla, now wife to the Prince of Wales, who exuded sex appeal. Johnny says she was the sexiest girl any of them had ever met. We would follow the hunt when there was a local meet, usually on foot, and get hot and excited clambering up the downs or watching the hounds in full cry along Firle ridge.

At the end of the Colemans' property was a sandpit that contained Neolithic ovens, and the archaeological group once uncovered a Saxon warrior in full war gear, preserved by the sand as he had been buried but who fell apart when the air hit him. There were also badgers in the sandpit and we would lie up in the long summer evenings to watch them playing. To me all this was scarcely believable and wonderfully happy. I once found an old diary I had when I was fifteen; at the beginning it said 'most favourite place to visit' and I had filled in Selmeston without hesitation. By then I was a girl who had been many times around the world and stayed in the finest hotels my parents could afford, but while Christine coveted my designer jeans I yearned for an old pair of landgirl britches. I tried to go there as often as I could and it must have hurt my mother that at every opportunity I was off. She was very long-suffering but when she called me home I resented it and thought she was being unreasonable. Now I can see that she was alone in the house with my father and although she had many friends of her own she loved her home, having never had one that she could remember as a child, and didn't much want to go away despite the tensions.

Of course I couldn't be in Selmeston all the time and at home things were no better. My sister Heather had reintroduced herself into our family life by appealing to our mother during one of the various periods of personal crisis Heather went through. Naturally, Mollypop responded immediately but it caused still further problems with my father. Heather lived with Jack in Green Street in Mayfair in great style. Whatever faults my sister had she never lacked style, and was always immaculately made-up, coiffured and turned out.

My father was now over sixty with retirement from the hospital looming. His beloved god-daughter Pat Rennie, child of his boyhood friend, had died horribly young of cancer leaving a small child behind. My father, obsessed with collecting for cancer research, became treasurer of the Imperial Cancer Research Fund and was out every night speaking for large fees, which he donated to the Fund. As he was still operating all day he turned even more to alcohol to keep him going. I believe that he single-handedly raised £8 million, a huge sum then, by speaking and collecting donations. His blackmailing tactics were legendary: he frequented nightclubs where rich businessmen took their mistresses and with no more pressure than a raised eyebrow would extract cheques for large sums. If the drink wasn't his friend it certainly wasn't ours either. It is difficult for me to calculate exactly how many bruises and cracked or even broken ribs I suffered at his hands. One night coming home very drunk he threw me to the floor and started kicking me and was only stopped by my mother hitting him over the head with a chestnut pan. Strangely, the violence becomes the norm but my father had a bitter tongue too. He had exercised it with great effect on the three eldest, telling Heather she was so ugly that no man would ever want her, a comment that led to behaviour intended to prove him wrong. He said the same to June when she was lying, possibly crippled, in a plaster case following a terrible car crash and what he said to Anthony caused an inferiority complex that lasted a lifetime. I felt no affection for my father, only hate, and was therefore perhaps freed from the effects of his venom.

Finally the Jack Taylor bubble burst, when my parents were in Sydney at a BMA conference. My father was vain about his publicity and had his cuttings agent send them wherever he was. A large package arrived on the hotel breakfast table, and apparently my father removed his folding scissors from his waistcoat pocket and opened it; his colleagues, seeing the size of the package, surrounded him asking what had he done now? He ripped back the paper to disclose a banner headline which read 'Queen's surgeon's son-in-law arrested at New York airport'. I don't think my father was ever able to live past that moment. Jack, long involved in various property scams and even accused of burning down a hotel he owned in Brighton, had fallen foul of the law and was sent to prison yet again. My sister Heather successfully sued the paper that falsely alleged she was involved but that was little consolation to my father.

Things deteriorated further in the family and any attempts at normality were abandoned: we no longer went on family holidays, my father was never home till late and meals were even more unpleasant. I travelled with my mother, and we went much to Spain, where one of Mollypop's best friends, Antonia Alvear, lived. She was a widow whose husband had died in the Spanish Civil War and she ran the Alvear sherry firm, and spent her time between Madrid and Seville. We had first gone to Seville for Easter when I was seven and attended all the Holy Week processions; it was an extraordinary sight with the men (including at least one of Antonia's sons) in their hooded robes carrying the giant figures of Christ, the Madonna, various tableaux and of course saints. It was Catholicism at its highest and with 'such great clouds of incense rise that even God must close his eyes'. The cathedral altar screen was all gold, brought back by the Conquistadors 500 years before. My father, who hated all such things, was particularly bad-tempered and used to goad me for being afraid of the stuffed wolf with a bloody lamb in its jaws which lurked in one of the back corridors; it had been shot by one of the family at some earlier date and indeed I was quite alarmed by it. Happily that was the last time my father ever came to Spain with us.

One of Antonia's daughters was married to a son of a famous bull breeder, the Marquis de Villamarta, and we went to *tientas* designed to test the young heifers' bravery and consequently their suitability as future mothers. The heifer was put into his private bullring and the young men would vie to play it with capes. Heifers are quite clever and feisty so a lot of the lads were tossed. Gypsy boys from the surrounding country would come to exhibit their skill in the hopes of being spotted by a bullfighting manager and so get their chance to become a matador. I loved it all and Spain became my favourite European country and remains so despite the damage wrought by the expatriate communities on the Costas del Sol and Blanca. When I was about ten we went to a tiny fishing village where the only excitement was the donkeys bringing the sand up from the beach for the foundations of the first multi-storey hotel, the Pez Espada: the village was called Torremolinos!

At home during the school holidays the three of us still sat down to breakfast and lunch together. It was always tense and sometimes savage rows would break out, usually over Heather. My only means of communication with my father was the exchange of information; he was a born teacher and we talked about everything from history to the makings of a magnesium bomb. *The Times* used to run a Historical Quiz on Saturdays and I would be grilled on it; it was a quiz for adults but no matter. There was a television game called *Junior Criss Cross Quiz*, which was a game of noughts and crosses with general knowledge questions to score points. I desperately wanted to be on it, but every time I failed to answer a question in *The Times* quiz my father would tell me I was too stupid. Strangely, I knew I wasn't stupid as I got good marks at school, and was often praised by my teachers. I just became determined to be cleverer than my father but as he was undoubtedly genius level this was always unlikely.

The other thing we talked about harmoniously was food, which perhaps explains a lot about what I have become. My father had his pigeons flown in from Cairo via the diplomatic bag because he found the squabs raised specially for the table the tenderest and juiciest. My father numbered many Persian patients among his list and so caviar was commonplace; the only type we weren't allowed to eat was the golden variety reserved for the Shah and his family, which my father kept for himself. I still love caviar but despite the price can never think of it as a luxury. St John's Wood in those days was a real village; we had two butchers and one kosher one, three greengrocers owned by a family of Sicilians called Salamone, a MacFisheries and a proper fishmonger called Mr Brown. In those days every London fishmonger had a tank of live eels and because of the Jewish community Mr Brown also sold carp and gefilte fish. There was also, unusual for those days, a large delicatessen with barrels of pickled cucumbers and herring and all sorts of mid–European sausages. I was allowed to roam down the High Street at will, plaguing the shopkeepers with questions, and when my mother thought I should come home she would ring one of them and the message was passed that I should go back. Curiously both Henrietta Green and Libbie Foster, who won the Rural Retailer of the Year award with her work at the

Sulgrave post office, grew up in St John's Wood at the same time so it was obviously a good place for foodies.

I am appalled in writing this book that I have no recollection of what became of Louise, as she was such an important part of my childhood, of all our lives and even an inhibiting influence on my father. I remember that she got appendicitis when I was first at boarding school, and I suppose she retired, but she may even have died. Certainly we never heard from her again. My mother never offered an explanation and I don't remember that I asked. An alcoholic world is so full of horrors and secrets that often the miasma in which one lives just closes round things and one doesn't ask. We now had a Spanish couple called Carlos and Isabel who my mother had obtained from an agency. He had been a *banderillo* in the team belonging to Manolete (probably the most famous bullfighter of all) until he had been gored and had to retire. Carlos was very tall and walked with a limp, and he also played the guitar rather well. Isabel had been a dancer and she sang in the Spanish fashion so at parties they would entertain us. One evening my mother saw that there was a production of *Carmen* on the television and thinking they would enjoy it told them to watch it. We were aroused a little later by screams from the servants' sitting room and rushed down to find Isabel pursuing Carlos with a carving knife; apparently he had once skulked off with a gypsy girl and the opera had reminded Isabel.

When I was thirteen my father drove me down to school; this was unusual as, apart from coming to parents' day and being nice to the richer parents and Mother Bartells who had been something brilliant in the medical profession before she entered the order, he pretty well avoided anything to do with my school. However on this occasion he wanted to talk to me about my future plans. My father had long intended that I should be the one to go into the medical profession. He had rather brutally dissuaded my brother, but we were after all a medical family and all my cousins had taken it up. This was, I suspect, the reason for my constant visits to the hospital and even the occasional visits to his consulting rooms, to acclimatise and familiarise me with things medical. He began the conversation by talking about O-levels, the GCSE of the day, and asking me if I had thought of what subjects I would take. It was important, he said, to choose carefully to further my preparations for a medical career. I was happy to tell him that I was not about to select medicine but had decided to become a barrister.

My father was furious and nearly crashed the car. I knew that he hated lawyers and that he regularly chose to give evidence in negligence or even murder cases so that he could pit his wits against Sir Bernard Spilsbury, the pathologist, and against the great barristers of the day. What at that time I didn't know and not for many years to come was that he hated them because it was the career he had wanted but he had been pushed into medicine by his mother following his father's death. We had a heated argument all the way to school but I remained steadfast, knowing how much my choice would anger him and this in itself made me happy. I had another reason to want to study law: I felt it was my duty to protect my mother as best I could and it seemed to me that with legal weapons at my disposal I might find a way to halt his violence and abuse of her. I suspected, although she wouldn't tell me when I asked, that his behaviour continued when I was at school. After all, why would it stop? And there were unexplained bruises when she visited me. I foresaw a world when I wouldn't be around as much as I was and was desperate to find a solution. There were no lawyers in my family and I had never met a barrister; my friends Dippy and Carrots both had fathers who were solicitors and I was fond of both of them, but a barrister I was determined to be. My father's parting shot was that I would get no help from him, but as I hadn't expected any that didn't worry me.

School continued apace. I took my O-levels, eight in all, and got Honours in most and distinctions in the rest apart from my science, which was chemistry, where I merely passed; no danger then of medical advances! Our headmistress at the time was a Mother Joan Faber, a cold, curious woman prone to favourites of which I was not one. She was fascinated by the science of psychoanalysis and would spend happy hours grilling those of us who seemed out of sync. She was intrigued by the fact that unlike the rest of the school I clearly preferred school to holidays. Eventually I gave in to the pressure and told her that my father drank and beat my mother and myself. She reacted with horror, telling me I was a wicked, lying child to speak so ill of such a wonderful, good and famous man (remember that was how the world saw my father). I was dismissed from her office and she sat down and wrote to my father recounting my accusations; as you can imagine that ended in tears, blows and kicks. It took me many years to forgive her and many more ever to trust anyone again.

One of my problems was that I usually had access to information that others didn't. I listened at dinner parties at home to what was discussed and Heather was also a great source of London information. I distressed my classmates by informing them that the much adored Dirk Bogarde was gay, or that Elvis was addicted to prescribed drugs and deep-fried hamburgers. I clashed with the nuns when I refused to go to chapel to pray for Jack Kennedy's soul because I knew then what we all know now about his sexual mores and refused to hail him as a saint. To Mother Faber he was a Catholic President and therefore a good thing and she practically slapped me. It doesn't go down well when a teenager has too much information; come to think of it that one doesn't go away.

As I began my A-level course we acquired a new English teacher, Mother April O'Leary, who was also Mistress of Studies. April was to be one of the great influences in my life and remains a dear friend to this day. She was a marvellous teacher, reading the comic parts in Shakespeare in a Warwickshire accent and bringing Chaucer and Milton alive. Christine and I would often go and pester her for chores in her office just for the pleasure of listening to her and she would get us to sort the string box or some other such task and we would sit and discuss literature for hours. Her faith has always been total but without any attempt to ram it down one's throat and I do believe that the reason I kept my faith in God is largely due to her. Mollypop had her own version: the God of old Mother Aethelraeda had remained her friend and her faith was that of the child whose place was the kingdom of heaven. 'It is not for you, Clarissa, to define the parameters of what God can and cannot do,' she would tell me sternly as she walked away leaving her car parked on a double yellow line and I would suffer agonies during lunch watching parking wardens walking past the window of the restaurant, only to emerge to find an unticketed car. 'Leave it to God,' she would remark as we stood in a suburban street looking for a taxi at 2 a.m. and, lo, out of the murk would emerge the glowing yellow light of the cab. I would point out that God had better things to do and she would just open her eyes and say that as God was omnipotent one shouldn't try to limit him.

Mollypop's eyes were one of her finest weapons; the most learned scientist would fall at her feet and tell her at length theories she couldn't possibly understand just for the joy of talking to her. She remained faithful to my dreadful father all the days of her life but there were many men who fell in love with her and would have carried her off on a white stallion. She exuded happiness and good humour even in the darkest days of my father's abuse and I believe this was because she always had her friend beside her. My sister Heather compared her to Lucille Ball in *I Love Lucy* and it was a good comparison but below the daffy behaviour ran a much stronger soul. My father in one of the rare conversations of our life once said to me that my mother was the strongest woman he had ever met and he looked perplexed as he said it.

For fun, Christine, Carrots, Annette and I let chickens into the school on the last day of that summer term. They were supposed to remain quiet till morning, but of course someone trod on one and they all took off like firecrackers; the nuns had no doubt who the culprits were. We were shut into separate piano cells and made to write lines by way of punishment, but had to be let out for prize-giving later in the day as we had scooped most of the prizes between us. Despite this I was made captain of games, majoring in lacrosse, cricket and tennis. Christine and I were made next in merits, a sort of deputy prefect, but we never made it to the blue ribbon of a full prefect; it was not an honour either of us wanted and in my case I had enough responsibility at home with my self-appointed role of protecting my mother that I wanted none of it elsewhere.

A-levels came and I took History, English and Latin. The first two were fine but we had a new Latin teacher. For O-level we had had a remarkable Prussian nun called Mother Peirquet who had coaxed and bullied me through both Latin and Ancient Greek; she was a sensational vegetable gardener and would have us declining irregular Latin verbs as we weeded or helped her with her hot beds. When I passed she declared there must be some mistake and when it proved to be true she recited the Nunc Dimittis. Now, sadly, in the second year we were given a Mrs Knox, wife of a teacher at Lancing and preoccupiedly pregnant with her first child. Whether she would have been a good teacher I cannot tell but she wasn't that year. We loved going off to her house in Lancing on the train but in the event I only got a C in Latin and that wasn't good enough. Hove was due to close, and there was no sixth form the following year so off I was sent to Woldingham for two terms to resit. I was in a sort of limbo land. I had no friends there, but I had a car, the use of a horse, the Old Surrey and Burstow met on the school lawn and hunted in the area and we were allowed to follow. Woldingham owns 350 acres of prime hunting country. Mother Shanley innocently enquired why I hadn't gone to her school when the extremely expensive theatre lights which were among my mother's gifts to Hove were shipped to Woldingham and I was pleased to tell her. She had recently been quoted in the press as saying, 'My girls are being brought up to marry diplomats and bankers,' so after I smoked a pipe in the refectory I think she was glad I hadn't. I had learned to smoke a pipe while playing Ernest in a school production of April O'Leary's of *The Importance of Being Earnest* and as a result had found my first addiction in nicotine. I passed the last hurdle with an A and was finally out in the world at the age of eighteen. It was 1964, great social changes were taking place and I was young, single and free except for the handicap of home.

4

The lure of the Law

My father refused to pay for me to go away to university unless I agreed to study medicine, which I was neither qualified for nor desirous of doing. I could have gone to Oxford, although I wanted to go to Trinity Dublin with Christine. However with no money available or parental permission for me to go away and no grant forthcoming due to my family's wealth what I did was stay at home, study for the Bar at the Inns of Court and do an external Law degree at UCL. I had to find my own way into the Inns of Court as my father adamantly refused to help. Fortunately some friends of my grandmother's knew the librarian at the House of Lords, a woman called Pat Malley, who was friends with the Under-Treasurer (the CEO) at Gray's Inn, which accepted me. There are four Inns of Court which conduct the admission, education and regulating of barristers. In my day the rhyme ran: 'Inner for the rich man, Middle for the poor, Gray's for the gentleman and Lincoln's for the bore.' The last referred to the fact that Lincoln's Inn was the Chancery Inn and lawyers dealing with wills, trusts and probates were deemed to be dry as dust. Inner was the smallest of the Inns and most often joined as a second Inn by those already prospering at the Bar, while Middle had almost all the African students and one English student is reputed to have greeted another with 'Dr Livingstone, I presume.' It was the latter days of the Empire and the heyday of the Commonwealth and the Africans were a colourful crowd, many of them wearing their national costumes. Gray's had the Celtic fringe, with a great many Welsh students, some Northern Irish and a few Scots looking for a double qualification; it also had the most money as with fewer barrister's chambers within the Inn it had more commercial rents.

Middle Temple boasted a dining hall where Shakespeare had performed his plays and Lincoln's Inn's Hall had once been where the Lord Chancellor sat, but the Gray's Inn Hall had been bombed and rebuilt. Its greatest time had been the Elizabethan period and the minstrels gallery was the screen from the poop deck of a captured Spanish Armada galleon; portraits of Bacon, Cecils and Francis Walsingham hung round the walls and in the walks sprawled the catalpa trees brought back by Raleigh from the first Virginia settlement. It was in those walks that Francis Bacon developed the pneumonia that killed him while stuffing a chicken with snow to see if that would preserve it. Francis's statue stood in the centre of the Inn and we did unspeakable things to it in moments of revelry, with traffic cones, mummifying bandages – all very harmless really. The governing body of the Inn were known as the benchers and consisted of High Court judges and leading Queen's Counsel. A foreign student on being asked in a company law exam, 'What are debentures?' replied, 'De benchers are de governing body of the Inn.' But the real benchers were a powerful lot who at the High Table with their guests provided a cross-section of the governing establishments of England and indeed the Commonwealth.

One of the historical duties of the Inns had been to feed their students and every Bar student had to eat thirty-six dinners at no more than three a term before they could be admitted as a fully qualified barrister. You could dine every night if you wanted but only three of them counted towards call. Part of the aim of dining was to encourage young aspirant lawyers to think on their feet and on Monday and Wednesday nights moots (mock trials argued on points of law) and debates followed dinner presided over by a bencher or some senior lawyer. The standard was high as we were performing before those on whom our future careers rested. Teams went forward to the Observer Mace contests in both disciplines and I did well in both. On other nights a system of fines could be claimed for alleged breaches of the rules of dining judged by the senior barrister in Hall who would award a subsidised decanter of port to the cleverest claimant. For instance, one evening a friend charged another with being in breach of a statute of Oliver Cromwell because he'd been seen to eat Christmas pudding in public, which is still of course an illegal act. The defendant had to pay for the port. Other Inns didn't really participate in their fines nights but we loved them, and I have no doubt they were good practice for quickness of advocacy later. They also encouraged drinking but in a more organised form than I have seen in student communities since. Today dining nights are very subdued and students are given speaking lessons. All very proper but it sounds rather dull to me.

Of course things occasionally got out of hand: the night when some students in the gallery captured a female student and carried her away to their table as a trophy, and the evening (known since as the riot) ended with everyone conga-ing round the Hall on the tables to the sound of smashing glass. In those days you didn't need a law degree to study for the Bar so that there was a constant influx of people of different ages who had left one career to become barristers and young men with estates to inherit who merely wished to learn some law. Only about 2 per cent of people called ever intended to practise in the UK, with the foreign students returning to their own countries and many students using it as a training ground for City companies.

The England of the sixties was a peaceful and prosperous land. Trains ran on time and cheaply to every tiny village, there were friendly policemen on the beat, very few cars on the road and of course no supermarkets. There were still street markets selling fruit and vegetables and butchers and fishmongers. The National Health Service was still a young bright hope although my father had attacked it since its infancy saying it would drown in bureaucracy and freeloading; it only took forty years for him to be proved right. Lest you think I am being nostalgic there were also maintenance grants for those who qualified to go to university and no tuition fees; true, fewer people went but there were polytechnics to gain a technical degree and apprenticeships to learn a trade. There was a lot more law and order, the system, love it or hate it, worked and my generation was about to blow it apart. Take for instance the unions. I approve of unions and twice in my life I have been a union official but in the sixties they threw the baby out with the bathwater. The great London dock strike was a case in point. London had been a powerful port since Roman times; my father had a retainer from the Port of London Authority and would take me down to see the ships unloading or to visit the Chinese quarter or the colourful Jewish/cockney street market of Petticoat Lane. In the sixties the dockers struck and locked the tidal gates of the docks, so that ships couldn't move, the cargoes rotted, and rats ran everywhere. I remember going round the area in the PLA boat and witnessing this. Some years ago I heard Barbara Castle and the other high heid yins, or important people, of 1960s Labour on some radio programme admitting they were wrong, that the strike had been a mistake. It was one that destroyed a whole way of life and thousands of jobs, for few shipping lines were anxious to dock in London again and now the port is gone. The Red Clyde destroyed the Scottish shipping industry and I think that is one of the many reasons why I have never been tempted by socialism.

They say that if you can remember the sixties you weren't there, but that's not strictly true: to qualify you either had to be rich, musically talented or a gangster; universal sex, drugs and rock and roll didn't start to kick in till the seventies. One of the great class dividers had been clothes, and you could tell where people ran in the pecking order by their clothes and their shoes, not just rich or poor but new money or old. With the fashion changes of the sixties all this changed: if you could afford to buy Mary Quant or shop in Carnaby Street you belonged anywhere. The other great divide was the smell: the poor smelled musty, corduroy smelled of the dog shit it was dyed with when it rained. Old ladies smelled of lavender water and ill-washed clothes; fashionable women like Mollypop or Heather wafted clouds of scent and men still smelled like men with an exotic dash of bay rum or Trumpers West Indian Limes if you were lucky.

Young men preened in awful frilled shirts and bell-bottomed hipster jeans and we girls wore mini skirts, pussy pelmets as they were known, hot pants, thigh boots – all very sexy if you had good legs. Happily I was lucky in that department. We also did dreadful things to our hair. I had a beehive which entailed going to the hairdresser on Saturday to have it put up, two more visits during the week just for back-combing and adjustment and more Elnett Satin spray and finally on Saturday you had it taken down and put up again. Young men of the sixties were not encouraged to run their fingers through your hair unless your hairstyle was the other alternative: long, sleek and preferably black. I still feel deprived nowadays when I come out of the hairdresser with no back-combing and without gallons of spray. Everyone strived for an unusual look. Johnny Scott sported an Afro with a kaftan or afghan jacket and had to borrow hairnets to keep his hair under his bowler when out hunting. Christine made a fantastic Doctor Zhivago coat from an old school one complete with a fur edging. Carrots thrived in the flowing florals of Laura Ashley and I raided my mother's wardrobe for some of her wonderful 1930s clothes. Why did I do this instead of rushing off to the King's Road?

Well, the truth of it was that Mollypop and I had no money. My father paid all the bills but never handed out cash. Mollypop had an allowance from her mother, a generous one at that, but if for some reason or another it stopped – the war, currency dramas, etc. – there was no spending money. My mother had been known to borrow half a crown off the cook to go to the cinema. The new shops of the sixties didn't give credit like the old fashion houses so I was stymied. Why had the money stopped now? Well, in 1964 my mother had gone out to Singapore to see her mother who had decided to return to England with her for a visit, much against my uncle's wishes. Vivien had a firm grasp on my grandmother's estate and he didn't wish to loosen it. My mother's allowance stopped and Vivien made great efforts to get my grandmother back, and telegrams flew back and forth over the Bay of Pigs crisis suggesting it was unsafe for her to stay in Britain and my grandmother found herself unable to draw on her own accounts. Grandma's presence at home at least ameliorated my father's violent outbursts but he retaliated with financial sanctions. Every week my mother put out an accounts book listing expenditure for the servants' wages, sundries for me (everything from sanitary towels to bus fares), and my father would leave cash in the book. It was humiliating for my mother as it was meant to be. With no money to buy clothes in an age when fashion was king I managed quite well in my mother's racing silks and thirty-year-old haute couture. It became apparent that Vivien had been sidelining my grandmother's money and a trip to the Hong Kong and Shanghai Bank restored funds but by then I had established my own style and was reluctant to change my look or admit earlier poverty.

Shortly after this my grandmother suffered a fall and broke her hip. The shock of this rendered her non compos mentis and she was installed in the old nursery quarters looked after by a nursing nun and a professional day nurse with another nursing nun at night. As Mollypop and Vivien were in dispute she was placed under the Court of Protection who administered her affairs. Funds stopped again, and now we had the ludicrous situation of a large house with servants and every luxury for the table, my grandmother in exceptional comfort paid for by the Protection trustees and my mother and I in the middle in a gilded cage with no money. The wheel turned again after a couple of years and the sale of the Goodwood Park Hotel in Singapore brought in a large sum of money for my mother. This coincided with Heather's divorce from Jack Taylor and my mother was very generous in trying to help Heather re-establish her life. She bought her a house near Bray and paid for her to take up hunting in a fine way and to show working hunters. To be fair to Heather this indulging assuaged Mollypop's feelings of guilt and failure over the rearing of her eldest child and gave her a lot of pleasure besides. Always a lover of the horse world, Mollypop delighted in Heather's renaissance. Mollypop had always ridden and hunted side-saddle and Heather now decided she wanted to learn that discipline; she was in her late thirties by now and very diminutive and the horses she wanted to ride were too large for her to straddle. Off she went to Cybil Smith, who had taught the Queen to ride side-saddle, to learn the skill, with my mother happy to offer advice. I often think that if Heather hadn't been so driven by my father's horrible treatment of her she could have married a well-to-do hunting squire and been quite happy with her life; she liked children. The showing world was much as it is today, full of genuine kindnesses, petulant resentments and energetic sexual encounters in the back of horseboxes. This was the time of the fiery young Harvey Smith shocking everyone with his televised V sign, of Annalie Drummond-Hay with her great horse Merely A Monarch who always walked the course carrying her handbag, of Pat Smythe and so many other famous names. I was Heather's little sister in this world and neither of us much liked that fact and I was glad to escape back to the Inn of Court.

I attended lectures and classes at the university, the Inn of Court School of Law and the privately run College of Law. We had some strange lecturers, such as Mr Bulloch who taught us Tort and was a renowned Egyptologist. One day he called me aside and asked if I could persuade my father to let him have a human head for embalming purposes, as they wanted to try a newly discovered technique. Naturally I never asked my father and was somewhat taken aback by a newspaper headline some weeks later which read: 'Human Torso Found in Thames'! Nothing to do with Mr Bulloch, I'm sure. Mr Treleaven taught us Criminal Law and was a Druid; he gave me his recipe for Cornish pasties and I have used it ever since. There was Commander Padley who taught Roman and Divorce Law, and had been abandoned by his wife after having gone down with his ship in the Arctic convoys and lost most of the use of his legs; consequently he was a great misogynist. On one occasion he remarked, 'Miss Champion, if you were married to Mr Murphy and he left you for a gorilla on what grounds would you divorce him?' No answer came. 'Bestiality, Miss Champion, bestiality!' Debbie, who was rather a stunning girl, replied, 'But Commander Padley, wouldn't it be insanity?' at which even he had to laugh.

It is strange looking back to see how far the cause of women's equality in the legal profession has advanced in forty years. There were few women students and even fewer practising female barristers in the sixties. Our incursions into the profession were looked at with derision by the old guard and only the brilliant career of Dame Rose Heilbron, aided admittedly by the war which gave her previously unlooked-for opportunities, had given us any street cred at all. It was regarded as a valid reason not to grant a woman a tenancy that there were insufficient lavatories; it was still expected that women would settle down, keep house and raise a family and once that happened they seldom worked as well. I had no intention of marrying or having children. Nothing in my upbringing had led me to believe marriage was to be sought after or brought happiness and I think I instinctively knew I would make a lousy parent. When I was twelve I had made a sealed bet with Christine that if I was unmarried and childless at thirty she would owe me £10 and it was one bet I knew I would collect. Having made this decision I had no option but to go for a successful career and moreover I was well equipped to endure hostile behaviour. I was a firm believer in the adage, sticks and stones may break my bones but words will never harm me, and I was very ambitious, mainly to show my father. Hate is a great driver.

My life has covered the growth of rights movements, women, black people, gays all marching for their right to be included equally in society and the civilised world has seen huge changes for all these groups. As students we sat in and protested for a right to be heard on our courses and our examination procedures, but it was sometimes counter-productive. The African students were convinced that they were being discriminated against when their names appeared on exam papers and in answer to their protests the Council of Legal Education allocated all of us numbers to put on our papers. The celebrations were short-lived, as at the next set of exams most of the Africans failed. The examiners had previously been told to go easy on their grammar and non-factual mistakes, acknowledging the lower level of education in their countries! It was the time of the American war in Vietnam and we felt as strongly against it as I and so many others do against the war in Iraq; that is curious looking back as Britain was not involved. We not only marched but picketed the American Embassy in Grosvenor Square which led to quite dramatic clashes with the police on guard duty there. One law student who was also a policeman quit the force in horror at their behaviour at these protests. I was not however much involved in politics during my university days; the committees I was elected to were the debating and mooting ones and my love of rugby continued so I became Fixtures Secretary for the Gray's Inn Rugby Club.

Nor was I either a fan or a member of the feminist movement. Perhaps because to be fair to my father he was a man who approved of and understood education for women and so whatever blows we suffered at home were distributed regardless of sex. I have never really believed, nor indeed found any reason to, in the great sisterhood of women. I tend to regard people as people rather than put them in boxes of sex, sexuality, age or any other categories. Also just as it was the First World War rather than the suffragette movement that brought votes for women I believe that history has its own relentless pressure that brings about its changes. The feminist movement within the Bar was largely driven by those with political ambitions and I doubt wrought many changes. Helena (Baroness) Kennedy was one of its movers and shakers and a good friend of mine back then. In fact when I passed my Bar Finals it was Helena who rang me from the public phone in Gray's to tell me I had passed and to come down and join the party.

There was at that time an annual event called the Smoking Concert which was held in Hall under the auspices of Mr Justice Mars-Jones; this was a male-only event which was generally regarded as an occasion for free drink brought about by Mars-Bars' (as he was nicknamed) desire to play the guitar in public. There had been various attempts to infiltrate it: one girl hid under the tables but was soon discovered; and Nemine Lethbridge, a young barrister of some note who ruined her career by marrying one of her criminal clients, tried to attend dressed as a lion. Several of my male friends bet me I couldn't successfully attend. So off I went to Moss Bros and hired a suit, much to the horror of the very camp fitter who had to measure me and actually asked me on which side I dressed! Then on to Berman's and Nathan's to hire a wig and glasses. I borrowed a more masculine pipe and I was set. Only one friend was in the know, as someone had to buy me a ticket. I pulled it off without discovery. I have to report it was a very dull evening with much singing of songs such as 'There's a Hole in my Bucket' which was reminiscent of school outings, and while Mars-Bars had a beautiful Welsh voice it was not one that lent itself to the guitar or indeed to modern popular music. At the end I stood up, took off my wig and thanked everyone for a pleasant evening. A great roar went up and the rugby boys picked me up and carried me round the Hall to much cheering. Only when it quietened could Mars-Jones be heard ordering me to leave Hall. It was of course his duty to do so and he made no trouble for me after. In Helena's book she wrote that it was me who attended in a lion skin and that I was verbally abused and pilloried from the Hall. When I challenged her on this, we fell out rather badly over the way she represented the incident.

There were a number of the present Cabinet around, Tony Blair for one, although we called him Miranda in those days, and nobody ever thought how powerful he would become. He was regarded as a poor sad thing with his guitar and his rather girlish looks, and was also considered as something of a fantasist; his story about attempting to stow away on a plane to the Caribbean from Edinburgh was a source of great amusement as there were no transatlantic flights from Scotland back then. The boys I knew who had been at Fettes with him didn't have many good words to say about him. Much more impressive was Jack Straw, who we would have picked as a man destined for the top. I always rather liked him; despite his inflamed oratory and his passionate communism there was something rather honest and even kind about him, although with hindsight perhaps he wasn't ruthless or dishonest enough for the top. Peter Hain, even before he dug up the wicket at the Oval, was much disliked. He smelled of naked ambition without, as far as we could see, the talent to match and with an enormously high opinion of himself. Then of course there was Cherie, clever, hungry for success, for love, desperately needy, the product of another dysfunctional home. In those days she was very close with her head of chambers, Derry Irvine. I could tell you many stories about contemporaries but the witnesses are for the most part dead or on the High Court Bench so I'll leave it for another volume.

I enjoyed my student days. We were a lively lot full of ideas to change the world as students always are, it was the sixties and although we weren't into drugs as we had to keep our noses clean if we aspired to the Bench there was plenty of drink; it was the new sexual revolution so there was a lot of that too, although despite the safety of the pill it wasn't as wild as it was to become in the seventies. Of course that wasn't true of everyone: next door to us lived Linda and Paul McCartney, who had built a glass-domed building at the bottom of the garden ostensibly to watch the night sky. I could see into it from my bedroom balcony and through the waves of what smelled like marijuana smoke could see the languorous intertwining of bodies that symbolises the sixties!

Out of the blue my father decided he was not going to pay for my fees; although he had refused to help me with any introductions or in any other way, once I was accepted by Gray's Inn, up till now, he had paid up. My mother offered to hock her jewellery, but I had a better idea. There was a splendid woman called Edna Katz who owned a designer shoe shop in Baker Street called Les Jumelles; my mother bought lots of shoes from her but she was also a friend and lived in a mansion block nearby. She and her husband had no children and were very fond of me, so I went to her and asked if she would lend me the money for my fees. She was shocked at my father's behaviour and readily wrote the cheque, assuring me she would tell no one. I told her she had misunderstood and that I wanted her to tell the whole Jewish community. My father had many Jewish patients and the Jews are very keen on education for their children and would admonish him for his action. Grasping the point, she did so with gusto and within a fortnight my father had paid her back the entire amount.

In 1966 my grandmother died peacefully in her sleep at Circus Road and the Court of Protection was proved to have done a good and thoroughly professional job. They had sold up in Singapore at the top of the market and moved everything to Australia where things were booming. Having abandoned Singapore and no longer having a residence there and not having the mental ability to chose an English domicile she had reverted to her Australian one which was far and away the best for death duty purposes. There was a case in the Privy Council, British and Malayan Trustees v Manasseh, which established that Grandma owed no inheritance tax anywhere but Australia and the flow of money was restored. Sadly so was the combat zone. My father made up for all that lost time: he had had to control his drunken rages with nurses always in the house but now he went back to his beatings and bullying with a vengeance.

In 1968 I was twenty-one, and in April of that year my father sat down with me and said he supposed I would like a twenty-first birthday party. I was, as you may imagine, somewhat amazed. He was very gracious and said I could have as many people as I liked. I suggested a hundred and he said that was fine and I was to go ahead and tell my mother to arrange everything. I smelled a rat and told Mollypop to tell me what to order but on no account was she to speak to any suppliers or to sign for anything but leave all that to me. It was a great party, we had a discotheque out on the loggia with coloured smoke, delicious food laid out in the dining room and endless champagne. Friends and relatives of all ages came, bringing lovely presents and the only thing that marred the evening was my father's speech where he said he didn't know how he was going to pay for it and would have to stick his knife in a few more Jews. We danced the night away and saw the sun come up and breakfasted on kedgeree. Miss Fox, a wonderful old woman who had been a ladies maid from 1912 and had seen society at its highest level and now came in to our house to answer the telephone when the servants were out, had refused to be a guest but had a lovely time looking after the coats and attending to the needs of the women guests; she sniffed and said in her mistress's day we would have gone on to Skindles at Maidenhead for breakfast and that the young had no stamina. But it was a great night.

The next day at lunchtime I found my father in the library poking a fire although it was June; he did love his fires. I thanked him profusely, still glowing with the excitement of it all and perhaps foolishly thinking he had turned over a new leaf. 'Don't thank me, thank your mother; she ordered everything so she can pay for it.' 'Oh no, Daddy,' I replied, 'I did all the ordering and organising.' 'You pay for it then,' he snarled. It was a moment of triumph. 'No, Daddy, I'm not twenty-one till Wednesday!' At that time one was not responsible for debts incurred before the age of twenty-one, a fact my father was clearly unaware of. He pulled back the hot poker and struck me across the jaw with it, and I fled. I had a horrid burn along my jaw line and he must have chipped the bone, for it would flare up for years after. Even now my only reaction to this horrid event is, well, it was a great party and the bastard paid!

This however proved to be the beginning of the end. I was taking my Bar finals and was up to my eyes in work, sitting in my room smoking heavily to block out the world. One morning my parents and I were seated in the gallery for breakfast, which was at eight o'clock every morning and woe betide me if I was late. We were never allowed to touch my father's jug of fresh orange juice as it was laced with vodka and he would sit there looking at his list of private patients and working out the day's operations on the butter pat; when he had done he would stab the knife into it and leave. On this morning my mother was opening her post when she gave a gasp, dropped her coffee cup, clasped a hand to her heart and left the room. My father kept on eating his breakfast. I followed my mother and found her in the library looking shaken;

she handed me the letter. It was from a firm of solicitors telling her that her husband was filing divorce proceedings and would she please vacate the house in seven days. At this point my parents were still sleeping together in a fairly small double bed. Such is the secrecy that exists in an alcoholic household that there was no discussion or even mention of the letter between my parents. There is always the feeling that if you hold your breath, keep quiet and do nothing the situation will go away. My mother, against my advice, ignored the letter and things continued as normal for several weeks. Finally a second letter came asking her why she had not left the matrimonial home. Eric Parker, Dippy's father, advised her to go to Charles Russell and Co. and letters were exchanged.

Clearly my father's solicitors told him to move out of the marital bed because one night he came home only fairly drunk and announced he was moving to the nursery, the suite where my grandmother had been. My father wasn't really very sane at this point I think; he had driven himself burning the candle at all three ends, working all hours with medicine and his speaking engagements, drinking heavily and I don't know what else. In his bathroom cabinet stood a bottle of LSD, which people erroneously took for depression in those days. I once glanced out of my bedroom window and saw him look over his shoulder with a terrified expression and start running as if the hounds of hell were after him; he slipped and nearly fell but kept on running until he was out of my line of sight. On the night my father moved out of their bedroom, the bed in the nursery was not made up and my mother begged me to take up some sheets and pillows. I demurred, saying I didn't care if he slept on the floor but she persuaded me. When I went into the room my father was lying on the bed with no covers over him. I said I had brought him some bedding and he went berserk; he leapt up, grabbed me and tried to smash my head against the marble mantelpiece. For the first time I was really afraid of him: he looked so mad and I knew this time he wanted to kill me. I raised my knee to his groin, but ineffectively, and then my mother ran in and shoved a chair under his knees. He fell back, letting go of me, and my mother grabbed me; we fled and locked ourselves in but he didn't pursue us.

The next few weeks were very strange: my father slept in the nursery and I slept with my mother behind a locked door, like two scared children. We would hear him creeping around the house and in the morning objects such as the Epstein bust of Bernard Shaw or the gold coin collection Philip Harben had left him would be missing. One night he cleared out the whole wine cellar, a Herculean task; we would watch him out of the window going backwards and forwards across the lawn to his car. Another night my mother woke me to say that he was taking the pictures she had inherited from her father, the only things she had of him. We went downstairs in our dressing gowns; the front gate stood open with the car outside, its back door open; inside I could see some of the pictures but no sign of my father. I went over and started unloading the pictures as fast as I could. Suddenly I felt a heavy blow to my ribs, turned and there was my father grasping the umbrella with which he had hit me and broken two of my ribs. My mother came rushing out and grabbed the umbrella before he could hit me again and he punched her in the face. What might have happened then I don't know but a passing motorist stopped, said he had seen what had happened and ordered my father to go. He gave us his card as a witness and left. My mother and I hauled the pictures back into the house and spent the rest of the darkness huddled together. In the morning we called a doctor to make a report of our injuries. That was the last I ever saw of my father. He moved to his brother Douglas's house where he stayed with Douglas and Olive, living in their spare room for the next few years.

Looking back, I wonder how we or the thousands of others in similar circumstances endure it. The first sanctuary for battered wives was started at Fontevraud Abbey by Eleanor of Aquitaine in the twelfth century and she was condemned by the Catholic Church for her actions. Erin Pizzey was driven out of Britain by the feminists because she dared to say that women were often the arbiters of their own suffering by going back to abusive situations. Having lived in such a situation I can see the madness that one becomes caught up in and my only advice is go, run, sort out the pieces later. Go at the first incidence of violence and don't look back. I don't think that my poor mother could have left, with no help or support to turn to but she was something of an exception with her family miles away and the war intervening. Things are different now: there are places and people in authority to turn to. I know it is hard to overcome the co-dependency and the shame that the battered wife thinks belong to her, but go. You can't heal the drunk but you can heal yourself, and please go to Al-Anon, the partner fellowship to Alcoholics Anonymous for those who are affected by others' drinking. My parents never got divorced; the pleadings sat on the file, and there were various maintenance orders which my father never paid.

Looking back over the years living with my father it is easier to see the progression of his illness; although he had struck all of us over the years there had been times when he would sit down for meals and talk about history, rugby or cricket in a rational way. We never talked about feelings or emotions or even really about plans and hopes for the future. It was an uneasy atmosphere. As my father got older and the others left home he would come home drunk more often. By the time I was thirteen or fourteen he was never at home for dinner and we would look to see where he was speaking; if it was a Variety Club dinner or some such theatrical charity the odds were that he would come back very drunk and abusive, but less likely if it was the Mansion House or a medical event. After his retirement from the hospital in 1962 there was a huge upsurge of violence. From then onwards my mother and I, then aged fifteen, were bashed about on a weekly basis, sometimes just bruises, sometimes broken or cracked ribs, and always verbal abuse when he came home. Living in the gyre one didn't really see its onward march but by the time my father left home at the age of seventy-one he was far from rational. I felt a huge sense of relief when my father had gone; it was as if a gale had stopped blowing or a great black cloud had passed over. My mother felt a failure as a wife and lover but even she came to terms with the fact that life was so much lighter.

5

Happy days

The years that followed my father's departure were happy ones. My grandmother's death had freed up money for my mother and Anthony had come back into our lives, having finally left his first wife Angela, driven out by her excessive drinking and its accompanying behaviour. He had run away with Marah, the wife of Angela's first cousin. Shortly after this, in 1971, he suffered his first heart attack and Marah rang my mother telling her if she wanted to see her son alive she had better hotfoot it to the King Edward VII Hospital at Midhurst. Off we went, to find Ant was in intensive care, which didn't deter my mother, who simply sent for Matron and soon we were standing by Ant's bed. He lay there surrounded by drips and beeping machines and looked surprised to see us after so many years. It had been thirteen years since we had last seen each other. Mollypop looked down at him and pronounced, 'Anthony, we don't have heart attacks in our family, what you have is a bad attack of wind. I shall expect you for dinner at Circus Road in, shall we say, three weeks and bring that nice young woman. I only hope you've got it right this time.' With this she swept out. I looked at Ant who raised an eyebrow and we both smiled. 'Three weeks it is then,' I said and followed Ma out. It was nearer six weeks but he came.

I passed my Bar exams at twenty-one and was called as the

youngest female barrister at that date. At Call night in Gray's Inn the men all wear white tie. I have always thought this the most formal of evening dress and it was remarkable to see how even the toughest of rugby forwards looked beautiful in such attire. I believe I still remain the youngest woman called to the Bar. I also passed my degree and was successful in various debating contests. My favourite motion remains the Observer Mace one: 'This House wishes the Plymouth rock had landed on the Pilgrim Fathers!' I had various boyfriends and there was dearest David. I think his father and my mother hoped we would marry but it was not what either of us wanted, though we spent many happy hours going to auction sales at Battle in Sussex to buy silver, cashing in on the silver boom of the seventies, and buying wine in anticipation of the claret boom or simply wandering around London at night after many splendid dinners smelling the roses. Every barrister on qualifying has to spend a year in pupilage; for the first six months one is not allowed a right of audience in court but spends the time following one's pupil master learning the ropes on no pay. I found a pupilage thanks to the auspices of another member of Gray's Inn who sent me to see Neil Taylor, the head of Chambers at 2 Dr Johnson's Buildings; it was a general Common Law chambers but Neil was one of the leading divorce barristers of the day. He was about six foot five in height, the tallest man ever to win the Diamond Sculls at Henley and had trouble with his back as a consequence.

One of the questions a barrister is most frequently asked is how do you defend someone if you know they are guilty, and the answer is you don't. The only possible way you can actually know someone is guilty is either if you were there, in which case you would be a witness and disqualified from appearing, or if they told you, in which case you would have to advise them to plead guilty or refuse to appear for them. If there is an issue of law you can run a not guilty plea until the end of the prosecution's case and argue the law or make a submission on the law or the lack of evidence; what you cannot do is appear for them knowing they are lying. You can think what you like of them and their evidence but that is your opinion and not fact or knowledge. A barrister is not meant to refuse a case but if you really feel strongly there are ways out; after all, what client wants a lawyer who is clearly not on their side? Barristers do not earn wages but are paid a fee for each case by their instructing solicitor. If you look at the back of a barrister's gown you will see what looks like a small sack; in times past the solicitor would drop coins into it as the case progressed, thus ensuring his continued performance. Barristers and solicitors do not discuss money: that is all handled by the barrister's clerk, a powerful person in chambers who advises solicitors which of the young barristers he should instruct and in my day took 10 per cent of your fees. A good clerk was vital to the success of chambers and could make or break an up-and-coming practitioner.

I had been working during my studies for the first free legal advice centre in the country at the church in Upper Street in Islington. It was the brainchild of Bob Marshall Andrews, now an MP, and Andrew and Doris Urquhart and celebrated its thirtieth anniversary a little while ago. Islington at that time was still a poor area but was beginning to be invaded by the professional classes. Robert Carrier had just opened his first restaurant in Camden Passage and the antiques shops there were becoming more upmarket, but there were still a lot of clients for the centre. At the time of my call Doris was expecting her first child and had decided to give up practising so she sold me her wig which was excellent as it was an old one with a good colour; new white wigs showed you up as starting practice and old horse-hair ones, which were far more comfortable, were much sought after. Doris had done pupilage in Nëil's chambers too under a man called Jimmy Davies and I had gone and helped her take notes on a most extraordinary case, Celantano v Celantano. This was the last case of restitution of conjugal rites ever heard. This was an action whereby only a man could sue his wife to obtain an order that she be restored to him for purposes of sexual intercourse. Mr Celantano's wife on everybody's admission had left him because she disliked anal intercourse and he wanted her returned to his bed. It was a cause célèbre in the tabloid press and was heard by Mr Justice 'Scotty' Baker, the President of the Divorce and Admiralty Division. Scotty, giving judgement against Mr Celantano, earned himself banner headlines by translating the old legal adage '*ex turpi causa non oritor actio*', i.e. no action arises from a bad cause, into the ringing 'the dirty dog will get no dinner here'.

Nearly forty years ago it was a different England: the country was predominantly white, the West Indians who had come over and settled in the fifties were hard-working and law-abiding, nobody thought of multiculturalism and there weren't even many Chinese or Indian restaurants; there was no thought either of political correctness. I can remember one judge, Mr Justice Melford Stevenson, who sat as a red judge – that is a senior judge who is distinguished by his red robe – at the Old Bailey, and when he processed in his robes he always carried his black cap, as we said just in case. A black cap is what a judge places on his head when passing sentence of death and I remember one hardened old lag I was representing who on seeing this clutched my arm and said in awed tones, 'They don't any more, please tell me they don't, miss.' Melford lived in a house called Truncheons! One case he heard concerned two West Indians who were fighting over a woman; one of them was a crane driver who waited until the other had gone into the Portaloo which he then picked up with his crane, hoisted it up and dropped it, breaking both his rival's legs. As the prosecution was opening to the jury Melford was heard to mutter, 'It's really a case of eenie meenie mini mo, isn't it?' This referred to a nursery rhyme which continued, 'catch a nigger by his toe, if he hollers let him go . . .' Counsel ignored him and the jury tittered. Imagine if that happened today! It was a more robust world then. The police in the sixties were still trusted and well regarded but not for very much longer; the seventies saw *Dixon of Dock Green* go and entered the world of *The Sweeney*, the violent cop who would stitch up anyone and was as often as not corrupt.

Various areas of London were gangland; the East End round the docks was a prime example where a number of gangs were vying for domination, with the Kray kingdom becoming increasingly powerful but each area of criminality had its own gangs. All this meant there was plenty of Criminal work. These were also the days of the old divorce legislation where the petitioner had to show cause and as often as not the agreeing parties would set up a fiction with a professional co-respondent in a hotel room in some off-season seaside town. I remember on one occasion no fewer than five divorces cited the same co-respondent, an air force officer. The judge asked Neil where this energetic man was that afternoon. Neil replied that he was at the palace being decorated by Her Majesty and the judge suggested we have a minute's silence for the safety of the realm and then sing 'God Save the Queen'. On Friday afternoons the Queen's Proctor would stand up and challenge any of the week's decrees that he thought showed collusion but strangely never in my time did any of these clearly structured adultery cases feature.

Neil shared his room in chambers with another barrister and

his pupil, a Nigerian called George with a totally unpronounce-able surname. We spent a lot of our time drafting divorce petitions, which I found very easy and once I got good at it Neil would pay me part of his fee. George, from his African viewpoint, had problems with these petitions: he would think it more cruel to tear a telephone off the wall than to break a jaw bone, the rationale being that the first prohibited the victim from calling for help and deprived her of the use of modern technology whereas the broken jaw would mend. We would spend much time arguing over this type of matter when our masters were out of the room.

My day started at eight thirty when I would sort Neil's papers for the day in court and collect any books of authority we might need into a strap for the clerk to take across either to the High Court opposite or to Somerset House which at that time housed the Divorce Registry. Neil would arrive and often we would go and have breakfast together at the ABC coffee bar. Days were long; sometimes there was no time to go to Hall for a quick lunch and we made do with just a sandwich if we were lucky. Court finished at four thirty then we went back to chambers for conferences either with just solicitors or clients as well. Then it was time for paperwork. Neil was a kind man and treated me rather like a puppy being trained with rough affection and the occasional cream bun. The first set of affidavits I drafted for him he threw straight in the bin without even looking at them. When I protested he said that whatever I had tried to do I would do better next time round. I didn't know that he had looked at them when I was out of the room. He smoked an extremely smelly pipe using a very pungent tobacco called Charter; it was so strong that when I finished my pupilage I burned all my clothes. I was devoted to him after he told me my father had rung him up and tried to dissuade him from taking me on and that he replied that my father's behaviour in trying to scupper my chances of a career at the Bar had convinced him, telling my father that if I could survive that sort of abusive treatment I was clearly tough enough for the Bar.

One case that came back to me while I was writing was the curious one of a man who was charged with sexual assault on a train. He had been asleep, flown with wine, and when he woke up grabbed a woman sitting across the carriage and started kissing her. She fought him off and when the train stopped in a station he was arrested. In conference he kept saying, 'I thought she was my wife.' When we got to court the victim was the complete doppelgänger of the wife – they could have been identical twins. I called the wife and the jury acquitted.

At home things were good, at least for me. It is difficult to judge how my mother really felt; although she had lived through forty years of bullying and physical and verbal abuse there is no doubt in my mind that she still felt something for her husband and the father of her children. As always she made the best of things. We no longer had a cook as my father wasn't paying the maintenance and my mother's money was still frozen following her mother's death so my mother, who hadn't cooked since the incident in Bickenhall Mansions when she was newly married, made a stab at cooking. There were certain things she did very well, a surprising cross-section. Her roast duck was superlative: Boris Chaliapin, the son of the great opera singer, once ate a whole one at the end of dinner saying it was so good. Her stuffed breast of veal (don't ask me why this dish) was delicious, as were her minestrone and her fish pie, and her curry, which took all day to make, was amazing but that was it. Apart, of course, from roast beef which she taught me how to cook and with which I have never failed since. Discovering housework in her sixties this elegant woman, whose clothes came from Paris and who wore the highest of high heels, would polish parquet or clean chandeliers with a verve that most English women save for their gardens. I had never cooked either but if we were to have dinner parties I would have to try and so I discovered my one true talent. All of us have something we can do, some more than others, but everyone has a natural gift; it is just a question of discovering it.

We had supper parties, dinners, al fresco lunches or just eats. My friends, my mother's friends, it didn't matter: out came the best glass, the green and gold mid-nineteenth-century Venetian and the mid-seventeenth-century Cork and Orrery, which had always been locked away for fear of my father's rages. My friends were a talented lot: we wrote reviews for the Inn and practised them on the drawing room piano. I can still see Ernst Horridge, six foot five, half Swedish, reciting his 'the police officer who arrested Moses' and inadvertently setting fire to a large bush in the process! I can see us kicking cancan style down the long gallery to 'She Had to go and Lose it at the Astor' conducted by Mollypop, or my friend Penny singing 'The Streets of London' to make us all cry. My friend Rashid, grandson of the Nizam of Hyderbad, would always come to dinner in his full national costume just to delight my mother and suddenly Circus Road was full of light and laughter. Christine had gone to Trinity Dublin but would still visit in the holidays with her soon-to-be-husband Douglas. Carrots was living in London and was the toast of all the good-looking young barristers.

It was the sixties so we played hard as well and enjoyed the freedom to have sex wherever and whenever. My most extraordinary venue remains behind the Speaker's Chair in the House of Commons during the summer vacation. My partner was an

MP who shall be nameless and who was not a boyfriend, just a good acquaintance, but who had suggested I might like to see the floor of the House. It was all rather hurried and breathless and was more about being daring than the joy of sex but the memory makes me laugh when I watch all those pompous politicians pontificating.

My mother had acquired an admirer who held her hand and brought her flowers and put a smile on her face again. Heather, now calling herself the Countess d'Almeida although no one ever saw hide nor hair of the supposed Jaime d'Almeida, had taken herself off to Ecuador to visit some cousins we had discovered out there. They were descended from a Captain James Wright who had gone as a captain of mercenaries in 1740 and whose house is a museum in Quito. I think she hoped for one of the sons, Stanley, who had been a Trappist monk but had quit; when she came back across the Atlantic she went to stay in Spain where my sister June was living with her young second husband and baby daughter.

Napoleon once asked of a prospective general, 'But is he lucky?' and in those days I felt lucky. Neil broke me in gently to my first appearance in court: he would leave me outside courts saying I was to do the case if he was late, then always appear at the last minute so that I was lulled into a sense of security and when the day came and I actually had to get up and speak it was all very easy. Once I was in my second six months I started getting work and being sent far and wide to Magistrates' Courts in the south-west on small matters. My first brief with my own name on it came from Carrot's father. It was a simple undefended divorce between parties who had been separated for fifteen years with no children, costs or property involved. It was scheduled for Monday morning so I went for the weekend. The excitement of seeing my own name typed on a brief was almost overwhelming. There is a picture of me in my wig and gown taken beside their grandfather clock looking unbelievably young and thin. I was good at dressing for effect in those days and it is hard to believe that other women at the Bar used to copy my clothes. I remember I was the first woman to wear pinstripes rather than just black and this was regarded as very daring.

London at that time was being rent by IRA bombings, and there were times when, had I been paranoid, I might have thought they were after me: David and I just missed the one that blew in the windows and wrecked the restaurant in Walton Street as we had decided to cancel our table; several at railway stations detonated just after my train had left; and finally there was the huge bomb at the Old Bailey. The women barristers' changing rooms were in the middle of the building with no windows, a constant cause for complaint but never after that day. The men's robing room with its high windows looking on to the street was a horror of flying glass with blood everywhere though thankfully no fatalities. A huge QC called James Crespie, who must have weighed nearly thirty stone, was on the steps and was blown off his feet and against the wall of the building but was otherwise unhurt. Vary bravely he quipped to the television cameras, 'I tried to interpose myself between the bomb and the Bailey but the bomb won.' Looking back, we just got on with our daily lives without the government trying to destroy the rule of law or whip us all into a frenzy. I remember two middle-aged country women up for the day on a bus just after the Harrods bomb remarking, 'Let's go to Harrods first and show them we don't care.'

I had a couple of pieces of good fortune that helped me to a tenancy in chambers, the first thanks to Princess Anne and Lord Denning. I was treasurer of the Debating Society that year and the two of them were guests at the society dinner. I was and remain a great fan of both of them. Princess Anne made a splendid speech, including references that couldn't have been written in beforehand as I had only told her about them before dinner. I also spoke, as did Alan Ward who was in chambers. He is now a rather high-profile High Court judge and remarked to Barry Madden, the senior clerk, how well I had spoken and how well I had obviously got on with my two heroes. Barry was so impressed and delighted that he changed his mind on my future as a prospective tenant and one more barrier was removed.

The other concerned a long fraud case in which Neil was junior counsel behind a QC called Muir Hunter. When a barrister feels that his practice contains sufficient senior court work he can apply to take silk, that is become a Queen's Counsel. Thereafter the only paperwork he does will be written opinions and any pleadings will be done by his junior. The junior is usually a fairly senior barrister who has not yet taken silk and if it is a complicated case with a lot of paperwork he will often employ a junior junior or just a noting brief. Neil gave me a junior brief in this case although I was still a pupil, which was a great honour. The case concerned the use of bills of exchange as security in the fur and skin trade. At that time London had a huge skin business involving thousands of pelts both native and imported, and people wore fur coats without the risk of having a can of paint thrown over them. They were warm, not made of manufactured material and they were very ecological. I sometimes think that when we are forced to stop confusing sentiment with Green issues we may all go back there again. There are not many carbon emissions in using natural products as opposed to man-made fibres.

In any event our client, let us call him Mr White, was a Russian Jewish immigrant who had come here at the age of eleven. He had been apprenticed into the fur trade and now had a highly successful company and was rightly much respected. On the other hand there was the villain, let us call him Mr Black. He had been buying up defunct companies that still had good credit ratings in the fur trade directory and issuing bills of exchange which he discounted on the market; this of course led to what is known as a snowball effect as new bills were issued to pay off the old ones when they fell due for payment. This was still all legal. The con came in that to get a higher rate of payment the bills were marked on the front 'for value in furs received', thereby claiming that behind the transaction was a bale of valuable skins. Nobody could really understand why Mr White had backed hundreds of these bills with his signature, implying he was involved in the transactions and lending his good name to the bill. Eventually Mr Black became ill from the pressure and the whole lot came tumbling down and in stepped the fraud squad. Mr White could offer no answer for his involvement in all this but there was no doubt it was his signature on the back of the bills.

I spent days and all my weekends working on the huge volume of papers and eventually there came a time when Mr White, a solicitor's clerk and myself were shut in a room with his ledgers in an attempt to match the bills against any genuine transactions. With the ledger facing me I asked him to point out where minks and sables were recorded on this page. He pointed confidently and without turning the ledger to an entry that said quite clearly leopards and ocelots; in my brain something clicked. I thanked him, waited a few minutes more, then turned a page and asked him to show me the entries for musquash; again he confidently pointed to an entry reading silver fox skins. I looked him in the face and said very gently, 'Mr White, you can't read, can you?' His whole face crumpled and he burst into tears. 'The shame, the shame, you mustn't tell anyone, promise me you won't. What will they say in the synagogue?' This was a man who entirely on his own merits had built up a successful business, he was literate in Russian and Yiddish but not in English at all, and he was more ashamed of admitting this fact than of going to prison for a crime of which he was completely innocent.

I told Neil who called Muir Hunter and the real villain of the piece was unearthed. Mr White had an accountant, who knew his shortcoming, and was hand in glove with Mr Black and had exploited Mr White's weakness and the fact that he couldn't read the damning 'for value in furs received' clause. Our client was rightly acquitted, the villains condemned and after thirteen long working weeks in a hot Old Bailey we won. It always reminds me of the Somerset Maugham story of the Verger of St Peter's Eton Square. As a result of this I was much praised. Muir Hunter wanted to give me a red bag. Barristers carry their robes in a cloth bag which is usually blue, and each QC is allowed to award two red bags in his lifetime to juniors he feels have shown special merit. It was a huge compliment; the only problem was that as I was still a pupil I couldn't accept it. Barry Madden was impressed and after the next chambers meeting I was given my tenancy. It was 1969 and life was brilliant.

My room in chambers, which I shared with another lady barrister, Cynthia Cruickshank, was in the annex next door, where there were two large bright rooms overlooking the Temple Church, and the other was occupied by a brilliant young man called Peter Leighton. In the hot days of the long vacation the High Courts shut for all of August and a week either side, and County Courts shut for August. The Bailey still sat but with a reduced number of courts and the senior barristers and silks took their paperwork to the country. It says all you need to know about the increase in crime and litigation that not only are there many more courts but there is no longer a long vacation; they'd never catch up with the backlog. We juniors stayed in chambers hoping to pick up work in the Magistrates' Court and from various emergency applications and injunctions that might arise. It was all agreeable and leisurely and we played scrabble or croquet if the weather was fine; Peter had tunnel vision which made him a demon at either croquet or snooker. We took long lunches and argued about anything and everything. The rooms were above John Mortimer's chambers, and he has always been a man I have much admired for his liberality of thought and his wit both written and spoken. I would often meet him on the staircase in the morning and we would sometimes have a cup of coffee together.

My luck continued. I had two cases recorded in the All England Law Reports (the leading authoritative reports at the time), one concerning a remarriage adoption. This was before the Children's Act and if the new spouse wished to adopt the child from their partner's previous marriage they had to obtain a court order excluding the rights of the other parent. With the Children's Act still in parliamentary discussions there were a number of such cases backing up so that there would be a judicial precedent to advise the Commons committee. I was given Re B, a minor, one summer day because I got back from the morning lists before anyone else. Off I set, not knowing that this was one case that would take me all the way to the Court of Appeal. Representing the mother and her new husband, we won in the Magistrates' Court but the father, who had barely seen the child since he left in its early infancy, decided to appeal on the unsatisfactory basis that he might one day want to see the child. Ours was first out of the hat, we won again and I made the law reports.

The other case with which I made the law reports was all about a stud stallion called Kuai King (pronounced Cow King) who won two legs of the American Triple, was syndicated for stud and tore a tendon in the third leg. His owner was a Kentucky horse breeder straight out of a Remington painting with a stud manager to match.

My client was a handsome, well-born Indian with a blood-stock agency, and the whole case hinged on the American habit of putting the month before the day when writing a date, most famously as in 9/11 which we would write 11/9. This was an important definition for international trade. I will not go into the particulars of the case but there is one charming vignette I would like to describe. Both the owner and his stud manager during their turns in the witness box had testified that they had spent their lives around horses from the ages of eleven and nine respectively. When it was my client's turn I asked him the same question. He pulled something from his inside pocket and handed it to the clerk who passed it to the judge. I was quite mystified. The judge let out a snort of laughter and asked me if I had seen it. I said I had not and it was handed to me. I found myself looking at an old black and white photograph of an elegant woman riding side-saddle on a horse; on the non-stirrup side of the saddle was strapped a pannier out of which emerged a baby's head. The caption read: 'Hassan [my client] aged 3 months'. Despite such humour we lost both there and in the Court of Appeal but we put up a good fight and I got to appear in front of Lord Denning who spoke very kindly of my performance and said I would go far.

This was of course the glamour side of my practice. Most days I schlepped off to the sticks with a handful of applications or undefended divorces or endeavoured to persuade young criminals that actually they were wasting their lives. Sometimes it was funny, sometimes it was tragic, but it was all part of the career path to Queen's Counsel and High Court judge that I saw very clearly. I was persuaded to stand as Hall Representative for Gray's Inn on the Senate and was elected by a huge majority vote; this was my first stint as a trade union official but I am afraid I failed to achieve very much.

I have always been an admirer of the English judiciary; of course it isn't perfect, nothing is, and as Neil said to me in my first month of pupilage, 'Don't expect justice other than from the Almighty.' Thomas More, a man who died as much for his belief in the legal system as for his faith once said, 'The laws of England are like a grove of oaks, cut them down and what will you do when the wind blows.' In the reign of James I and VI the Chief Justice of the King's Bench sent Lord Cooke to the Tower rather than bow to pressure from the King to give a corrupt judgement, thereby finally establishing the independence of the judiciary. Of course judges are human with all their frailties. I remember that when Sir Arthur Bagnall, known as 'Bangwell' because of his sexual energies, was appointed to the Bench of the Divorce Division Scotty Baker wrote to welcome him, saying now we will have a judge who truly understands the definition of adultery! But Bangwell was a fair judge none the less.

The greatest judge of my lifetime was undoubtedly Lord Denning. Parliament had to pass several statutes to codify the changes in the law he had established as precedent. Denning's great gift was his ability to find quirks in the law that allowed justice to prevail; I'm talking about civil not criminal law here. He invented, for instance, the incredibly complicated doctrine of equitable estoppel which so plagued my studies. Briefly, you could not use your own negative action to attack someone with whom you had struck a deal; estoppel was a shield not a sword.

Denning was the son of a Hampshire shopkeeper and his father had been an agricultural labourer; he was one of three brothers, all of whom rose to dizzy heights in their fields, and when he was really taking the mickey out of pompous counsel his Hampshire accent, not usually noticeable, became broader by the minute. I remember Jeremiah Harman, a most unpopular and pompous man, pontificating for some time about a duck pond in a Rights of Way case; he then moved on to some other feature and had just launched into this when Denning looked over his glasses and in broadest Hampshire remarked, 'Oh, Mr Harman, Oi've just found your duck pond.' Collapse of pompous party.

I could stay talking about this part of my life for a long time. I was focused, happy, praised and life was good. In 1973 my father, then aged seventy-seven, who in the interim had been living with his brother Douglas and Aunt Olive in London, suffered eleven strokes in nine minutes while lecturing in South Africa. It should have killed him but they rushed him to the Groote Schuur Hospital, arguably the best in the world at that time, and saved his life. Sadly they did him no favours, as he became virtually a cabbage from then on. My mother offered for him to come home as we did have the quarters that my grandmother had occupied but Uncle Douglas declined and my father spent the next three years in the Lindo Wing of St Mary's Paddington where no doubt he felt more at home.

Derby Day fell on 6 June 1975, as in those days the race was run on a Wednesday and skiving off to attend added an extra dimension to the fun. I don't go any more but I can't imagine it to be as good. I went to the Oaks a few years ago and it was all corporate entertaining and crowds who one didn't feel were that keen on the racing. It was Grundy's year, a horse my mother had much admired as a two-year-old and throughout his third year and she had invested early in his ability to win. We were all there to watch him and my mother had a lovely day with success on all the races. We floated home on a sea of bubbles. Heather, by then living in London, was rather drunk and Mollypop asked me to take her away so we went out to dinner. When I got home just before midnight the lights in Ma's room were on so I went in to say goodnight. 'Wasting electricity again,' I quipped as I walked towards the bed; she appeared to be sleeping peacefully until I noticed the slight rictus of the mouth and the lack of breath. She was dead and cold as any stone.

6

Darkness begins to close

Even after all this time it is impossible to describe what I felt; all sorts of analogies of seven swords piercing my heart come to mind and fall flat. It was not just that my mother was dead and I was only twenty-five, it was, I think, that Ma and I had fought so hard together for safety and sanity, we had endured the buffets and blows, the verbal cruelty from my father, and now suddenly when things were improving she had gone. I felt I had no purpose in life any more and that I had failed in all I had tried to do. I was enclosed in this searing white light that was emotional pain and I couldn't bear it. I rushed from the house to David's flat and fell through the door gasping out the horrid fact. He offered me a cup of tea but I asked for a large whisky, poured myself four fingers and as I gulped it down the white light faded. Here, I suddenly realised, was the answer to everything, the key to the universe, the abatement of pain. David rang Anthony and back we went to Circus Road. Anthony met us there and we spent the night with all the paraphernalia of sudden death – the police, the doctor, the coroner's office – and whenever the pain showed signs of coming back I reached for the whisky and made another cup of tea for everyone else. Finally, as the dawn was beginning to infuse the sky, they moved my darling mother out of the house we had struggled so hard to stay in for the last time and I went back to

Anthony's house. The next morning Marah offered me a Valium and I remember snorting that I didn't take drugs and pouring myself a strong Bloody Mary. I had found my friend.

We buried Mollypop with style. She was to be interred with her mother at Putney and we had the service at the Sacred Heart Convent at Roehampton thanks to the help of April O'Leary. Father Thomas Kewene, who had been our curate when I was young and to whom Mollypop had once given a car, took the service and had a special prayer to St Philomena, which was great as Pope John XXIII had declared she never existed.

Let me pause here to tell you about Mollypop and Philo. For some reason I never discovered, Ma had a thing for Philomena, a Roman martyr of the reign of Diocletian, whose tomb had been found in the catacombs in Victorian times under an inscription that read '*Pax tecum Filumena*'. The remains were transported to Mugnano del Cardinali, a small parish near Naples. Whether Mollypop was quite so attached to Philo before the papal deposition I can't really remember but she took up the cudgels with anarchic enthusiasm. Medals were stamped and Ma would give them to people, saying that if you had one in your wallet you would never want for money. She also declared that if you asked Philo you would always find a parking place. Strangely that one works. We even set off to Naples to visit the shrine. It was in the days of currency restrictions and our travel agent Mr Shirley James would arrange for Homburg-hatted men to deliver parcels of money to our hotel with great discretion. Ma and I set off for the shrine which was a typical gaudy Italian affair, where the Papal Guard were fighting running battles with the village youths in an attempt to remove the remains. Mollypop, the parish priest, the mayor and I sat in the village square like a scene from *The Little World of Don Camillo* toasting St Philomena and Ma snatched a good diamond ring from her finger and presented it to the priest for the campaign. There must have been a cardinal somewhere with a fine diamond and Philomena was duly reinstated. Anyway, you see how important it was to me to have her mentioned.

The chapel was packed, everyone came; even Arthur Porritt, my father's great rival who had been fond of my mother, came to the graveside. Pipe Major Robertson, who Ma had always engaged to play at parties and had always argued with me that he wouldn't play 'The Lament for the Chief' at her funeral because she was a woman and no chieftain, broke his vow and played with tears streaming down his cheeks. We had a great wake with champagne and lobsters, and as someone described it, 'It was Molly's last party.' Her school friend Goldfish remarked, 'Molly was always so thoughtful, halfway between Epsom and Ascot, what a perfect time for a funeral.' For myself I simply couldn't stop crying, the tears just rolled steadily down my cheeks but it was a great party. Afterwards Christine and her husband Douglas drove me back to Birmingham where they were living. I slept all the way.

I knew that Mollypop's will left everything to me; because the others were so much older she had made provision at different stages for them but the rest was for me. There were no instructions to look after my siblings or to share my inheritance with them; it was my reward for all our battles and it was not one I had wanted to inherit for many years to come. My mother was sixty-seven and she had died as she would have wanted; she hated the thought of age or infirmity and she had always said that God would take her with a bang. It all just seemed a little early.

The beginning of my drinking career was really rather enjoyable. I was rich, good-looking and kept the pain at bay on a wave of champagne and other drinks. My friends, knowing how bitterly I felt my mother's death, forgave me, made excuses for me and tried to protect me from myself. Circus Road was my home and the status quo remained. My father was still in St Mary's and despite rather feeble attempts to oust me from the house by Aunt Olive and Uncle Douglas while my father lived the lawyers kept things much as they were. I continued to practise at the Bar and at this stage was able to hold everything together. I was obliged to go out to the Far East and Australia to try to resolve financial affairs, since my grandmother's estate was still not sorted but there was no real emergency there. However what my dear kind friends didn't realise was that as far as I was concerned my life had no purpose any more; there was a great hole in my soul to which as far as I could see the only solution was to pour alcohol into it to assuage the loss. One of the by-products of my childhood was an inability to trust or confide in people. My ambition to succeed as a barrister had rested solely on two premises: one, to annoy my father and the second to make my mother proud of me. Now both of these were swept away. I had no doubt that I could succeed; it was among other things the age of the token woman and what I had to offer was better than most but knowing that I could diminished the desire to do so. I could hear the eulogies at my own memorial service at some future date inside my head and somehow it didn't seem to matter any more. I remember saying to God that as I had been brought up not to commit suicide we'd play Russian roulette with the alcohol and that was the last time I spoke to God for a very long time.

One of the good things that happened was that Christine gave birth to her first child, a daughter Sara, my beloved goddaughter. Chris was exhausted after thirteen hours of induced labour and I went up to help look after them. Douglas was working and they were both glad of my help, although had they known my actual alcohol intake they might not have been. All was well, however. I cooked nourishing, appetising dishes and got up in the middle of the night to do bottle feeds and change nappies. This is the only time in my life I have ever done this and it felt like a dream; the baby slept in a cot by my bed and I loved her dearly as I do to this day. I am still convinced that the reason she can't sing is that I used to sing her lullabies in the middle of the night and, believe me, I can't sing either.

On the surface I kept up a good face. I was still staying at my brother's house because I couldn't face sleeping at Circus Road but I went over to sort things out. I used to have lunch parties and barbecues for my friends and the general view was that I was holding together. An assortment of things changed all this. On returning from the Far East I discovered I was bankrupt, not insolvent as I was theoretically worth £2.8 million. I had given the contract for the funeral champagne to the new husband of a friend and shortly before I left for the East she had rung me and asked for the address of a really tough firm of divorce solicitors, which I gave her. She didn't say and I never thought it was for her. The debt wasn't even strictly speaking mine, it was Mollypop's estate's but in anger her husband had issued, in strict order, a writ, a judgement, a bankruptcy notice and finally an order against me which had expired the day before I returned. These were all served by post on my chambers and were there on my desk waiting for me. Bankrupt and all for less than £1,000. It wouldn't happen now; they changed the law because of my case but back then once you were caught in the gyre there was no way out. The bank offered to pay but now I had to go through the whole process of an examination of my assets by an official working for the Bankruptcy Courts.

My examiner was Hungarian and a truly horrid man; not to me, he was rather afraid of me, but to little people. I would sit at the far end of his room waiting for my appointment, reading my files and listening to him bullying them. One day when he was being particularly unpleasant to a middle-aged plumber who had gone bust because his clients hadn't paid him so he couldn't pay his suppliers, I flipped. A great wave of anger rose in me and I stalked across and intervened. In answer to my question about his war service the plumber told me he had been a desert rat. I turned on the examiner and told him that but for people like the plumber he would have had no safe haven to flee to and would have been languishing under the Russian boot and that he must apologise for his rudeness. This, I am happy to say, he did. I can be quite alarming at times. After my own interview, a short one in the event – are you surprised? – I left to find the plumber waiting to thank me. Informing him that in my case I was only bankrupt not broke, I swept him off to the Seven Stars for a drink. This was a tiny pub in Carey Street with no lavatories; funny the things you remember. I never wanted for a plumber as long as I stayed in London. The examiner eventually killed himself so he must have had problems of his own but it didn't really excuse the way he treated people.

I also had to have a public hearing before the Trustee in Bankruptcy sitting as a judge. I remember he asked me what I was living on if everything was frozen. Rather than say, 'Oh, you know, the odd Persian carpet or piece of silver,' I looked coy and said, 'We are to be married, you know,' which embarrassed him so much he shut up. It was a good trick and it worked. I was not of course about to be married to anyone. Bankruptcy back then still carried a stigma but did not preclude me from continuing to practise. Barristers aren't fund-holders like accountants or solicitors and neither do chambers incorporate themselves. Eventually my solicitor, of whom more later, sorted out a way to get my frozen inheritance released to him to pay the debts in full. I had to pay £13,000 in fees to the Bankruptcy Courts. I also had to disappear to avoid Heather, who had received no bequest in the will and was trying to persuade me to give her money. She wanted to use an injunction to keep me in bankruptcy until I agreed, and had she been able to find me she would have served the papers. I fled to Christine's and soon it was all sorted, the bankruptcy was annulled and legally I was solvent and as if the whole thing had never happened. The wine merchant was closed down by the VAT people some time later.

I was still staying at Anthony's house but I realised I must move back when I returned from a weekend at Selmeston and discovered the locks on Circus Road had been changed by Aunt Olive. I flew round to the police station and the sergeant who had known me for years simply looked at me and handed me a list of locksmiths with a wry smile and a comment about possession being nine-tenths of the law. I was back inside within the hour. Marah's half-brother, the artist Harry More-Gordon, came to stay on an extended painting trip. He had several sitters for portraits. I commissioned him to paint both myself and my mother's study. I stood in my wig and gown leaning on the mantelpiece with my bust of the Duke of Wellington and a stuffed flamingo I had bought at Battle intending to sell on. Mollypop had fallen in love with it and so I gave it to her and she called it Albert because she said it looked like the gardener. I had once represented a man who was sleeping rough in St James's Park and had killed a flamingo while trying to have sexual intercourse with it; his explanation was that he had woken from a drunken dream and thought it was his wife! That has nothing to do with either the gardener or my flamingo but the mind takes curious leaps, doesn't it.

The other painting I commissioned was of the bit of my mother's study where we used to sit and play backgammon. Mollypop was a demon player having been taught by a nun at her school in Australia, where she had promised she would never play for money, but she loved to play and we spent many happy hours at the board. I always played red and I was always soundly thrashed. For the picture I set up the board so that red was winning; he who laughs last, I thought. When the picture was finished white was quite clearly winning. I remonstrated with Harry who replied that he knew nothing about backgammon and only ever painted what he saw down to the last curlicue in the Persian rug. I confronted him with the board and he just shrugged and replied that I must have changed it since. She who laughs last indeed. While he was there Olive and Douglas came to the house and demanded to be let in. I had told him on no account to let them in, so with his head stuck through the venetian blind, which he couldn't raise, he told them to go, and only later did he discover he had failed to lock the front door which was open to all.

Once Harry had left I couldn't face living in the house on my own. Christine's youngest brother and sister both wanted to be in London, Martin to study medicine and Jane to study opera singing so they agreed to come and live in the house. Martin paid his non-existent rent by brewing delicious beer for me and Jane helped with things around the house, mostly washing up after large and jolly dinner parties. One of the other people who came to stay was Avril Stoneham, an old family friend who we had lost touch with until Ma and I met her with her mother and sister in Harrods banking hall. After that I used to go and stay on her parents' farm in Cornwall and ride on hay wagons and help with the bales and we would all go swimming and sailing in the Carrick Roads. Avril then went out to the West Indies to cook on a charter yacht, and had come back to do a course at the Cordon Bleu School in order to earn more money cooking on the yachts.

Also in the house was a Bar student, Libby Arfon – Jones as she then was – who is now very grand and sits as a judge on immigration appeals, is chairman of the Welsh branch of the Lottery Heritage Commission and high up on the Committee of Women at the Bar. Still full of fun and exuberance, she was for a while an ambassador's wife when Brian was our representative in Ghana. Over time there were other people but this was the core. As long as I balanced my alcohol consumption, not drinking too much too early, and paced myself over the day to keep the pain under wraps, I was okay and enjoyed myself. I was still working in chambers and made some of my best jury speeches with a hangover. People supported me because they felt sorry for me and we all had a lot of fun. It is not unusual that my friends didn't challenge me. Most people don't usually confront a drinking alcoholic, presumably because they are afraid that they will lose them, that they will walk away.

Avril finished her course and took me back to the Caribbean with her for a holiday on the boat. This was a yacht called *Good Hope* built in the 1930s as the flagship for the commander of the New York Yacht Squadron and was a thing of beauty. She belonged to a Boston lawyer and Avril and Dave, her boyfriend, ran the charters for him as cook and captain. The yacht was based at English Harbour in Antigua and took charterers up and down the Windward and Grenadine islands. The West Indies in the seventies were very undeveloped for the tourist trade and it was really only a playground for the rich and for the sailing fraternity.

The Pitons at St Lucia, twin volcanic peaks, were completely unspoilt; one tied the yacht with a long line to a palm tree and winched it as close as possible then either swam or took the tender ashore. There was nothing there but a few shacks where one could buy fruit and vegetables from the locals. We climbed one of the Pitons, a hard climb through the breadfruit trees but with a wonderful view of other islands from the top. Now the space between the Pitons is a hotel complex, but then pigs ran happily in the bush and the West Indians lived off the bounty of the island; now I expect they wait at tables for a wage. I often wonder what makes people think they have a better life. For instance do the Amazonian Indians really want to wander round trying to shoot monkeys with blowpipes in order to eat and live short lives wearing only beads and on top of that have to endure the attentions of television crews and anthropologists or would they rather live in prefab houses wearing cheap designer clothes and watching bad television? It's all a mystery to me.

St Vincent was the island I liked best, mainly because it had a wonderful produce market, where old ladies, ribald like market traders the world around, sold fruit and veg, fresh fish, delicious home-made hot sauce and very good black puddings made with oatmeal. I have always loved food markets and would happily spend hours wandering about eating rotis, a form of unleavened wheat pancake wrapped round goat or chicken curry. Edson, the yacht's crew, bought conch (known locally as conc in the market) and prepared it for us; it had to be bashed like an octopus then cut up and marinated in lime juice and chilli sauce and I found it quite delicious. On that occasion we had to leave the island in a hurry: I had been adopted by a three-legged dog which followed me about, and when a rough boy threw it in the harbour I threw him in after the dog to save it. His father was rather large and very cross about it. In the West Indies I discovered morning drinking: a beer, or even two, after or with breakfast, added a nice golden glow to the day. Lots of people (well, so it seemed) did likewise. I came back totally in love with the islands and the yachts and arranged to charter *Good Hope* the following year.

In the meantime Aunt Olive had been busy: she informed the lawyers that my father wanted to come to Circus Road to sit in the garden. I pointed out that February was not the best time for a frail man in a wheelchair to come and do this but she was adamant. I was not to be there as this would upset him so we compromised on Miss Fox to be in attendance. Apparently he sat listlessly in his chair for about ten minutes then suddenly became very agitated shouting, 'Molly, where's Molly?' As he didn't really speak this surprised everyone, and he then became so disturbed they had to take him away. That night for no apparent reason he turned his face to the wall and died. I can never understand the weft of human emotions. There were my parents locked together for more than forty years in a maelstrom of alcohol-induced violence. They never seemed to have anything much in common, nor to communicate where they did. They both loved racing but would go separately to the same meeting with their own separate friends and never speak or exchange drinks or information and yet like the contorted ending of an Ibsen play there was some form of skewed love and dependency underlying it all.

I felt nothing when my father died, no sense of relief, sadness or even gladness; he had simply gone. My brother was very upset; he had always wanted to be recognised by my father in some way that would never have been possible and as the Irish say, 'A man doesn't become a man till the day his father dies.' Libby reminded me that on the evening I heard of his death I said to her, 'I suppose celebrations are in order. I'm going to teach you about claret,' and opened a bottle of 1962 Ducru-Beaucaillou (always my favourite) and a 1962 Lafite so that she could compare first and fourth growths. I must have drunk most of this, as I have no memory of this event at all.

There was a horrible funeral to which almost no one came at the Paddington Crematorium, with bad sherry at Olive and Douglas's afterwards and a huge memorial service at the church in Trafalgar Square. Arthur Porritt gave the address, which was ironic and made me very happy by talking eloquently about my mother. He was a good man, Porritt, though not the surgeon my father was. Some do say he was sent back to his native New Zealand as Governor so that my father could perform the Queen Mother's colostomy operation without offending protocol but if that is true it was New Zealand's gain, and possibly the Queen Mum's as she made 104.

Curiously, if my father had predeceased my mother as one might have expected I would probably be dead. I have always said if I'd had another hundred thousand I'd have managed to drink myself to death. On leaving the house my father had, oddly, made a will leaving everything to my mother with no arrangements for reversions in the event that she predeceased him. Following my mother's death nine months before, another will of my father's emerged leaving everything to Douglas and Olive and witnessed by various members of St Mary's medical staff who testified that my father was in possession of his testamentary capacities. Now it was not surprising that he disinherited Heather or me because we stood up to him, whereas June and Anthony had done nothing to warrant this behaviour. Indeed the will included quite a number of shares in my brother's company, which my father had invested in. Anthony invented things and this company included a patent for those tarpaulins you see on lorries with adjustable straps and a roll-on roll-off loading system for rolls of printing paper for newspapers, and was at that time successful. Apparently when my father took the shares in return for investment money he had told him they would be returned to Ant in his will.

Anthony therefore had to contest the will and on counsel's advice we all joined in the action. Unfortunately Olive and Douglas were caught up in the whole gyre of hatred and refused to make any offer of settlement and so the court appointed an administrator *pendente lite* in the form of Cork Gully. Now my father had many overseas patients and operated abroad, especially in the Arab states, quite regularly. He begrudged the taxman his share and deposited the money abroad in Swiss banks and in the countries where he was paid, sometimes in gold ingots. The administrator had a hay day and between his fees and payments to the taxman the whole estate was eaten away or simply lost. I am sure there are other offshore bank accounts that will never be found, to say nothing of the house in Baghdad. My father had the dubious honour of saving Saddam Hussein's life, operating on him for a severely torsioned gut when he was still a young officer, and in thanks Saddam had given my father a large house in the palace district of Baghdad. If the Americans haven't destroyed it the ensuing civil unrest will render it worthless and in any event I don't think the deeds were ever found. What else was lost in the débâcle we will never know.

In any event when it became obvious that there would soon be nothing left Olive and Douglas finally decided to settle and after Anthony had got his shares back six of us received £26,000 each from an estate estimated at well over £3 million. The strain of it all proved too much for poor Douglas who died of a massive heart attack within a week of signing. As they both had plenty of money and no children it was all a rather pointless battle but I think it was driven by Aunt Olive who had always been jealous of my mother, believing, rightly, that Douglas had carried a torch for my mother. Mollypop told me once that when I was born Douglas came and sat on her bed and told her that he supposed he now really had to give up hope. Ma told him to go and marry Olive, the daughter of a rich antique dealer with a good business of her own and who worshipped him. I don't doubt that somewhere over the years Douglas told her this, for she never liked my mother.

How strange that my father, always the miser, should have worked so hard all his life and have squirrelled all this away from everyone only to lose it to the taxmen and the accountants he hated. I wonder who he thought would get it all in the end? Or maybe misers don't think and the compulsion to hoard is enough. My parents were poles apart in this as in so much else: Mollypop was a generous person who gave of herself and of her possessions and is still remembered by so many people I meet whose lives she touched. Christine said that you had to be careful what you admired at Circus Road or you would go home with it. My father, on the other hand, was mean and crabbit; he gave of himself only to his patients and then to be honest it was unstintingly, but he never gave of his possessions. Once when I was sixteen he gave me a present, a picture of a fish painted in sepia ink in the Japanese manner. I was very surprised, put it back in its case and into a drawer and it was only after his death that I realised he had done it himself. He never said that he had painted it or explained why he had given it to me and I still don't understand the gift.

So now I had no one in the world to prove anything to, no one to fight and no one to defend. My ambition, which had been powered by these motives, disintegrated almost overnight. I had money, looks and with the drink I never felt alone. For a lot of my life I have had more money than my friends and I have discovered it is actually quite hard to get your friends to allow you to pay for things. Often I have had to rely on a win on the horses or the fruit machines before I can persuade people to accept some treat. It is probably why rich people are surrounded by hangers-on: they have long since despaired of getting real friends to accept things from them. If you have money and want the best I find it rather irritating to eat in a cheaper restaurant or stay in a cheaper hotel so that your friends can pay their share. I was now about to embark on a period of extravagance, lavish expenditure and debauchery that was to last the best part of a decade and I wanted my friends to share at least the first two aspects of it. For my charter trip on *Good Hope* that I had booked the year before, none of my close friends would accept my hospitality. Thus the party consisted of Penny Cowland, now Hamilton, and her husband Nick who I finally managed to persuade to come with me and two friends of theirs who I didn't know well. I was paying all the expenses on the trip. We had a lovely time seeing islands that other boats didn't go to then. We took a day run out to Martinique to visit the distillery at Les Anses d'Arlets which produced Vieille rum, a well-matured product. Dave, the captain again, advised us to drink no more than one or at the most two, which advice I took with great disdain and had six. I do not remember being carried back to the boat! We also stopped at Bequia, Edson's island, where they had just killed a whale so we had great bowls of whale stew; it is the only time I have eaten this meat which is very like lean beef that has not been hung long enough. Nowadays I'm all for saving whales.

The routine of the day was breakfast, then set sail and this was the time for sunbathing, with care as you could get badly burned, and helping with the yacht if you were so inclined. We trawled a line off the stern and caught king mackerel, but you had to be quick or a shark would take it and you would be left with just the head. At about one o'clock we anchored for lunch, usually in a cove or bay but sometimes out at sea. We had a cold lunch and a swim before sailing on to our evening mooring. Usually we ate on board but if there was a jump-up or a particularly good eating place we went ashore. Jump-ups were barbecues with a steel band and we would dance long into the night. I felt really at home and loved the perpetual presence of the sea, the wind in the shrouds tinkling me to sleep, the markets, the humour of the people.

Later that same year for fun I went back to work as passage crew on the run north to the summer chartering grounds of the north-east coast of America. Dockyard Day was the end of the West Indian charter season, a sort of pageant cum village fête on the harbour. One race required the entrants to cross the harbour on some kind of raft which must not have cost more than $5BWI, about £2.50. The crew of Baron Bich's yacht swam across the harbour with their rear steps as a raft but were disqualified because the steps were over the permitted value. The crew of *Taiconderoga*, the winner of the 1977 American Tall Ships Race, crossed on a plywood raft, and each of the men had the following words on their backs: England: Expects: Every: Man: To: Do: His, and every woman wore the word Duty! They were declared the winners. Much rum punch was drunk and we all had a splendid day. It's a funny thing about rum: I always enjoyed it out there in the daiquiris, punches and pina coladas but I could never enjoy it back in England. We then sailed north. Working as passage crew is quite punishing, the turns are four hours on, four hours off and because it is the start of the hurricane season one has to be on a constant lookout for squalls. The watches were for two people with the captain on permanent call, and when off watch you hit bed and fell into oblivion very quickly. One morning I was on watch at dawn, my companion had gone below for some reason and I realised it was the anniversary of my mother's death. I remember saying, 'Come on, Ma, give me a sign you're okay,' and suddenly a single dolphin broke surface and kept pace with the ship for some way. Dolphins usually travel in groups so I felt maybe it was my sign. We were becalmed in the Sargasso Sea, famed as the mysterious Bermuda Triangle, and hauled one of the weed islands up on a hook to the masthead so that we could see all the strata of wildlife living there, and frightened each other with tales of giant squids before starting the motor and moving on. It was a strange, still place, the Bermuda Triangle.

We were glad to see Bermuda and moored up in the Royal Dockyard to enjoy showers and clean the ship. I went to the club for a drink. Women were not allowed into the bar but would be served on the veranda. No one came. I can see myself now – apple-green Surf 'n Sand shorts over my swimming costume with a towelling waistcoat and an old panama hat and flip-flops – marching into the bar. An immaculately dressed man in perfectly creased Bermuda shorts stepped forward. 'Excuse me, ma'am, girls aren't allowed in this bar.' I roared with laughter. 'Good heavens,' I said, 'I can't remember when I was last called a girl and anyway I'm a gentleman by statute.' (Barristers are, you know.) He fled and the barman winked at me and poured me a drink; whether they thought I was a transvestite or just mad I shall never know. From Bermuda we headed north to Boston. I had hoped to get home for the Queen's Silver Jubilee but strong winds kept us out of harbour and so I missed it.

I flew home from Boston with a box containing live lobsters and steamer clams on dry ice and seaweed, to settle an argument with my brother over the quality of Maine lobsters. They went in the hold and were very lively going through customs. The officer asked me what was alive in my baggage and I told him lobsters. 'You can't take live lobsters into England,' he told me. 'Could I take them if they were dead?' I asked. Receiving an affirmative answer, I started to unpin a large brooch with a strong pin, and when asked what I was doing I replied that I was going to kill them. 'Not in front of me you're not,' replied this sentimental customs officer. 'Take them away and eat them.' So we did.

I became quite addicted to yachting, both in the Caribbean and to a lesser extent in the Aegean. I was determined that Christine and Douglas should come on a sailing holiday, but sadly the firm Douglas worked for would only allow him to take holidays in August which rather restricted sailing options. Finally I decided that we would go to the northern Greek islands, which were not so badly affected by the Meltami, the Greek version of the winds that blow through all the Mediterranean in August. Off we went, Chris and Douglas, and three other friends. There were currency restrictions in force and I hadn't obtained the necessary licence so I stuffed £10,000 in the back pocket of my jeans. Christine quipped that looking as I did I might be searched for vagrancy and the yachting agents at Piraeus were somewhat amazed when I hauled the by now rather sweaty and crumpled notes from my pocket. At that point the Greek government had decreed that all charter captains were to be Greek, so we lost the nice bloke Avril had recommended and got a very surly Greek and his even sulkier girlfriend. He was used to stink pots (motor boats) so was always reluctant to put the sails up and she was even more reluctant to cook. We went past the temple of Sunion and up through the Corinth Canal to Skopelos and Skyros. It was strange to stand by Rupert Brooke's grave and think this place of rough land and roving goats was his corner of a foreign land that was forever England, and stranger still to think such a great war poet died of an infected mosquito bite and not a bullet. We made the best of it and had a great holiday, despite our crew. Meals improved once I took over the cooking and Douglas, who is a keen fisherman, caught lots of sardines which we barbecued on the beach.

Back at Circus Road I realised I had simply been living in the bottle, frittering things away. I was still a member of chambers but had done little work for a long time. I was bent on self-destruction and an absence of pain and I had no desire to leave the soft glow of the gin. Things had moved on and the time had come to leave. With both my parents dead and their estates settled I could not justify staying on nor did I really want to; that part of my life was over. I was thirty years old and I had lived there all my life. In 2004 I had a strange visit back to the house. I was driving past, the gates were open and builders were moving around inside. I parked the car and walked in, expecting someone to stop me but no one did, so I went into the house and wandered all over it and as if I were a ghost no one spoke to me or enquired my business. The house was full of vulgar changes: marble; gold leaf; the loggia had been closed in as a rumpus room; and the gallery had become the main entrance with an ostentatious chandelier that would never have fitted in the original house hanging from the elevated ceiling. That visit made me very sad but at least it laid my ghosts to rest; however rich I might become even if I won the Lottery I could never go home any more. Aunt Olive haunted my footsteps in the days when I was packing up, offering me money for pieces I didn't want to take with me. We never discussed the battle over my father's will and she was a sad lost person without Uncle Douglas. To escape I would seek sanctuary in the newly opened Chinese restaurant in the High Street and eat dim sum to the strangled renderings of 'Any Old Iron' or 'You Can't Make Willy Go Where Willy Won't Go' in Chinese.

I had a huge leaving party. One day gazing at the Pitons I had seen this sow with piglets rootling on the edge of the beach. Avril had exclaimed, 'How sweet,' but I remarked, 'How delicious, let's have one for dinner.' When she demurred I said I would cook one for her in England. For this party I dug up part of the path and built a barbecue trench, Christopher Coleman provided a sheep part-cooked in a baker's oven and we had four suckling pigs. The barbecue was a great success and was a terrific send-off from my childhood home.

7

Wild days

I had been going to rent Johnny Coleman's house as he and his wife were going to India, but in the event it didn't happen and in the late seventies I moved into the small cottage at Little Bells which had been a chicken house in my youth. It had two bedrooms and a sitting room cum dining room, a kitchen and bathroom and it looked out on to the Ouse Valley with the sheep grazing almost to the bedroom window. I was where I had always wanted to be but sadly I did not behave well and drove myself out of Paradise. I spent my time commuting to London for cases or if I was lucky being briefed in the Lewes or Brighton courts.

The later seventies was probably one of the most corrupt periods of CID policing but convincing a court or a jury that the police had stitched up your client required fairly definite proof. On the one hand you had the gangs giving backhanders right, left and centre, and on the other you had frustrated policemen who couldn't find enough evidence simply inventing it. For instance one client, an Oxford don accused of stealing books from the Bodleian, burst into tears in the witness box at the appalling English in his supposed confession. 'I have dedicated my whole life to the beauties of the English language and I would never, whatever I had done, be guilty of so abusing it,' he sobbed. The jury believed him. And I had a case where two police officers swore blind they had seen my client drive a lorry into a lock-up. The vehicle was found with another driver and the stolen goods five miles away on the following day. The evidence against my client was refuted only because the lorry was three feet too high to go through the garage doors. I like to believe that things are different now but I am in no position to judge.

It was at Selmeston that I first had occasion to cook peacock. I had a vegetable garden outside my window and would shoot the rabbits that wanted to deprive me of my greens, and I got quite good at cooking rabbit. One morning, very hung over, I heard a rustling, took aim and was rewarded with a loud squawk. Thinking I had potted an out-of-season pheasant I went to look and found a very dead peacock, which had strayed in from the estate over the road. Mortified, I invited the neighbours to dinner and looked out some rather good wine. By the time we got to the main course we were all well flown. They pronounced the dish delicious and asked what it was. When I told them they roared with laughter and announced that I could have as many as I liked as they were overrun with them. Apparently if peacocks breed they do it very efficiently except that they produce a heavy proportion of males.

The pub I favoured was the Yew Tree at Chalvington, where we had always gone in my adult visits to have a drink and watch the cricket. So enthused was I by umpiring Sunday cricket matches that I took a qualification to become an accredited umpire at village league level run by the MCC and umpired regularly at weekends. Johnny Scott used to play cricket there and I can still see him with a bandana tied round his head to hold back his Afro curls. The old publican Charlie Baker had kept open hours, only closing the pub when he felt himself falling asleep. The pub had been sold on Charlie's death and I had thought of buying it, but fortunately for everyone's sake I didn't.

This photo of Molly, my beloved mother, was taken when she was 14 years old.

She grew up largely in Singapore and Australia. Eden Hall, now the Residency for the British High Commission in Singapore, was the house built for my grandmother.

My formidable paternal grandmother, universally referred to as 'Muddy'.

My father was a brilliant surgeon but a deeply troubled man.

My parents married
in Paris in 1927.

Both my parents rode. This was taken in Rotten Row, Hyde Park, in 1932.
My father is the second on the left and my mother is riding side-saddle.

My grandmother
Elsie, seated, my
mother, and my sister
Heather, who is 19
years older than me.

Me and my mother, who was 39 when I was born.

Going to the circus with friends, aged about 7.

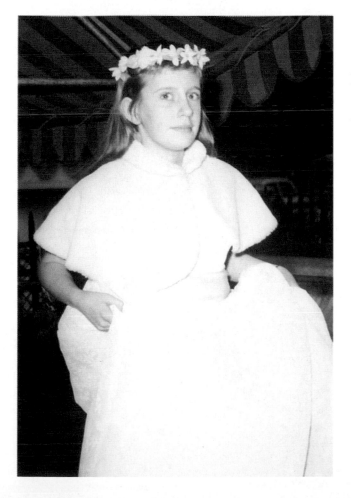

I was ten when my brother Anthony got married in 1957.

Playing Ernest in the school production of *The Importance of Being Ernest.*
That's me in the bow tie and stripy jacket.

My school friend
Christine made this
sketch of me when we
were both 16.

This photo of me was published in the *Evening News* on
the occasion of my 21st birthday.

I was the youngest
woman ever to be
called to the Bar.
This was taken on
the day I received
my first brief in my
own name.

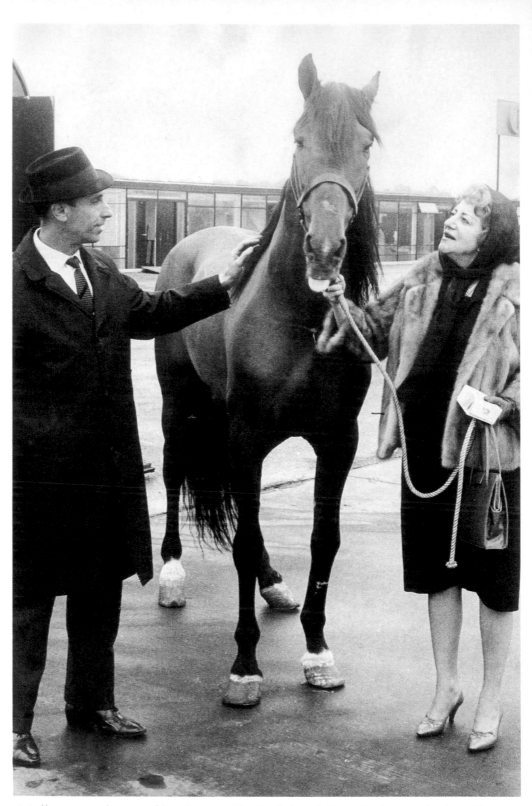

Mollypop with one of her horses, Ruisiñol and Pepe Forbes in the late sixties. When she died in 1975, my life spiralled out of control.

Driving through the back lanes I was unlikely to be stopped, and I am afraid to say that drink-driving was the norm for me. I was delighted to discover that the new owners of the pub were Jim and Rhett Comber who had been with me at Gray's Inn. I deposited the mug I had been given for organising the Gray's Inn Common Room Bar at the pub and spent most of my evenings there. On my arrival I would be offered my usual, which was four double gins and two small tonics with ice in my pint mug. Throughout the evening people would add an extra gin and sometimes I would buy an extra tonic but by the end of the evening I would have drunk nearly a pint of gin if not more. This was not of course my only alcohol intake during the day. Surprisingly, such is the human body's capacity for the stuff that I was not rolling drunk or falling about, though heaven knows how many times over the limit I was. I had not yet started drinking in the mornings or shall we say not before the pubs opened at eleven and then not if I was working.

Johnny's father Sir Walter was a benefactor and patron of the Yew Tree, and he was a great breeder of Jack Russell terriers. His arrival was always heralded: the pub door would open and through it would burst a spray of terriers, snarling and scuffling, followed by Walter, at which point every woman in the know would pick their handbags off the floor mid-conversation; if you didn't you would probably get a rather wet handbag as terriers feel it their duty to pee on everything. I spent many happy hours discussing food with Walter, who was an enthusiastic cook and gourmet.

I decided to organise a rugby match between Gray's Inn and a team of my own which I would call the Dickson Rioters. With Walter's help we erected rugby posts on the grass field next to the cricket pitch, I had T-shirts printed with a Gray's Inn griffin holding a rugby ball in one hand and a pint mug in the other with the fixture details below. I booked the Selmeston Village Hall and arranged for someone to roast a pig. It was a splendid event, Gray's Inn trouncing my team as I would have hoped but not too overwhelmingly. We drank the pub dry of beer and moved on to the party. The pig was delicious and Miss Lamb, the former village school teacher who was stern and formidable and held the keys to the hall, was so entranced at being asked to dance by so many nice polite young men that she let us stay well past the midnight deadline. Sixteen people, among them the local copper, travelled down the village in or on my Bristol, and although arrangements had been made for local beds I awoke next morning to find fourteen people sleeping in or around my cottage, including the fly half who was sleeping like a knight on a tomb on top of the narrow upright piano. I set to cooking breakfast for a rather fragile crew.

It all sounds great fun and at a certain level it was, but by now my chambers were getting fed up with my continued absences and offered that I should keep my name on the door but vacate my room, a polite way of telling me to leave, that really meant that if I was sent work of my own they would clerk it for me but I would not be provided with work from chambers. Did I care? No, not really. My ambition and plans for my career were long gone. It was merely an incentive to go off and spend more money, on more yacht charters, hiring private aeroplanes to go to the races at Deauville, on visits to the Cipriani, the Ritz in Madrid and Paris and expensive restaurants: amazing how the money goes. People ask, was I miserable? What did I feel? The answer is nothing. If you spend your waking hours cocooned in alcohol, if the moment there is the sign of a feeling or a critical thought you reach for the bottle you don't feel, you aren't afraid. I may have been spiralling downwards into a welter of destruction but I wasn't really aware of it and if I ever was I didn't care. I existed from one drink to the next and my entire world was focused on where that next one was and where and possibly with whom I would drink it. Finally Aunt Olive took out an injunction to stop me dealing with my own money until Circus Road was sold and everything froze. I suddenly had no money again and instead of explaining this to the Colemans I ran away. I simply left everything and went. I didn't pay my rent, my tradesmen's bills, I just ran.

Ran back to London and into the arms of William, known as Bill or Billy. He was another lost child; his parents had been the glamorous couple of London society before the war, his mother had been deb of the year, and theirs was the wedding of the year at Hanover Square. Then came the war; his father, imprisoned with the Guards Brigade at Calais, spent the war as a POW, while his mother did war work being over-friendly to Americans. Father returned and soon departed with a girl groom, leaving Bill and his sister Vicky with their mother. Like so many Old Etonians nothing afterwards ever measured up to school. Bill had a brilliant palate and was top of his profession as a wine merchant until his business partner David Grand was decapitated by a flying hawser in a sailing accident and Bill's affairs took a nosedive. Bill had already spent his mother's inheritance: her grandfather had been Lawrence van de Weyer, the man who invented Belgium as a fiefdom for Prince Albert's brother Leopold and to whom Queen Victoria had given a house in Windsor Park so he could be near her. Bill existed by selling wine now and again and by the kindness of his friends in general and his sister and brother-in-law in particular. Bill was a wild child, tall, well built and looked rather like the young Churchill, his sole aim in life being to enjoy it. He carried a torch for the skier Davina Gallitzer but when she went off with his old school mate the Duke of Fife he had no hesitation in assuaging his broken heart and his thirst by selling the story to William Hickey. He did mad things. After my last Circus Road party he and Bill Bentley, of wine bar fame, went off to the Dorchester for breakfast and in a vain attempt to order scrambled eggs with manzanilla (I never discovered whether you were meant to drink the sherry on the side or cook the eggs with it) were served scrambled eggs with maraschino cherries which, though deeply horrible, they insisted was a new gourmet dish.

It was Bill who introduced me to the world of St James's bars and after-hours drinking clubs. Back then pubs opened between 11 a.m. and 3 p.m. and reopened between 6 p.m. and 11 p.m. These regulated hours had been brought in during the First World War to keep the munitions workers away from the drink and to circumvent them there had sprung up a raft of afternoon drinking clubs, such as the Colony Club, made famous by the antics of the artist Francis Bacon, or Muriel's, portrayed in the Simon Raven novels. In Shepherd's Market there was the maisonette owned by the famous Ruby Lloyd, who had been a deb but had married a Dublin gangster who died young, as such people often do, leaving her the house. And all over London, up dingy stairs or in basements, there were such clubs; there was even one supposedly owned by a retired voodoo witch. There was a great vogue for society to mix with the world of gangland villains, not just for sex as in the Christine Keeler or the Lord Lambton affairs but just for the edge, the desire to rub shoulders with dangerous people who thought nothing of inflicting pain or death. The Kray twins you may remember were fêted by Lord Boothby and a certain crowd of rich and titled people. The availability of drugs was made possible by such connections, and it was in these drinking clubs that much of the shoulder rubbing took place. The clubs weren't particularly glamorous, although some of them had grand pianos where out-of-work pianists tinkled the ivories but most of them were just large rooms with a bar at one end and chairs and tables to sit at when you couldn't stand up any more. Their main purpose was to supply drink and often other services to drinking people. Afloat on a sea of alcohol it all seemed deeply glamorous and enormous fun. The clubs' real heyday was during the Second World War when only a bomb would close them and lonely servicemen could meet society ladies for a little consolation, but they were still going strong until the change in licensing laws allowing all-day drinking finally rendered them obsolete.

Twenty-four-hour drinking was easily obtainable in seventies London. After the pubs closed in the afternoon, you moved on to one of the afternoon drinking clubs until the pubs reopened in the evening, then you moved to a nightclub which stayed open till 3 a.m.; and after that it was on to the pubs in the London markets, Covent Garden, Billingsgate or Smithfield, where the pubs were open to service the night trade of the markets. At the market taverns you rubbed shoulders with the traders, the porters and the ladies of the night in for a quick port and black, or gin and lime to keep out the night cold. You could get a very good breakfast in the market pubs, much needed blotting paper in the hard round of balancing your drinking so you didn't fall down drunk. Usually we staggered home to bed with the dawn, for the hardest time to find a drink was between 8 a.m. and 11 a.m. and even a dedicated carouser has to sleep some time. The high spot of St James's drinking was Jules Bar in Jermyn Street where the manager Paul Lilly was rightly reputed to make the best Bloody Marys in London. Bill loved this world and he was a man who found fun everywhere, whether it was talking to Bill Cracknall who had been Starter Assistant at Newmarket and told me my father had once advised him to take his Long Tom (stockwhip) to Piccadilly where he would make a fortune, or some titled old school chum like 'Lucky' Lord Lucan or the millionaire jeweller Anthony Edgar. Lord Lucan was a dour rather humourless man whose sole interest in life was gambling, mostly at backgammon. A member of my chambers had been representing his wife at the time of the murder and London was full of mad rumours, one of which was that he had died and been fed to Aspinall's lions; one day we shall know what happened to him, perhaps.

I was renting a flat in Fawcett Street which was perfectly okay except that my aged landlady, who I suspect had incipient Alzheimer's, would come down the back stair and appear in my bedroom in the middle of the night to discuss her boundary dispute on a property she owned in Kent. I didn't mind if I was on my own and would give her a cup of tea and send her back upstairs but it was rather unnerving if Bill was there, especially as she would pretend not to notice him. Bill used to describe himself as a Capulian by which I think he meant happy-go-lucky. Sometimes we would go out to dinner with no money and he would grandly call for the bill and sign it, to be sent a bill at a later date – he vowed he was driven to do this by his alter ego Colonel Signinton-Smythe – and would draw a picture of a dome-headed moustachioed individual at the bottom of the bill as proof. Usually these bills would catch up with him months later and were generally paid by his long-suffering sister Vicky. At some point in our relationship Bill's father died. They hadn't spoken for many years and Bill's only bequest in the will was his grandfather's revolver which came with a note attached; this read: 'If you are a gentleman you will know what to do with this legacy.' Meaning shoot yourself. Bill sold the revolver, took a whole group of us out to dinner on the proceeds and then, yes, you guessed it, signed the bill. On this occasion we went to a casino afterwards and Bill had a run of luck which I managed to hide in my handbag and persuade him he had lost it so at least the next day we had £500 to play with.

We went to Raffles nightclub perhaps four nights a week, never Friday nights which Bill swore was hairdressers' night out, meaning there were too many people. I was a great dancer in those days and we would dance the night away. I had a passion for Boney M and on my birthday Bill persuaded the DJ to play 'Ra Ra Rasputin' seven times in succession. I think we were thrown out that night. I am fairly sure Bill wasn't a member, nor was he one of Hurlingham where we would go to play croquet and in my case swim but such was his air of confidence that no one ever gainsaid him. This wasn't true of Annabel's, Mark Birley's exclusive nightclub on Barclay Square; for excursions there we had to rely on Bill's friend Freddie Sinha, the Raja of Pikepara as Bill called him, who was an accountant with Touche Ross and a bona fide member.

When Freddie and Bill got the flavour and went on the toot it was mad fun but quite exhausting. Here is a verse I wrote at the time, which really sums it up.

The Sermon on the Mount

Be like a little child they said, or the lilies of the field
The birds of the air and the grasses that seek no earthly yield.
I have two friends that follow that to the very nth degree
With every precept in that speech they really quite agree.
If there's no cash for food or drink do not be glum or ill
Just summon up the best in town and sign another bill.

They must believe that God will pay to risk so much on spec

That great divine Bank Manager who never bounced a cheque.

They laugh and dance their way through life in a charming childlike way

But woe betide anyone who'd sleep or doesn't want to play.

Repressive conventionalists they disapprove and frown

They've all misread their Bibles and seek a different heavenly crown

But they will be the ones who're barred with a millstone round each neck

By Raphael the manager at the heavenly discotheque

And my two friends will be wined and dined by the man from Galilee

I only hope for his own sake he's got more stamina than me!

One of our greatest achievements of going where we weren't allowed was at Longchamps racecourse on the day of the Prix de l'Arc de Triomphe. The perimeters of the French Jockey Club are closely guarded, but Bill and I, looking totally English and with very little money in our pockets, marched past the security guards talking loudly with glassy vowels and total sangfroid and were admitted with an enthusiastic salute and no questions. We had a lovely time drinking free Pimm's and watching the racing from the best possible venue; inside we saw several friends who were too polite to ask what we were doing there. I backed an outsider, young Walter Swinburne, still a qualified claiming apprentice, and I followed him dedicatedly and successfully after that, feeling him a lucky star for me. I backed him in the last race and won a lot of money so we had a very jolly evening. I have noticed that Old Etonians always bring too much luggage: on this trip I brought a small valise (shades of Muddy you might say) and Bill a cabin trunk with every change of clothes he might need.

Another companion on our excursions was David Morris, my solicitor, who had been discovered as a bright young man by the head of a top firm of London solicitors, Thicknesse and Hull, whose offices in a beautiful building behind Westminster Abbey had a steel plate in the door inserted after the Barnaby Rudge Riots. We used to joke that we might need this against my sister Heather who had once broken in the front door at Circus Road with the starting handle of a car. Bill and I taught David all about the good things in life – where to buy his clothes, what to order from a wine list as a change from Bolshevik Bollinger – and in turn he did his best to keep us out of trouble.

It was during this time that Heather decided to sue me for a share of my mother's estate. She came up with a totally bizarre and unworkable premise that Mollypop had left her out of the will because Heather was bankrupt at the time my mother made it and so she had created a secret trust for Heather. This would have failed in law for illegality but somehow she found counsel who wrote an opinion that got her Legal Aid. The other tenets of her case were that I had kept her apart from my mother, over whom I had exercised undue influence in Heather's absence, and that I had promised to give Heather money. The latter instance was true but an offer of a gift is scarcely binding in law, and ridiculously I probably would have given her money if she hadn't sued me. We ended up occupying five days of the High Court's time; the secret trust argument and the promise fell early but Heather's counsel plugged on with the undue influence. Heather went into the witness box and swore blind that I had prevented her from speaking to my mother, shedding the odd tear at the thought of being separated from Mollypop. That evening David Morris was re-examining the files when he found a letter wedged into the fabric at the back of one. This was a letter from my mother to Eric Parker, Dippy's father, who had been her solicitor at the time and had drawn up the will. To paraphrase, it said: 'Dear Eric, I enclose the telephone bill which you will see is for the horrific sum of

£500 but you will also see it is made up mostly of reverse-charge calls from Heather in Spain. You might say I shouldn't have accepted them but what should I have done when the dreaded alternative was her getting on a plane and arriving here to demand yet more money.' Collapse of Heather's case, we won and obtained full costs against the Legal Aid Fund. I was now able to sever all ties with Heather, the residual guilt I had inherited from my mother around her behaviour was swept away and I was glad to be shot of her venom and abuse. Apart from my brother's funeral I have never seen or spoken to her again.

It was one evening when Bill, David Morris and myself had gone to Jules Bar prior to going out to dinner that I first saw Clive, the man I was to love more than any other in my life. I had heard Clive stories for years, such as how he had found a policeman's bicycle outside Jules Bar (the policeman had been having a quick fag in a doorway) and mounted it to ride it up the street for a laugh. The policeman had run out shouting and Clive had pedalled up Jermyn Street the wrong way with the policeman pursuing on foot. Reaching the doorway of St James's Piccadilly Clive discarded the bike and rushed into the church shouting, 'Sanctuary, for God's sake sanctuary.' Clinging to the altar rail he was very downcast to discover that that option no longer existed in twentieth-century England. The magistrate who dealt with it found it very funny and offered him the choice of walking to Dover carrying a lighted candle and leaving the country for ever or paying a £10 fine. I knew that Clive had been successful in the insurance trade, his family having been involved in Lloyds since its inception in the eighteenth century, but he had left to set up Abbey Life with Mark Weinstock and had done very well.

On entering Jules Bar I saw a man in his shirt sleeves wearing a toque he had borrowed from one of the chefs doling out gull's eggs to all and sundry. Gull's eggs were a great spring delicacy back then and I love them, but they are harder to get now, as the open refuse sites attract gulls and there is a risk of E. coli. I asked Bill who that was and he said, 'Surely you know Clive.' He was a huge man around six foot five with a rather sinister scar down his face, the legacy of diving on to a rock while swimming. I was introduced and asked him why he was giving gull's eggs away. He told me that the day before at the Stafford Hotel he had seen an American devour several with the shells still on and had decided it was his duty to educate people. I persuaded David to ask Clive to dinner too and we all went to the Poissonnerie on Sloane Avenue, which still serves excellent fish to this day. During dinner Bill and I started bickering, probably over his proposed trip to Sri Lanka, and Clive, saying that he had enough in his life of domestic wrangling, left abruptly. I thought him quite wonderful and most attractive.

Bill had some very iffy friends and was invited to go to Sri Lanka to try to set up a casino as it was thought he might have some influence there: he knew the Bandaranaikas, a leading political family. The people behind this scheme were quite clearly East End crooks although they had Frenchified their names and I knew that what they were really interested in was drug running. I told this to Bill who couldn't or wouldn't see it. I informed some of my friends in Customs and Excise and eight people were arrested in due course but not Bill who went anyway. I was proved right when he ended up in a Sri Lankan jail from which I was persuaded to go and bail him but by that time I had moved on. One had always heard rumours that Bill was AC/DC, and one night when I was not expected I went round to the ground-floor studio flat he lived in just off Knightsbridge. I let myself in and found him having it away with a rent boy. I was furious, picked up the naked rent boy and not knowing where to put him hurled him through the window into the street beyond. As I was remonstrating with Bill I heard the boy on the phone in the hall trying to call the police. I rushed outside, grabbed him with one hand and ripped the phone off the wall with the other, then dragged the boy whose name was Terry into the flat. Bill had fled into the bathroom and locked the door so Terry and I found a bottle of brandy and his clothes and spent a pleasant night sitting and talking about life and drinking; at one point I made us omelettes. Bill spent the night cowering in the bathroom listening to the laughter, and in the morning he had a dramatic black eye where I had hit him. So that was the end of my affair with Bill but we remained friends, thank God, as you will see later. I don't think I had been in love with Bill, I just enjoyed his company and his zest for life. We did wild and mad things together and we had the same drive to black out any pain with our alcoholic drinking.

8

Sunk in gin

I didn't see Clive again until some months later, when I was about to take over the food side of an afternoon drinking club. I had given up practising as a barrister. Chambers had decided quite rightly that I wasn't pulling my weight and had asked me to give up my seat and in any event I was bored with the legal world, having no parent left to show off to. After my experiences in the West Indies where I was so enthusiastic about the food I had decided without too much thought that food was a path I wanted to follow. The club was called Wilde's Club because it occupied premises in St James's Place where Oscar Wilde had once had a pied à terre for entertaining his young men. This sometimes led to confusion but it wasn't a gay club but an original First World War drinking club. The doyenne at the time was a woman called Valentina Houliham, who must have been a great beauty in her day and still had beautiful skin and cheekbones despite a diet consisting almost solely of brandy and soda. The club occupied a long bow-windowed room in a Georgian house. It had a piano and banquette seating at one end and a very long bar with stools filled the rest of the room; there was also a tiny kitchen, an office and storage space at the back. Val had had enough of club life and wanted to retire and a Northumbrian called Jerry Dempsey had made her an offer. At that time there was hardly anywhere to eat in St James's outside the gentlemen's clubs and it seemed a good idea to attract new members to the club by doing food. In nearby Ormond Yard there was another such club called Eileen's run by two Irish sisters from rural Tipperary who had come to London as young women to make their fortunes. It had a television set, an uncommon addition to drinking places in those days, and attracted the racing enthusiasts who watched the sport over drinks and sandwiches. On this day, leaving Jerry to deal with things, I had gone over to Eileen's for a drink with Freddie and to my surprise found Clive at the bar. I was in a frivolous mood and wanted to buy everyone a drink so I announced, quite untruthfully, that the drinks were on me as I had had a winner the day before. Everyone congratulated me except Clive who questioned me about my winner. To my flustered response Clive delivered a put-down about my meagre supposed winnings, which made me feel very stupid. I ignored him and paid for the drinks.

Wilde's Club was my first commercial cooking venture. Collins the publishers owned the building, indeed most of the street, and Jerry had offered group membership to them, and also to Christie's and the *Economist*, which proved a brilliant idea. Most of Wilde's existing members, although they paid by direct debit, which provided a nice platform of income, were ageing and didn't come to London that much so we needed new blood. The main drinkers came in at around 3 p.m. after lunch for a liqueur or some champagne or just to while away the afternoon and then another wave swept in on their way home from the office and stayed until we closed at 8 p.m. In my tiny kitchen I would cook a huge vat of chilli con carne every day to be served with French bread. Though I say it as shouldn't you would be hard put to find better than my chilli. I also cooked a dish of the day, quite often steak and kidney pudding which I would make in pressure cookers. The benefit of this is that they only need two hours not four to cook and once the pressure is up you can move the pans off the heat and they will stay pressurised and cooking for some time so that you can make several at once. I only had two rings, a Baby Belling oven and a salamander grill so I was glad of my experience with the limited space and facilities of a yacht. I would also make proper Cornish pasties from the recipe given me by Mr Treleavan, but I had very little oven space, and of course grills, chops or steak sandwiches which were very popular. The Collins kitchens sold us quiches every day and Joan their cook would come in and drive us mad by ordering a rainbow cocktail, a drink with stripes of different coloured liqueurs which are kept separate by their specific gravity, once a week as her reward for her help. We always got the first one wrong so she had that for free. Ploughman's lunch or Stilton and biscuits were also popular as were omelettes in summer and cold ham on the bone or oxtail in winter. The first wave of lunchers were the Collins sub-editors who always arrived shortly after we opened at twelve and virtually lived on chilli or so it seemed. I used to use the knife I had chopped the garlic with to slice the butter and it was an easy way of producing a subtle garlic-flavoured butter for their bread. Most of them went on to be senior editors, many in the cookery world, so I caught up with them again later in my life.

We stopped serving food between four and five in the afternoon to give me time to hop on the bus and go down to Brewer Street market to buy meat, vegetables and fish. We didn't serve much fish but offered smoked salmon or smoked mackerel pâté and occasionally fish pie. On my way back I would often go via Fortnum's to buy ingredients and pop into Eileen's for a quick drink. I was not really aware that I did this to see Clive but I did. Likewise Clive, who hadn't really patronised Wilde's before, would come in about six and stay till closing and a group of us might then go across to Duke's Hotel to talk to Gino the nice Italian barman or up to the Blue Posts, the local pub. One day out of the blue Clive asked me if I wanted to go racing the next day, Saturday. I accepted happily and we arranged to meet at Paddington Station.

I was by now living in rather better premises, in a house owned by a man called Barry Sutcliffe, a large ebullient man with a Roman nose who had the food franchise at the Old Vic. He was an excellent cook and on non-matinee days when the restaurant was closed would organise private lunches where his friends would pay a nominal sum for the food, and the drink consumed supplemented Barry's income. He was required to wear evening dress every night and I used to reduce my rent in exchange for ironing them. I always knew when he was in hot pursuit of a lady friend because he would ask me to iron his boxer shorts as well! Barry and I rubbed along very companionably; neither of us fancied the other so we spent many happy hours reading recipes to each other, and discussing wine. Barry was also a friend of Freddie's and on the day I was to go racing Freddie rang early in the morning. I answered the phone as Barry was in the bath. Freddie said I was to tell Barry that he would come over to watch the racing as he had been intending to go with Clive but had been told that Clive was too hung over to go. Freddie was quite peeved but not as cross as me. So I stayed in and watched the tele with Barry and Freddie.

Monday dawned and I went to Eileen's expecting an apology from Clive. What I found was six foot five of towering fury. Clive, it emerged, had missed the first two race trains waiting for me and had only taken the third at the last minute. I had, it seemed, made a fool of him as he had told his friends he was waiting for a girl who had then not turned up. I was speechless and recited Freddie's tale of woe as explanation. This did nothing to pacify Clive who said that he hadn't wanted Freddie along playing gooseberry. You could have knocked me down with a feather. I said we really had to talk about this, but both of us had dinner engagements that evening. I was dining with a friend of Freddie's called Mohinda who was good fun but had a passion (unreciprocated) for me, and Clive with a group of friends. Fate intervened as it happened. Clive and his friends and Mohinda and I all turned up at the same restaurant. By the time we had reached pudding Clive had detached himself from his party and joined our table, much to Mohinda's annoyance, and wouldn't leave. Finally he announced to Mohinda that as he and I were going the same way we would all share a taxi and drop Mohinda off en route. I was somewhat surprised at this, as I knew Clive lived in Belgravia and Barry's house was in Brondesbury Park. It was, I suppose, a *coup de foudre*; no sooner was Mohinda out of the cab than Clive and I were locked in a steamy embrace. He took me back to Chesham Street to see his hunting buttons and that was how it all began.

Clive, who was fourteen years older than me, had been married twice. His first marriage had ended abruptly when his wife had died leaving him with a small daughter and he had married again fairly soon as he couldn't cope on his own, looking after a small child. As a young man he had been devastatingly handsome and had been Captain of Cricket at Harrow but the drink had struck fairly early and like me he was a dedicated alcoholic. By his second wife Ann Clive had had two more children, Francesca and Richard, but some years before I met him Ann, fed up by his drinking habits, had left him for a Rhodesian dentist. In fact she had stayed in the house with the children and

Clive had moved from Oxfordshire to London and hung up his riding boots. His mother had apparently been an amazing person. She was born a Grenville, known as a wild lot, that family, ever since Sir Richard intoned the lines, 'Sink me the ship, Master Gunner – sink her, and split her in twain/ Fall into the hands of God, not into the hands of Spain', or rather something less poetic and sank his ship with all its crew somewhere off the Azores in the reign of Elizabeth! Clive's mother, a magnificent horsewoman, had produced two illegitimate children by different fathers, the first a famous racing driver and the second of whom left her a racing establishment at Newmarket where she spent her summers. Finally she settled down, married and produced Clive and his brother Martin, and all the children were raised together. Her whole life was devoted to horses and so it was with Clive, who, despite his size, hunted and even point-to-pointed. Eventually the drink took away his ability to ride. Everyone in the Bicester country knows the story of Clive's lawn meet where, hounds gathered outside his house, he rode across the lawn and slowly toppled out of the saddle drunk as a lord, curled up and went to sleep with his horse cropping the grass beside him. When we were together we went to the races at least once a week, mostly on Saturday but sometimes an evening meeting during the week.

Clive and Ann had the most civilised divorce I have ever come across and this spread to access to Francesca and Richard, his two younger children, who would come up every other exeat and for half the holidays. They were put on the coach at Oxford and Clive would meet them off it. I would cook for them and we would go off to Hurlingham together. The club had seen me so often by now they were convinced I was a member and we could all go swimming or play croquet or tennis. Clive was always well behaved when the children were up and we moderated our drinking accordingly. He had a friend Norman who had worked for P&O and often we would all take day trips to France courtesy of Norman.

However at other times we were quite wild. Clive loved practical jokes. I remember one evening we were at Nikita's, a well-known Russian restaurant, when Clive went to the loo and discovered the hoover. Tying a towel into a very passable charlady's bandana, he plugged it in and came out hoovering round all the tables. We were asked to leave rather quickly after they had managed to detach him from the hoover. A further prank was when we were walking back to the flat and he saw some road signs which were designed to direct the traffic round a hole in the road. We were both rather drunk and Clive directed the arrows so that they would have taken you down the steps to the basement if you were fool enough to follow. At this point a police car drew up and we ran off and into the flat. I put on my dressing gown and when the police came knocking said there was no one else there, at which Clive walked out of the bathroom where he had taken cover, stark naked, saying he had a letter from his son Richard. The police ignored him and gave me a lecture. He also thought it a huge joke after Epiphany when the Christmas trees were thrown out to acquire them and arrive at various establishments dragging one, which he would then leave behind. Clive loved jazz and we would go virtually every week to the 100 Club on Oxford Street to hear the greats of the jazz world, Humphrey Lyttelton, George Melly, Kenny Ball, Acker Bilk and many others. He was also a good friend of Mike Mackenzie, the tiny, crippled, brilliant black jazz pianist who used to perform at the Dorchester Piano Bar. We often went there and when Mike saw Clive he would immediately start playing 'As Time Goes By', which was Clive's favourite and even after all these years I can barely manage to listen to it without weeping. When Mike had finished Clive would just pick him up and carry him to his car.

I shall never forget Grand National night 1980. I had backed the first three horses in a triple and stood to receive a lot of money when the cheque arrived. I promised Clive dinner at the Ritz and he said, 'Why not tonight?' I pointed out that I had to wait for the cheque and he said I could pay him back. Off we went, already with (as the Irish say) drink taken. When we got to the Ritz we met this Armenian admiral friend of ours. It was the admiral's birthday and we had to stop and drink several champagne cocktails before going in to dinner. By this time we were feeling no pain and asked to move our table three times because we couldn't hear the band. There was no band! There never was on a Saturday. At the end of dinner Clive asked for a house cheque with which to pay the bill. Sadly the Ritz had just changed hands and had stopped this facility. Clive said he'd just pop round to the office (it was in Pall Mall) to get a cheque book and told me to stay till he came back. He explained this to the management who were quite happy. I ordered another crème de menthe frappé and another cigar.

When you are drunk time either goes very slowly or very fast. After a while it seemed to me that I had been there for hours so I said I was leaving and asked for my coat. They replied that I had to stay until my friend returned. I again asked for my coat, where-upon they threatened to call the police. 'So call the bloody police,' was my reply and they did. When the police arrived I clamped my hands inside the arms of the *fauteuil* I was sitting in and under the seat. They could not get me out of the chair without breaking something. It took eight policemen to hoist me and my chair and carry me rather like the Pope out of the restaurant and to the waiting van and then again from the van into

Vine Street police station. By this time I was beginning to think this was not a good idea and asked the station sergeant to ring my solicitor. He pointed out that it was 2 a.m. to which I replied, 'That's what they're for,' and gave him David Morris's number. They told me David was on his way and again I tried to leave. They told me if I did they would put me in a cell so I told them to get on with it. Once again eight policemen carried me and my chair to a cell. I found myself sharing the cell with an underage pregnant girl who had been picked up for soliciting on Piccadilly.

At this point both Clive and David arrived having met at the Ritz, the bill had been paid and I was free. I finished telling the girl her rights and left her with the chair. I never knew what happened to either of them. Clive was deeply apologetic; he had got to the office, sat down and fallen asleep. David thought it all a huge joke and took us to the Cavendish for breakfast. It was by now 3.30 a.m. In those days the Cavendish served breakfast all night with alcohol served in a teapot at a price and the Jermyn Street tarts used to fight each other in the ladies loo, pulling each other's hair out and drawing blood with fingernails and nail files. Now it is a smart Greenall Hotel though the food doesn't measure up to what it was in Edward VII's day when one of his mistresses, Rosa Lewis, ran it and served him snipe pudding and baked onions stuffed with chicken livers, brandy and cream for his breakfast.

The club was doing rather well, but in the beginning we had had to deal with a lot of debts. The bailiffs would come round before opening time and I would cook them breakfast served with a pint of beer and they would tell me how to deal with the latest set of problems. I have always been rather fond of bailiffs: treat them right and they will tell you all sorts of options I never learned in the Inns of Court and funny stories too. I remember one telling me that the actor Dennis Price had tried to climb out of his loo window to escape and got stuck and they had had to take the window out to release him before they could serve him with the process. Johnny Noble of Loch Fyne fame was still selling wine in those days, not yet having come into his inheritance. He was the first wine merchant to import good quality foreign wines into the UK; before that it had either been French or some hocks and Rieslings. His offices were a few doors up from the club and he would look in at the end of the day with something to try in exchange for a steak sandwich. I became good friends with him long before he inherited the Ardkinglas estate and soared to success and the Queen's Award for Industry.

Collins had started bringing in their authors to entertain them and I remember telling Gerald Durrell that I had eaten lammergeier, a type of bustard known as the Egyptian stone breaker and a very rare bird, and he was not very amused. I forget that people don't share my enthusiastic desire to taste things. I often wonder what dodo tasted like that it was eaten to extinction. I also spent several hours entertaining Peter Townsend who was the most delightful and charming man; no wonder Princess Margaret yearned for him, although one must remember she didn't yearn enough to give up her claim to the throne. It wasn't that she couldn't marry him, just that she couldn't have her cake and eat it. One of my longest running pleasures, however, was a delighted young author who had just signed his first contract. He was dying to splurge on champagne but he wasn't a member so he couldn't buy it, so I socked him a bottle. I said I would look out for his books and I have bought every book Bernard Cornwell has ever written and all in hardback.

I even spent a curious two weeks working for Collins. Robert MacDonald, the brilliant head of Natural History who had saved the firm's bacon by persuading David Attenborough to contract with them for *Life on Earth*, wanted the overseas rights job to go to the girl who later became his wife. She had to give notice to Virago and Collins were not prepared to keep the post empty so I went and ran the desk. Everyone was clamouring for rights to *Life on Earth*. Collins had just published what then seemed to me to be a very boring book called *Flight Patterns of Birds of the Western Archipelagos* and I would amuse myself by telling would-be bidders that they had to bid for that as a twin package, and many of them did.

We had all sorts of members: some were from the Guards band that played at St James's Palace and they would come in and bring their instruments and we would have impromptu jamming sessions, and some were from the Artists Rifles which you may know is part of the SAS. At the beginning of my time at the club we had, as was and probably still is usual, a visit from the local heavy boys demanding protection money. As I was still slim and blonde I looked helpless and asked them to come back that afternoon since I was only the cook. I then rang Reg the Doctor, so called because he lectured on how to survive on lichen and earthworms and he came round with a couple of friends, including one who made Clive look petite and they waited in the office. When the heavies came back I sent them down there. I never heard a sound and I never knew or asked what happened but we were never troubled again!

On Oscar Wilde's birthday we used to have a party, when all the staff dressed up, Jerry as Oscar, Liz, who ran the bar and was very pretty, and myself as Edwardian demi-mondaines. We gave green carnations to all the men and served a cocktail for which I had found a recipe in Oscar's diary. It was made up of gin, parfait d'amour, blue curaçao, orange curaçao and lemon juice and properly mixed was vivid emerald green. We gave away as much of that as you wanted but even the most hardened drinkers couldn't face more than three, after which all you wanted to drink was champagne. David Morris recalls me saying to someone of this cocktail, 'If that is champagne this is real pain.' During my time at Wilde's Prince Charles married Princess Diana and we brought in a TV and had a huge breakfast party with kedgeree and Buck's fizz or black velvet. We were just up the road from the Mall so people came and went. All great fun but let me give you an indication of what drink does in excess. For the start of the eighties we had a party, to which thirty people came: of those thirty ten are dead, ten are in recovery and where the others are I do not know.

The therapists say that a relationship between alcoholics can never be a real one because of the presence of the drink as a constant third party, but all I can say about Clive and me is that there was always enough to go round so it never came between us and we both had a mutual dedication to protecting our supplies. We had only one row in our time together; it was a bad one and I walked out. I who never wrote letters wrote to him telling him I loved him, although we were back together by the next evening.

However alcoholism is a progressive illness and reaps its own harvest. Clive went off to Madeira with Norman for a week's holiday and when he came back he was orange. He went to the doctor who told him that he must go to hospital after Cheltenham week, believing that he had picked up a virus in Madeira. I don't know whether it was the extra week that killed him. We went every day to the festival and it is difficult not to enjoy it; we drank champagne and ate smoked salmon sandwiches. I've no idea if Clive felt it would be his last time but he threw his cap over the windmill even more than usual. I was in the stands after Clive had put £1,000 on his fancy and was standing next to a chubby Irish priest who had backed a different horse; their horses were neck and neck in the last furlong with each of our heroes egging on their favourite. In the event the priest's horse won by a short head and Clive, ever the gentleman, turned to him and hoped he had had a good bet. 'Oh I did, my son, I did,' cooed the priest. 'Sure didn't I have two pounds each way!'

On the Monday following the festival I took Clive to hospital. As we walked through St James's Piccadilly, Clive said he had always wanted to ring the church bell so we did and ran off giggling like naughty children. The hospital was the Central Middlesex out at Acton, which served as an isolation hospital and they wanted to isolate the virus. I went out every day and the Lloyds boys, as we called the young men from the City who favoured the Antelope on Eaton Terrace and stopped off at the club after work, went out every weekday. They were great admirers of Clive. Two weeks down the line it was Grand National Day, the year Grittar won and the jockey Bob Champion was the same age as Clive. I said I would go back and clean his racing boots as he would be so thin on his release he could go back to race riding. He seemed really well that day; he had grown a beard and looked a bit like Edward VII as Prince of Wales. He was longing for a bath and I got permission to give him one, and we fooled about a bit and I was sure all would be well.

On the Sunday I was godmother at the christening of Penny and Nick Hamilton's eldest son and didn't go in though we spoke on the phone. On the Monday I went to visit and they broke the news that they had put him on a drip to bypass his liver and his kidneys were packing up. I asked if they were going to put him on dialysis but they said no. The reason for this was that he had done the damage himself with his drinking and was not a preferred patient; this was the first time I had come across this attitude in medical practice and I was livid. Clive was very piano but I stayed with him as long as I could. The next morning I woke at 5 a.m. with a dreadful premonition, and rang the hospital but they said there was no change. At six his brother Martin was hammering on the door saying the hospital had rung him to say come quickly. I rang Imogen who also came out. Martin had once driven racing Bentleys so it was a very speedy trip. Clive was in a coma when we got there and died soon afterwards; in the breast pocket of his pyjamas was the letter I had written him. The darkness that I felt closing around me was a long time lifting.

His ex-wife Ann was very kind and said I must stay with them for the funeral as the children would want it. I don't know how I spent the days between the death and the funeral. I drank obviously but otherwise I have no recall. Clive was cremated and his ashes scattered on Bredon Hill where he could watch the hounds flying by and had spent so many happy days hunting. I went back to London on the train when it was all over, met a friend at Paddington Station and went on the toot. I unloaded him at his club at midnight and carried on for three days before falling senseless to bed.

I don't know how long I stayed in that bed, only getting up to go to the off-licence round the corner to buy more gin, where the sweet young manager Tom Gilbey would close the shop and walk me back to my door lest I fall under a bus. Sometimes I would wake up in the bath wrapped in my duvet with a pillow under my head and the side of the bath strewn with carefully arranged garlic bulbs and chillies; what strange thoughts had taken me there I shall never know but it certainly wasn't any desire to wash. I grew rank and fetid and wept bitter tears. One day there was a crash and the door burst open to reveal Bill who had come to rescue me.

My absence and refusal to answer the phone or the doorbell had worried all my friends. Good old Bill got me up and made me eat and persuaded me to go out and about again. I suppose he saved my life but at the time I could not find it in me to be grateful.

The lease on the club was up and Collins were selling their building. In any event I didn't have the heart to continue with it. I had loved Clive more than any other lover I have ever had and to this day he remains the one real love of my life. We were completely happy together, both of us larger-than-life characters with reputations for wildness but when we were at home in the flat, playing backgammon or just relaxing it was, as Clive said, lovely just to be us. My heart would leap and I would go weak at the knees when he entered a room. Our mutual interest in horses and racing gave us a natural bond but it was more than that, it was the most I have known of love. Yes, we were both alcoholics and we drank too much but that never really mattered. I have had other lovers since but they have never measured up, nor have I looked for anyone to do so. Once for me was enough and those who came after, however much they may have been friends, have really only been to fulfil a physical appetite. It is Clive who has my heart.

Following Clive's death I was involved in various other clubs and it was while connected with a club in Warwick Court called Grays that I became caught up in a series of events that led to my disbarment. An acquaintance of mine called Barrington J was involved in a court case and brought his solicitor to lunch at the club to meet me. Somewhere after my tenth large gin I remember saying that if he sent the papers down to the club I would look at them. I was no longer a member of chambers so this could only have meant on a voluntary basis. The papers duly arrived in the form of a brief, which I thought was a huge joke, and after looking at them in a rather cursory fashion put them in a drawer. In due course the case went to court and I of course wasn't there. I was reported for practising without chambers but by this time I had moved on and the command to explain myself to the benchers never reached me. Some time later I was told that notice of my disbarment had been published in *The Times*. Did I care? At that point I was so sunk in gin I wouldn't have cared if the world had ended. Later in sobriety I applied to the Bar Council who lifted the order.

If the next stage of my story seems rather garbled you must forgive me, for the five years that followed Clive's death were a mishmash of blackout and unmanageability.

He died the day the war in the Falklands was declared in 1982 but I knew nothing of it. One day some time later I was standing in the rain under an umbrella, and there was a parade going past and I asked a young man standing beside me what it was for. Smiling, he replied that it was the Falklands parade. Mystified, I asked him whether something had happened in the Falklands, and not surprisingly he fled. After I was a few years sober someone gave me a book on the eighties: I don't even remember the Pope being shot because I spent the first six years of that decade with my head in a gin bottle.

My drinking now occupied all my waking hours. I could not get out of bed in the morning without a third or half a bottle of vodka. At this I shook uncontrollably and it was a chore to drink as waking brought with it retching and dry heaves which made it difficult to keep it down. On one occasion I had run out of drink at home and staggered to the Antelope, and by the time I was served I was shaking so badly that a friend had to take me behind a pillar and force-feed me gin until I stopped juddering. I spent the first year working my way through my remaining money. Barry was dying of cancer and had gone to the country but I still had the keys to his flat as well as Chesham Street. The emotional pain was so bad some days that the drink wouldn't kill it; Clive's was, if you like, a death too far. Barry's flat was in Brondesbury not far from the Kilburn High Road. There is a piece in the *Big Book of AA* which says we seek out dark and sordid places, and in my case add the word dangerous to this. The troubles in Northern Ireland were in full swing and many of the Irish pubs on the Kilburn High Road were ringed with balaclava-clad figures holding candles and collecting tins. You can imagine it was no place for someone with my name and my English accent but when the pain got too bad I would take myself off there and go drinking. This was not my only reason however. I had added a new addiction to the drinking in an effort to kill the pain: sex.

Before now sex had been merely an appetite, something to be enjoyed with someone of your choice who you were fond of, in a relationship with or merely as a form of extended friendship. I was not particularly promiscuous but I was a child of the sixties, the daughter of a mother who whatever else had enjoyed a good sex life with her husband and I was for some reason free of Catholic hang-ups on the subject. Now sex became something much darker and more destructive. I would go to these Irish pubs not only to drink in company dangerous to me but also to pick up men who I would take back to Barry's place. They were invariably Irish and given the location Republican sympathisers, and when I read in some Fenian's biography that he evaded police searches by picking up a woman and going to her place I often wonder if that was me. They were men with no faces, no names as far as I was concerned, often fairly uneducated, rough trade you might call them and they were there for only one thing. Once one of them threatened not to leave the next morning and I picked up a claw hammer and told him to go before I knee-capped him. He went. I expect I seemed quite mad sometimes. I would go to the Gaulty Boy Dance Hall on the Kilburn High Road, a place of fights and drinking, and take some Irish country boy home, so there are marriages in Ireland that will have benefited from some lad having learned more than the missionary position. The God who looks after idiots and drunkards must have watched over me, for I was unscathed. Perhaps the aura of violence from my childhood was so familiar to me that I was unafraid and that may have protected me, or it may simply be that stored in my memory are all the verses of 'When Rhodri Macaulay Goes to Die on the Bridge of Taum' which I would often sing with great gusto and no musical ability to the assembled horde.

Eventually the money ran out and Barry died so I spent my days round the pubs of Belgravia. As long as I had my entrance fee, i.e. the price of the first drink, I could manage to drink for the rest of the day on other people's largesse. It was hard work, being entertaining, offering legal advice and generally being amusing but I managed it day in, day out for many months, usually finding the price of a bottle of gin from somewhere for the night. At this time a friend I had known from childhood, Tommy Mathew, was busy fighting a case over his brother's estate and in exchange for my advice he funded a lot of my drinking. His wife Olga became a friend and I spent a great deal of time in their flat, where such was my drinking that her three young children nicknamed me 'Gin' and the little girl Poggy learned to count to five by putting ice cubes in my drink. Olga was a Romanov and we used to joke that if she came into her own she would give me a council house in Siberia. When I was turned out of Barry's flat I fled to them and spent the night on their sofa. Olga, obviously alarmed that I might never move on, spoke to another friend Martina who allowed me to stay in a room in her flat.

Martina had been a student lawyer with me, and in one of our revues she had to perform an entr'acte where she walked on to the stage in a silver lamé dress and gumboots reciting, 'I must go down to the sea again, the lonely sea and the sky/I've left my bra and knickers there I wonder if they're dry.' She was somewhat taken aback at the riotous applause, for when the light hit her it was quite obvious she was naked beneath her dress! Martina didn't practise but cooked directors' lunches for a living and would happily feed me on leftovers. She was very good to me but sadly she fell for an ex-con with one eye who was into sado-masochistic gay practices. Often in the middle of the night Martina would receive a call from the Colherne or some other gay pub asking her to come and fetch him as he had passed out. Martina would wake me and call a taxi and off we'd go to collect him. You can imagine the impact on the other habitués of the pub when in walked two women and started carting out one of their number, albeit totally comatose. What used to fascinate me was the number of people one recognised from the law or politics in these heavy leather pubs, many of them deeply in the closet with wives and children. Martina married Luke and things didn't get any better.

I finally decided to move out when after one party from which I had absented myself I returned to find my bed clearly had been used for energetic sex and my wastepaper basket was full of faeces. Where to go? At this point my sister June had returned from America with her daughter by her second marriage, Christina. June's husband Hank had been a draft dodger and they had lived in many remote countries, in the Sierra Madre or the Pyrenees, even Turkey, so Christina's youth and education had been scrappy and peripatetic, although June, who should have been an Oxford don, had taught her well. June offered me the chance of living with her but though I was fond of her I didn't think it a good idea. June remains the only person ever to have confronted me with my drinking and until I got sober her words always rang in my head: 'Look at you with your great red moon face. What would Mummy have said?' And of course she was right.

9

Homeless

I was now homeless. I spent my time travelling between my friends, Christine, Carrots, Avril's mother in Cornwall, usually journeying by coach as the cheapest solution. When people look at Alcoholics Anonymous, usually known as AA, they are often surprised at the camaraderie between recovering alcoholics but I always found the same among drinkers. I had made friends via the Antelope with a couple called Titchy and Colin who lived in one of the Peabody flats off Chelsea Hospital Road, and they were endlessly kind to me, often letting me stay either in their spare room or on their sitting room floor if Titchy's ma was visiting; I would bring some drink and we would eat whatever there was and spend many happy hours whiling the world away. On only two nights did I sleep rough. Once I started the night at Victoria Station but the benches are specially designed to prevent sleepers and the Transport Police move you on; David Morris's offices were on Buckingham Palace Road at this time so I made my way to what had been the coal cellar in the area and slept peacefully on piles of old files till morning. The second time I managed to hide and was locked into the waiting room of the Victoria Coach Station where I slept on the benches till morning. It is not a lot of fun sleeping rough in winter: you get very stiff and cold, there are problems going to the loo and it is impossible to wash.

One day I was sitting in David Morris's office hoping to cadge lunch off him when I picked up a copy of the *Lady*. For those of you who don't know it the *Lady* is the specialist magazine for jobs in domestic service. I had my answer. I remembered how well our servants had been treated, eating the food we ate and living in comfortable rooms. I could cook and I would have a roof over my head and wages in my pocket: perfect. I have never understood the aversion to domestic service; the choice between living on the dole in some horrible hostel surrounded by people who will rob you as soon as look at you or living comfortably in a pleasant environment working for someone you might actually like and respect is to me no contest. I am not sufficiently bourgeoise to worry about my place in the class system and if you don't understand this, well, that's your problem. I had no sense of downshifting; maybe I should have had but pragmatism is the saving of many an alcoholic. I found an advertisement for a cook/housekeeper in Sussex. I phoned the number and spoke to the advertiser, a woman called Rebeka Hardy at Danehill and made an appointment to go for an interview the next day. David Morris marched me over to the railway station and bought me a ticket, not wanting to risk just giving me the money lest I drink it away, and then treated me to lunch. In the evening I went to the Antelope and fell in with a man who lived virtually next door to the pub; we went back to his place and spent most of the evening in his jacuzzi with a bottle of champagne which must have washed the smell of stale gin out of my pores and in the morning I took the train to Haywards Heath.

The Hardys' house, old and mellow, stood high on the Sussex Weald and the land fell away to a lake at the bottom of the hill. Lawrence owned the brick works; there had been brick works there since Roman times and when you looked into the lake, which had been created from a flooded working, you could see stones with Roman numerals chiselled into them. Rebeka was an energetic, sharp-tongued redhead; some of the staff on the estate were afraid of her but I thought she was great. The job included helping with the pheasant rearing for their family shoot and I remember Rebeka asking, 'You do know about pheasant, don't you?' I replied cheerfully that I had learned all I knew at my mother's knee. This was not strictly a lie as I knew nothing and the nearest Mollypop got to a pheasant was with a knife and fork! Although my father had shot them and we had hung them in the game cellar the butcher had plucked and dressed them. It was early spring and the hens had just been gathered into the rearing pens, so we went and looked at them and I tried to appear knowledgeable. Rebeka said she would let me know and put me back on the train. As she was leaving she remarked that they always liked to have a cake knocking about in case of visitors or peckishness. She refunded my train fare so I bought a bottle and went round to Titchy and Colin's to spend the night. I had given their number to Rebeka as a contact and at 10.30 the phone rang. It was Rebeka apologising for calling so late but they hadn't wanted to risk losing me: I had the job.

Now the remark about the cakes came back and I took fright. I was a good cook but my last attempt at baking had got me thrown out of the Brownies for adding anchovies to chocolate cake, a cake that even without the Brownies resembled a frisbee. After Louise left we had bought our cakes, since the advantage of living in St John's Wood with its Viennese Jewish refugees was that we had wonderful patisseries. I rang Christine in a panic and she told me to come up for the weekend and we would have a crash course. Telling Rebeka I couldn't start till the following week I cadged a ticket off David Morris again and shot north. We baked tea bread and scones, sponge cake and boiled fruit cake as well as ordinary fruitcake. Thanks to Douglas's passion for good baking Christine had become a talented baker. So I set off to Sussex with a light heart.

On my first evening Rebeka said they didn't want to tire me so they'd just have a cheese soufflé; again I froze, as this was not something I had ever made. The only book I could find was Robert Carrier's cookbook and I shall be forever grateful to him for what he wrote. Basically he said there was a lot of rubbish talked about soufflés, and if you could make a white sauce you could make a soufflé. As a child of my generation of course I could make a white sauce and he was right: I have never looked back.

I also have a great debt of gratitude to Rebeka. When I went to Danehill I was a good cook but when I left I had been pushed by her insistence that of course I could cook any dish into something much better. She never freaked if she came home and there were ten pints of cream in the fridge but only enquired what I was going to make with them.

The minutiae of raising pheasants took up quite a lot of time too; pheasants are nasty, unpleasant birds and I would defy the most dedicated fluffy bunnier to feel fond of them after spending any time with them. At the end of the shooting season in February the hens are collected along with some cock birds. Cock pheasants are not nice creatures and engage in gang bangs. Hen pheasants are bad mothers so the eggs are collected every four hours and hatched either under bantams or in incubators. The Romans introduced the pheasant to Britain but they do not really thrive in the wild and without shooting you would see very few. Game crops carefully planted to hold the birds also supply food and homes for many small birds. Pheasant shooting not only provides employment for keepers and beaters alike but also, as with all field sports, brings extra money into the area for both hotels and shops. The Hardys had a small family shoot putting out a few thousand birds but we reared extra birds to sell to other shoots. I obviously learned to cook a lot with pheasant, which is a good and healthy meat much better than most chickens you can buy. I can never understand why chicken is labelled the healthy option, given the proven direct link between MRSA and Third World chickens, which is mostly what you buy in supermarkets, and in any event they are raised in conditions you would not wish on your worst enemy and certainly not something you would want to eat. Enough, I am not yet a food champion. That is some way ahead; here I am merely a drunken cook.

There is a splendid cartoon I saw recently of a country couple in bed covered by dogs, and one is saying to the other, 'Put another dog on the bed, I'm still cold.' I was much reminded of Rebeka who always slept piled high with dogs in winter. I would hear her going downstairs early with the dogs and after she had walked the pheasant pens she would go back to her room. This was my time to take her her breakfast and my notebook and any cookery books I thought suitable. We would have a cosy time discussing menus and proposed parties, dinner or otherwise. On one occasion she decided I should cook a Gâteau St Honoré for a dinner party. I pointed out that St Honoré was the patron saint of pastry cooks and this was the dish that *pâtissiers* made to qualify for the French Pastry Chef's Guild. Such arguments held no sway with Rebeka so I made it anyway and I am happy to say successfully. I missed Clive dreadfully of course and was forever thinking of things he would have enjoyed but my old friend the gin kept the worst of it at bay.

So what, I hear you asking, is happening on the drinking

front? Well, with all the extra exercise and interest you would think that my consumption might have abated, but not a bit of it; I merely had it balanced, drinking steadily throughout the day and spending all my wages on gin. I had one partial day off a week, which started mid-morning and I would drive over to the Yew Tree, my old haunt, to spend the day drinking. I tended not to go much to Little Bells, although the rift with the family had been healed, but went instead to Christine's brother Nicky and his wife June who had a pig farm not far from the pub. Nicky was two down from Christine and had a smashing den he had built in the spinney complete with fireplace; once I cooked chips on the fire there, which tasted rather of the kerosene we had used to get them going but we pronounced them excellent. I would return from the Yew Tree with a bottle and often something to eat and when the pub reopened would try to persuade them to come back with me. Later we would all have dinner and I would spend the night on their sofa, getting up very early to drive back to Danehill. Their young daughter Charlotte would sneak into the sitting room earlier still to talk to me, play a game or worst of all play her recorder to me. One tune, 'It's Raining, it's Raining Again I Can't go to School Today', is still burned into my brain; she would at my request pour me a gin and tonic after which I could go on. June is a great cook and we have spent many happy hours cooking together. At one point they were living in a static caravan while building a house and the oven door had to be kept closed by one or other of us leaning against it which led to much mirth. When there was a large party at Danehill she would come over and help me. This actually led her to a career in catering.

In the morning I would be back at Rebeka's in time to cook breakfast. She did once remark to me that if on the day after my day off I was so hung over I couldn't work I was actually stealing her time, which was a point well made. She must have known I was drinking heavily; for one thing there was the smell but I suppose people associate cooks with drink and as long as they get good food served on time they will tolerate it.

I was still having a lot of blackouts and I produced the best meal I have ever cooked with total lack of recall. It was the engagement party for their son Allen and it was a very ambitious menu, ten courses for ten people. All I can remember is picking up the first saucepans at about two o'clock in the afternoon and then I woke in my bed the next morning, in a state of panic. I rushed downstairs and there was a beautifully clean kitchen, which looked as if nothing had been cooked there for days. I heard Rebeka coming towards the kitchen and froze like a rabbit in the headlights. In she swept. 'Clarissa, such a triumph, the whole county will be talking about it green with envy.' I smiled weakly and muttered that I was glad she was pleased. I had no memory of what I had cooked but could scarcely ask for the menu. Some six years later when I was a few years sober I met a man who said, 'I know who you are.' I winced but he went on, 'You cooked that brilliant dinner for the Hardys.' I asked him if he remembered what he ate and he replied, 'Every mouthful,' so I asked him to tell me. Here it is. Prawns in chau-froid and aspic; game consommé with tiny herb dumplings; fillets of wild salmon wrapped round a mousseline of trout and smoked trout with a champagne sauce; English partridge with watercress salad and bread sauce; a medley of tomato, champagne and mint sorbets; hare with wild mushrooms flambéed in brandy; a salad of endive and walnuts; assorted puddings, pot au chocolat; apple jalousie and queen of puddings; cheese beignets with a piquant sauce. Wow! I rather doubt I could do it today. I had had a helper from the village, hence presumably the clean kitchen, and I remember she seemed to have found nothing wrong with me the next time I saw her.

On my weekend off I would often go to Birmingham. Christine now had two children: Sara, my goddaughter, was seven and David was four; to them I was darling Kissa or godmother Gertrude who came with a suitcase full of snow because it snowed when I went there. You may have noticed that there seem to be a lot of children around at this time in my life. Well, I suppose my friends were at that age and while I have never wanted children of my own I like other people's and they seem to like me. From my point of view I can put them back in the cupboard and I expect from theirs I am not quite like other people. I have never really grown up and I talk to them on their own level. In any event all these children and others are now adults and still seem to seek out my company, send me text messages and tell me their worries. Society has overlooked what you could call the aunt syndrome, the importance of the adult with whom the young feel safe and who knows the whole family picture but who will not as far as they are concerned leak their secrets to their parents. Sara would creep into my bedroom, sliding along the top of the staircase so that David wouldn't see her and leap on me with great glee, as her favourite game, which she called buffing buffaloes, involved bouncing up and down on my stomach. It was vital that I woke up before she did, so that I could imbibe sufficient spirits to prevent myself from being sick or getting the shakes.

The shooting season came and I found myself with a great many pheasants to pluck. I became very deft at it and could do them in my sitting room with a plastic sack and make no mess at all. As is always the case it was hard to sell them for any sort of money so I would take them to the pubs in the area and sell them to the publicans and to guilty punters to take home to their wives! I earned many brownie points for this and the rest went into the freezers for future inventions. Although it was only a family shoot there was a lot of extra work with shooting: breakfast; lunch for the guns and beaters; tea and dinner for the house guests as well as helping with the shoot itself. One day I got back to the house to discover all the power was off and I was at a loss how to heat the stew for lunch. Remembering the under-keeper had Calor gas in his caravan, I climbed in through the window and cooked the meal. He was heavily into taxidermy and was furious lest I had disturbed his carcases! It was with this young man that I had laid up to shoot a fox that had got into the rearing pens and taken out 600 poults in a feeding frenzy, just biting the heads off and tossing the carcases aside; unlike most hunting people I have never really liked foxes but I still felt my mother's ghost breathing down my neck when we shot it. Town people think foxes are sweet fluffy animals but they are cruel dedicated killers and I wish they could see the damage they do to lambs and poultry. Those poults had involved hours of care and work; one might argue that they would have been shot in the end but they provided wages for several people and would have supplied food for more had they not ended their lives in this needless fashion.

The Hardys had several gun dogs but the top dog was a black labrador called Ben, whose grandfather, father and litter brother had been All England Field Trial Champions. He was bred by Jim Comber's wife at the Yew Tree and I was keen Rebeka should breed him with a little blonde bitch of the Sandringham strain called Amber. She wasn't keen but after much manipulation I persuaded her and the match took place. Amber used to spend a lot of time with me and I knew she was pregnant, but Rebeka and the vet were convinced it was a phantom pregnancy. I was proved right when, coming back from the village one night, I found Rebeka on the floor with Amber and two little black blobs; there were four in all and one of them became my Shadow, the sweetest dog I ever had and it broke my heart when I had to part with him, but more of that later.

Back at Danehill things were not so simple. I had developed a habit of flipping cars into the ditch, and once when Christine's sister Jo and her small son came to collect me, William, aged three, looked with puzzlement at the upside-down car and pronounced, 'We drive our cars the other way up.' I did this twice with the Hardys' cars and each time was quite unhurt. I would remain in the car with my bottle of gin and my book until I finished the gin or the book or the light faded, at which point I would extricate myself and wander off to find a pub and a telephone. The Hardys were very long-suffering: overtaking a line of traffic I nearly killed a canon from Hailsham who was driving towards me and it was only his quick-wittedness that saved us. Finally I was stopped on the Uckfield bypass for driving too slowly. I then punched the policeman in an attempt to get myself arrested so that I could not be in charge of the vehicle when I was breathalysed (I had once won a case on this point of law). The policeman, with a swelling black eye, asked me what he should tell his wife. I replied, 'Say it was another woman,' which he found so funny that he didn't charge me with the assault. I had been breathalysed twice before and had passed negative which had more to do with my lung capacity than any hint of sobriety. On one of these I had hit a Royal Mail van and leaving the bemused policeman with the negative test in his hand had fallen into a taxi and told him to drive as I had just passed the breathalyser. I later had to send a telegram to the driver of the mail van to find out where the accident had happened so I could collect the car. Finally, after two and a half years, the Hardys had had enough and I was asked to leave. I rang an agency; and armed with a carefully worded reference from Rebeka I went off to get another job. Both Rebeka and I were sad to see each other go; she had tolerated my drinking saying it was rather like her addiction to chocolate and we had shared a love of food.

My new job was for a man called Graham Greene, nephew of the author Graham Greene and chief exec of the publishing house Jonathan Cape. He lived at an amazing place called Wotton Underwood near Thame. The main house had been built by Sir John in the eighteenth century and stood on the site of an earlier dower house for the Dukes of Buckingham; the gates, which were from this house, were by the ironsmith Tissot and were quite splendid. In the 1960s the local council had been about to pull the house down when Mr and Mrs Brunner of the Brunner Mond family went to see it with a view to buying some statuary (Brunner Mond later became ICI so there was no shortage of money). The Brunners fell in love with the house, bought it and saved it from the wreckers' ball and lavished love and cash on it so that when I visited it was magnificent. The surrounding buildings were let out: Graham Greene lived in the old brewhouse, John Gielgud in one of the pavilions and a rich Swiss lawyer in the other. I occupied a bungalow in the old walled garden, which had two bedrooms, a large sitting room, a kitchen and bathroom. In other circumstances it would have been a smashing job and I bitterly regret what a raw deal my employer had from me.

Shadow and I arrived and were duly installed; at that time Graham was estranged from his wife and lived with his son in the house at weekends. This meant that really I only had to work hard from Friday night to Sunday; there was a gardener/handyman and a domestic to do the cleaning who came in from a nearby village.

During the week I was meant to clean up from the weekend house party and shop and prepare for the next one. I also used to test recipes for the publishers who had a good list of cookery authors including the newly discovered Madhur Jaffrey. What of course I did was drink; sometimes I even leapt into the car they provided and Shadow and I would escape to Sussex to June and Nicky. This became particularly attractive after I discovered that Greene King breweries, with which the family had links, owned the local pub in Brill and my every action was reported back. I just about managed to hold it together at weekends and of course the cooking was okay; I had accounts with the shops in Brill and carte blanche on what I bought. My only tour de force during my time there was a dinner I cooked when Rab Butler retired as Master of Trinity. I had designed a splendid menu but sadly Graham's ex-wife returned and rejected it out of hand and we ate a meal of kipper pâté, boeuf bourguignon and elderflower fool, which was not what I would have chosen. In any event the dinner in high summer was a great success and I was quite amused because half the guests, including Annie Mallalieu, had been at the Bar with me and hailed me with great glee. I sometimes wonder and like to think that the Greenes were brought back together because Graham couldn't cope with his nightmare cook.

It was Shadow really who kept me alive, because the need to feed and exercise him got me out of bed during the week and he was my only and true companion. I had always wanted a dog of my own and he was the sweetest friend. I was bitterly unhappy, and would talk to my gin bottle, asking each new one I opened if it was going to be my last. Death, such an old friend to alcoholics, had never seemed more attractive; it wasn't that I wanted to kill myself, I simply wanted it all to be at an end.

Wotton was a strange place. Mrs Brunner, who was a great old girl and took tours round the house herself, must have been rather anti field sports, since the place was overrun with foxes because she would neither allow the hunt through nor order them to be shot. When you came up the drive at night their red eyes peered out at you from the bushes and I was forever having to wash Shadow who was at risk of mange from rolling in fox shit. The foxes had killed every living thing and were even trying to dig up the moles they were so hungry; the only survivor was a peacock whose mate had been killed by the foxes while she sat on her eggs and spent most of his time standing on various rooftops crying piteously for another. The Chinese say peacocks are the spirits of lost souls crying constantly for their lost companions, and in my madness and paranoia I would wake to his cries and think he was my father's spirit. You can imagine how that delighted me! Once again I flipped a car; they say it is quite difficult to overturn a mini van but I managed it.

One day Mrs Greene, who was down for the weekend, had gone strawberry picking with her son, and had put the fruit on to cook with some sugar and left it on the heat; she told me this and asked me to keep an eye on it which of course I promptly forgot. The jam bubbled over and spilled on to the quarry tiles of the kitchen floor. I don't know if you have ever tried to scrape up burned jam but when you consider that the metal plates at the side of Thomas Telford's magnificent Pontcysyllte aqueduct have been held together for 300 years by burned sugar you will get the idea. There I was down on my knees weeping with frustration and shaking gently; it was the first time I had been on my knees for years and, because I was, I prayed to a God I hadn't spoken to since my mother's death. 'Please,' I begged, 'if you're up there do something. I really can't go on.' I, who had once had boundless energy, was sick and tired of being sick and tired and couldn't even manage to clean a floor. Of course there was no crack of thunder and I got to my feet and went on with dinner.

The next day was Friday and Christine came over to see me with the children who loved playing with Shadow and they went off with him and the Greenes' son. Christine and I were sitting in the sun chattering when a police car drew up; following the flip with the mini they had run a check on me and had discovered there was a warrant out for my arrest for the Uckfield bypass breathalyser for which I had never turned up to court. I had left the area and had forgotten all about it. They had come to take me away to London to be dealt with. Poor Christine was rather taken aback and the children, who had come running over at the sight of the police car, were in tears as darling Kissa was borne away from them. I had rushed in to fetch my handbag and thrust into its capacious centre a bottle of gin and a copy of the works of Saki, my other constant companion at the time.

Off we went and as we proceeded down the drive we passed the house party coming up it for the weekend. I waved weakly at their astonished faces as the cook swept past them. Christine packed up my things and disposed of my store of empty gin bottles into the boot of her car. I confess I never went back to find out what happened. They took me to Aylesbury police station to await collection by a car from London and as I was only in transit never checked my bag so I sat in a cell for the afternoon sipping gin and reading short stories of black humour. Eventually I was collected and taken to Chelsea police station, where they found my gin and took it away and I was put into a cell with my book. Both Bill and Titchy tried to smuggle in gin to no avail but another friend succeeded and I spent the night with my book and my bottle in a cell with a magnificent parquet floor and so far had my world narrowed down that I, the girl once most likely to succeed at the Bar, was really quite content.

Next day I was taken to Horseferry Road Magistrates' Court in a Black Maria, the only other occupant a heroin addict, a pretty young woman who was shaking and shuddering with withdrawals. Fortified by my gin I gave her a lecture, telling her she mustn't waste her life like this. She must, I told her, ask the judge to send her to a treatment centre even if she subsequently had to serve time in prison. She looked at me with astonishment. David Morris came to court and eventually I was released on bail to appear at Uckfield at a later date. Out into the sunshine I went and straight to the Antelope to celebrate my release; one doesn't immediately recognise divine intervention after all. Of course I had to leave Shadow behind, because I had no future and his was a much better one with the Greenes. I later learned that he had been sent to Mrs Greene's brother in Italy and had been killed by a motorcycle; of all the disasters in my life his abandonment and death is the one I still most regret.

I had really burned my boats now. I knew no one was going to make excuses for me or give me references or even lend me money. I was horrible to look at: my face was bright red, verging on mulberry, with grog blossoms, as drinker's spots are called, appearing regularly. The whites of my eyes were a pale yellow tinged with red, piss holes in the snow I think it's called. I was very bloated and my hands shook with a gentle tremor however much I tried to control them. I smelled horribly of recycled alcohol. I was a mess. I felt nothing because I drank any feelings away but I looked like a lost soul. I had no real desire to stop drinking but I thought that if I said that I wanted to people would be impressed and say, 'Good old Clarissa, we must support her.' I didn't dare go back to Wotton, I had upset Christine and I didn't really know what to do. I threw myself on the mercy of Christine's mother, Josie Coleman. The only person I knew in AA was the Colemans' local priest, whose altar boys had complained that there was no wine for them to get squiffy on as he consecrated grape juice and they had seen AA literature around his house. I had once taken him out to lunch but had got pissed and so we had talked about the weather. Now I telephoned him and asked him if he didn't think it was time he did something about my drinking. He replied quite correctly that it was time I did something about my drinking.

Josie contacted Amberstone, which operated mainly as the detox centre for people prior to admission to Hellingly Mental Hospital, and their psychiatrist came to see me. I told her what I drank, the half bottle of vodka before I got out of bed, the two bottles of gin a day, the beer and wine with meals and anything else I could stay awake to drink and all this for ten years. She told me she didn't think I was an alcoholic, it was simply a nasty habit I had got into when my mother died, and after I was detoxed at Amberstone I would be all right as long as I counted my drinks, and I was duly given a date for admission. Dear heavens, what does one have to do to prove one's an alcoholic? Amberstone didn't support the AA message, as shown by an organisation called Libra started by a former patient which did not involve total abstinence. I went to one meeting and argued so I wasn't allowed back. My priest friend then took me to my first AA meeting. I thought they were all lovely people but that I had gone too far, that I had passed the point where I could make a recovery and that I was in a worse state than any of them and so would never be able to attend meetings. Years later I heard the story of the woman who had given the chair at my first meeting; it was incredibly like my story but clearly I wasn't listening.

On my first afternoon at Amberstone I was shown into a sitting room where there was another girl with bandaged wrists, and after a few minutes she gave an eldritch shriek and hurled herself against the window. This must have been unbreakable glass as she bounced off it, regathered, tried again and a cluster of men in white coats rushed in and bore her away. A mental hospital is a strangely liberating place, where you know that you will never be held responsible for your actions. One day another patient came into the refectory wearing my clothes, which were dripping wet as she had taken them from the washing machine. I was furious and made her strip to her underwear there and then. Life as a patient there was deadly dull as there was absolutely nothing to do. I had an embroidery on linen of the Bayeux Tapestry and people would come and sit around me to be lulled to sleep by the sound of the thread going through the cloth or simply to watch. On one occasion I got permission to give a cookery lesson – obviously no knives were allowed so I taught them to make a Victoria sponge – and it was the only activity we had during the ten days I was there. I never saw a doctor or a counsellor during my stay and was given hemeneverin, an addictive drug in its own right, which was supposed to stop me having a fit. Later I learned quite how dangerous and addictive it was but fortunately it didn't grab me. I palmed it and didn't take it. I had given Anthony's address as my next of kin and to my surprise Marah arrived to visit. As I wasn't dead I couldn't understand why she had been contacted but I was pleased to see her and it was arranged that I should go and stay in their basement when I was returned to the world after the ten days that are all a detox takes.

On my release I contacted an agency that provided short-term care, with no more than two weeks on a job. My first position was with an elderly widow in Edgbaston who was regarded as difficult. I didn't find her so and we got on very well and I persuaded her to go back to the golf club nearby and reunite with her friends. She really liked me and wanted to offer me a permanent job but I knew I couldn't keep it up and it was better to leave her in a positive frame of mind so I went. My next job was with an elderly man who needed a bit of help while his wife was in hospital; he lived virtually next door to Sissinghurst Castle and we spent a happy time driving round the Romney Marsh. He had lived there all his life and was delighted to show me all its secrets; it was not an area I knew and I grew to love its special quality.

After I left him the agency had no work for me so I answered an advertisement to stay with a Mrs Cohen aged ninety-nine, heading for her telegram and living on the Edgware Road. She was a dreadful old girl; if that's what it requires to make the ton I shall be glad to go at sixty. I was entitled to a daily walk after lunch which Mrs Cohen begrudged me, asking if I couldn't walk on the balcony by which she meant the fire-escape. The food was bought by her niece and there was so little of it that I actually spent part of my wages on food; the woman who came in to help with the housework told me that she had been Mrs Cohen's maid when younger and that she used to count out the cornflakes! Sometimes in the middle of the night she would rush into my room, jam her stick under the bed and demand to know if I had a man under there. One day she asked me if I was pregnant, telling me she had once had a servant who was and she had worked her till the seventh month then sacked her without a reference. For all that, though, it must be hard to have lived so long and outlived everyone. To my surprise when I came to leave she was very upset and said she would miss me. I had managed not to drink but it was white-knuckle sobriety and the world was an awful and frightening place without it. A friend of Marah's took me to AA meetings occasionally but I wasn't ready to listen to any new way to live. I just existed much as I had when drinking but with a constant feeling of fear, afraid of what I didn't really know.

My next job was for a Mr Garrod at Great Common near Woldingham, a rich man who was distressed to discover that my father had also been a member of the Garrick Club, and he felt uncomfortable employing someone from my background as a cook/housekeeper. He was always calling me to watch him swim and trying to persuade me to wear a uniform and I think he had a tendre for me. He had a pair of King Charles Cavalier spaniels which went everywhere with him and an alsatian which was frankly dangerous. The dog had already flown at the gardener and torn out his bicep and only a large payment had assuaged the poor man; he had also attacked a guest at a lunch party who had left the dining room to go to the loo. I spent all day with this dog and quite honestly didn't feel comfortable with him. One day just at dusk I was coming back from the dustbins and I saw the creature rushing down the path towards me with his fangs bared and his ears back. I shouted his name but with no result, and as he sprang I remembered my grandmother saying that if you hit a dog on the right hinge of his jaw you would knock him out. Nothing ventured, I took a swing and connected; bang, over he went backwards. I thought I had killed him, but when he came to I was his pack leader and he was as good as gold with me. So there I was: I had now knocked out one ex-Waterloo prop forward, one ex-flying squad officer and now an alsatian dog!

It was just before Christmas when I remembered Dr Hutton's words. I was run to a frazzle and I thought, Well, count your drinks. I had one gin and tonic and very quickly I looked again and somehow I had finished the bottle and then the next one. I remember I had failed to defrost the turbot, but there was one of those self-cleaning ovens that heated to some ferocious temperature, and through the haze I thought that it might do the trick; they had pasta for supper that night. The job was bound to go soon now that I was drinking, and just before New Year my employer became rather over-amorous and I put my knee rather hard where it hurt. Marah came and collected me the next day.

I tried to pretend I wasn't drinking or that at least I had followed Anthony's advice and was only drinking spritzers. Indeed I was in Motcombs wine bar with David Morris one evening, telling the assembled company that I was now only drinking spritzers, when my handbag tipped over and opened and a forty-ounce bottle (the sort of big one they put on optics) rolled out and along the bar. I scooped it up, thrust it back into the handbag and continued what I had been saying. No one said a word!

Marah didn't believe me but I kept going to AA meetings. I would declare how wonderful sobriety was and people would look at me wryly and say, 'Keep coming back.' I didn't see how they could possibly know though I must have reeked of gin.

April O' Leary, my nun friend who had been my Mistress of Studies at school, was based at a retreat centre up in the Brecon Beacons and I decided to go to visit her. I suppose it was some sort of cry for help. The centre was about eight miles out of Brecon on a hilltop, where there had once been a temple of Druidic priestesses so as April said it was a holy spot. I was very black and wrote a great deal of melancholy poetry, mostly highlighting the difference between the convent and the war planes that flew over the hills where the SAS exercised. I pretended I was only drinking tonic water until April took a swig out of my glass by mistake and realised it was almost neat gin. She didn't say a word but just looked at me quizzically and I walked away.

Leaving Brecon, I went to another job, this time in High Wycombe, primarily to cook for a funeral. An elderly couple had left the house and moved into an old people's home, then the husband had died and the wife had come back to bury him from their marital home. She had once played lacrosse for England and proudly showed me her team red dress, which hung in a cover in her wardrobe. The son of the house was an alcoholic too and I remember he passed out on the drawing room floor in the middle of the wake. This made me think and once again I prayed, telling a God I still doubted that he hadn't done much after the last time we spoke but please to do something this time. The next day, carrying a tray of glasses down the stairs, the rods came out of the stair carpet and down I went, hitting the newel post at the bottom. They carted me off in an ambulance thinking I'd ruptured my spleen and put me in a scanner. I waited to be told that I had only a short time to live; after all, my maternal grandfather had died at thirty-eight from the effects of alcohol, and I was now thirty-nine. Had they told me this I would now be dead because I would just have kept on drinking. Very few alcoholics stop drinking from fear of death, since the grave is usually more attractive than the abyss and by the chronic stage death has become an old friend, or at least it had to me. Curiously, I hadn't damaged my spleen and there was nothing wrong with my other organs either; tough as old boots, that's my body.

10

Dark night of the soul

I left the hospital and ended up in a small hotel on the Pimlico Road called the Lime Tree, and here I had my dark night of the soul. I had my bottle of gin but it wouldn't work, the drink had no effect and I was terrified, realising I wasn't going to die soon and that all the other alcoholics in my family had dragged themselves on to much older ages getting sadder and madder and badder. I didn't think I could face it. I seriously thought of the Embankment: life would be so easy just concentrating on the next drink and how to get it, and I had all the physical skills to survive such a life, so why not go there? I now see that the Embankment is a place in your head, and the desolation and self-destruction of such a life is the ultimate rock bottom before the grave but that night it was just a place. What stopped me was the thought that if there was a Christian heaven one day I might see my mother again and how could I face her, and if she was looking down on me how could I inflict such shame on her? With this thought I finally fell asleep.

The next morning I went to the Duke of Wellington, the pub at the other end of Eaton Terrace from the Antelope, not to drink because I didn't want company but to collect my Saki short stories that I had lent to the landlord. There was a message to ring my brother urgently should I go there. This was mystifying, for as far as Ant was concerned I was still working in High Wycombe. Anthony's health was deteriorating badly by this time and he had had several strokes and even more heart attacks brought on by his own drinking so I feared the worst. I rang the house and Harry More-Gordon, Marah's half-brother, answered the phone. He said that Ant had told him that if I called I was to get in a taxi at once and go straight to the house and he would pay the fare. Convinced of the worst, I went. Ant was okay but he had had a terrible premonition that something was desperately wrong with me; he said that I wasn't the only one in the family who was psychic, a thing I had never looked to hear him say. I was at my wits' ends and sat down with Marah, asking her what I should do. Her friend, the famous yoga teacher Mary Stewart, was god-mother to Guy, a doctor who was in practice with Robert Le Fevre, who ran a recovery centre in Kent called Promis. He had visited Hazeldene, the top American centre, and, impressed by their methods, determined to open one in England. In order to fund it he had learned to speak Arabic, which had brought him in a number of private patients and he had invested that money in a large house at Nonington in Kent and opened it as a treatment centre.

An appointment was made for me to see Guy and off I went at 9.30 a.m., the theory being that that early I would be sober. Ha! By now I was so in and out of blackout that all I remember was arriving, meeting this nice-looking young man, introducing myself, saying I was an alcoholic and I didn't know how to stop. I said I had been to AA and that hadn't helped and I needed to go into treatment. The next thing I knew I was leaving with a card telling me to go to Promis by 2 p.m. the next day. I rushed off to tell Marah who bit her tongue when she was about to ask who was going to pay. Promis, like most treatment centres, only had two assisted beds a year, and as the average time for treatment is eight weeks that meant at the most only thirteen people a year were funded by the NHS. The cost of keeping one heroin addict on methadone in any London hospital for one week would have funded an assisted bed for a year! In order to qualify for an assisted bed you had to be clean and sober for four weeks, almost an impossibility with so few detox places whose treatment in any event only ran for ten days. Private patients could of course go straight in; it was a hideous and deadly imbalance. I, as we know, had no money so how did I get there? Well, apparently I had told Guy that my Australian trustees would pay. I of course had no recollection of this, nor did I have any such trustees and I later assumed I had an assisted bed.

On the morning I was to enter the clinic I went off to the Belgravia pubs where I had some measure of credit and drank that credit. I think it was some form of insane logic to ensure that I would have no drink available to me when I came out, but maybe it was just a desire to get drunk. I got back to Marah's and off we set. In the car I remember wondering whether there was anything I could do to help myself and decided, having no resources left, that the only strategy was to tell the truth. I had as you will remember always loved the lie but my family motto is *Veritas Vincit*, which translates to 'truth will conquer'; I had always joked that it meant that if any member of my family ever managed to tell the truth they would undoubtedly conquer. Well, I decided to give it a go.

It was 9 April 1987 when I went up the drive, and I noticed that the rape was sprouting in neighbouring fields. I don't remember much about my admission process but once I had signed the form I was taken over to the main house.

All the group were out on a walk except for a large man called

Malcolm, who had not gone with them as he was suffering bad panic attacks due to benzodiazepine withdrawal. Malcolm was about fifteen years older than me and gay; he had been a very famous theatrical designer in his day and was now head of the Theatre Design School at Wimbledon, arguably the most renowned in Europe. At around the age of forty he had had an alcoholic breakdown and been found in his bath frozen with fear. In the mid-sixties Valium was the new wonder drug and he had been prescribed it and spent the next twenty years being prescribed a higher and stronger dose of the various benzodiazepine families. He had tried everything to stop his panic attacks, from Freudian psychiatrists through light and music therapy: you name it, he'd tried it and all to no avail. Finally he had started drinking on top of the pills and had gained a lot of weight. A friend of his, in early recovery himself, had sent him to Robert saying he was a brilliant diagnostician, a correct diagnosis was made and now on the last crumbs of Valium Malcolm had come to Promis. As you will see that was a great help to me and he became a dear friend. He made me a cup of tea and we chatted until the others returned.

After supper I returned to the nursing station where I was to spend the night and be monitored. I still had a lot of alcohol in the system so could not be given any drugs to prevent a possible fit. I heard Henk, the doctor and chief medical practitioner, say to the nurse that if my blood alcohol levels hadn't dropped significantly by midnight they would have to give me a drink instead. How I prayed. Here I was determined now to stop drinking: what a terrible irony if I hadn't had my last drink after all. In the event the levels dropped, I was given a Librium and fell into a fitful sleep.

Promis is what is known as a Minnesota method treatment centre, which means it advocates the various twelve-step programmes that are the basic foundation of AA, NA and OA (alcohol, narcotics and eating disorders) and takes each patient through the first five steps. These five steps concern admitting your addiction and learning about yourself, while the other seven are dealt with once you are back in the world. These are to do with your willingness to change your behaviour, making amends where possible to those you have harmed, and guiding you through the rest of your life in recovery in conjunction with AA meetings and literature (see Appendix).

Our day began with breakfast at 7.45 a.m. followed by morning meditation with readings, then we went into group session. There were twenty-two in the group when I arrived and it seldom fell below that but at tops was twenty-seven. Malcolm and I were the oldest, but the rest came from all walks of life from titled and gilded youth to East End gangsters. The youngest of us was Scott who was only sixteen and a solvent abuser and glue sniffer; there was even an Arab prince who had had so much trouble finding a vein by the end that he injected heroin into his eyeballs. Our addictions ranged from Class A drugs, through alcohol and prescribed pills to anorexia and bulimia, with variations on all those themes. Whatever paths we had taken, whatever our personal backgrounds, we had one factor in common: we were all addicts and consequently all the same underneath. This was a new discovery for me and a fact misunderstood by most of the medical profession and the social services. If you are an addict you have to guard against all mood-altering substances; you cannot for instance take anti-depressants instead of alcohol or cannabis, as you will simply transfer your addiction to them. If you are a heroin addict there is no point in turning to pot or alcohol because you will transfer your habit and it will probably lead you back to your original addiction. There were quite a few eating disorder sufferers as at that time Robert was the only twelve-step centre that would treat them. His theories on white flour and sugar as triggers in the brain for eating disorders were revolutionary back then but have since been largely accepted.

After group we were free for half an hour or so until either a lecture or a relaxation class. This latter was designed to help relieve stress and the breathing problems that come with addiction; it was a gentle form of yoga and I was held up as a model of perfect breathing, and I felt at least I had something I did right. The lectures were on various aspects of the addictive illness, or the physical damage caused or the history of recovery: you get the idea. There was then lunch followed by another group session. If we didn't have a one-to-one session with our individual counsellor afterwards we were free till tea. We were allowed to go for a walk in the surrounding countryside provided we went in a group of three or more. After tea we watched a Hazeldene video or listened to a tape on some aspect of the illness or on one of the twelve steps. Then it was supper and after that we were free till bed but couldn't go up to bed until after 9.30 p.m. The reason for this latter rule is that of course sleep or even duvet diving is another form of escapism from reality and they wanted us to stay in that state that we had all spent so long avoiding. As you can see it was all pretty intense and we were tired at the end of the day. You shared a room with at least one other person, I suppose so that we could keep an eye on each other. My first room-mate was a girl called Liz who came from a titled background and who had in her early teens thrown up with Princess Diana; apparently vomiting in company is not uncommon among bulimics.

Eating disorders are a curious group, where recovery is much harder because while alkies, druggies and gamblers can rely on total abstinence sufferers from eating disorders have to eat every day. Starvation and of course vomiting inflict pain on the body, which in turn stimulate the endorphinal glands; these glands supply painkilling heroin-type substances to the brain, which is the object of the exercise, providing a barrier between the addict and reality. Most eating disorder sufferers are familiar with the calorific and nutritional content of every edible thing and I have known bulimics who benchmark their eating, lining the stomach with ice cream then eating something red so that they can see how effectively they have vomited. I shared a group with one woman who would drive from Rochester to Queensway, buy thirty-two dishes from the all-night Chinese takeaway, consume them in lay-bys on the way home then rush into her bedroom and throw up out of the bedroom window. I'm glad I'm simply an alkie, especially as sufferers from eating disorders don't like food.

The point of an addiction treatment centre and more especially of the group sessions is to break down the individual's carefully constructed façades and barricades and help the individual to shine a light on the reality they have been running away from. At that time the head of group facilitators at Promis was a man called Beechy Coughlin who was regarded as the best in the country. He went on to television fame and as so often happens became less good at his job but in 1987 he was at his peak. Sadly his ego got in the way. I believe he stopped going to meetings and looking at his own addiction problems and has since been struck off. There was one problem, however, as far as I was concerned. I had been done over by experts and survived and my mental and verbal defences were on a par with my pit bull physical ones. Each of us started by writing our life stories, which we read out to the group who pinpointed what they saw as your strengths and weaknesses, your vices and your virtues. Unfortunately I reacted to anything I saw as criticism by hitting it to the boundary with withering scorn and the group backed off, which was getting none of us anywhere. I was not aware that the staff were concerned with the group's inability to break through my defences and were thinking of sending me away. At the end of the first week I was allowed to go outside the property but no one seemed to want to go with me and I wasn't prepared to ask. Malcolm had not yet been for a walk and when I asked him if he wanted to try one, he said he would probably have a panic attack. I had no idea what this entailed but envisaging some sort of hysterics I said I could always knock him out. Malcolm, who was a large man and had at some point served with the intelligence forces, found this hilariously funny and so we got permission and set off. We had a lovely walk with lots of laughter and apart from sitting on a bank to have a breather nothing panicky occurred. On our return, I remember saying just before we went into group that no one was going to have the pleasure of seeing me a blubbing lump of putty.

When it was my turn the group went round being critical of me until it came to Malcolm who said, 'I was just thinking what a nice person Clarissa is.' I looked at him open-mouthed then burst into tears and I must have cried for weeks; if you'd had shares in Kleenex you'd have made a fortune. I cried away all the pain, hurt and grief of my life. The Chinese believe that tears contain different chemical make-ups that change depending on whether they are tears of grief or of physical or mental pain or even of laughter; and science has now proved that grief sets up a chemical in the brain that can only be removed via the tear ducts. I am sure that in those weeks I got rid of a huge amount of emotional toxins. The change in the group's behaviour towards me was also noticeable: now I was one of them, a person wounded by life with whom they could identify. Sobriety is a painful awakening, and the guilt and remorse of past behaviours come flooding in, remorse for things said or done. I would wake up in the early hours weeping for something I had failed to do. I grieved for my mother and Clive, but there is something we call the 'frozen chicken syndrome', which stops everything hitting you at once. You only thaw out gradually and feel the pain over a period of two years or so. The great benefit of early sobriety is that you start feeling physically well, mentally lighter and the world, at least for most of us, is a brighter, better place.

I had been at Promis about three weeks when Patsy came, and after four weeks in detox elsewhere but without any programme or therapy she was like a caged rat. Born in the East End of London, her mother was a Kray and her father a gypsy; she had seen her first boyfriend with his throat cut when she was fifteen and had had a lifetime of heroin, cocaine and prostitution. In the common room she was picking on all and sundry till I told her to shut up. 'Who the fuck do you think you are?' she snarled. I told her I wasn't scared of her and we glared at each other then both burst out laughing and became great friends. Patsy had horrid nightmares and would wake up climbing the walls and screaming so no one wanted to share a room with her. I, who could sleep through the last trump, volunteered and we would while away the time talking about our lives. Patsy reckoned she could bring down both Houses of Parliament and the Established Church single-handed if she wrote her memoirs, as she had run a very upmarket brothel for the twins, and some of her stories were mind-blowing. Patsy, who was in her late thirties, had huge charisma, but sadly she got clean too late and died of cancer brought on by her various addictions. I still miss her to this day.

One reads so often in the papers that this or that celebrity has gone into rehab and is now clean or sober that it makes it sound such an easy thing to do, but believe me recovery is incredibly hard work both in the primary stages and out in the real world. At Promis we were taken twice weekly to AA or NA meetings in Canterbury to get us accustomed to attending; this time I listened and I saw that that was where I belonged, that all the patterns of the illness were replicated in me. I don't understand why the medical profession refuses to recognise addiction in general and alcoholism in particular as an illness but persists in treating the damage caused or the symptoms rather than the core. I don't have a very high regard for the medical profession coming as I do from that world but in this instance there is a glaring ignorance. When an ordinary person has a drink the alcohol just flushes away and if you drink too much you will feel ill and hung over the next day. I believe, and there is increasing medical evidence to support this, that alcoholics are born not made and that at some time in their drinking career a trigger will activate an endorphinal gland which is, like the appendix, not in use in other people. Once started, the alcohol will liaise with the dopamine that we all have in our brains and this particular endorphin to produce a substance closely akin to street heroin; the body clamours for more of this and so the alcoholic continues to drink even to jails, institutions and death. This substance, known in its shortened form as THQ, stores itself in the fatty tissues of the brain. When the alcoholic stops drinking the substance is no longer produced but renewed drinking will set the whole process off again, which is why I and my like cannot take even one drink. There is the case of a doctor who after eleven years sober decided he owed it to science to see what would happen if he drank again. He took one glass, then the next day two and ten weeks later they found him in a motel room surrounded by empty whisky bottles having blown his brains out. Sadly he was far from alone in his experience and I knew many who followed a similar path. Sometimes people for various reasons, particularly grief, will drink heavily for a while but then they will come to their senses and stop. That is not the way for us alcoholics: once the illness has kicked in there is no way we can go back to controlling our drinking.

The first step reads: 'We admitted we were powerless over alcohol and that our lives had become unmanageable.' I had no trouble with the first part of that, but despite the fact that I had lost my professional career, all my money, my looks, my lovers and didn't own a roof over my head or even a bank account, I failed singularly to recognise that my life was unmanageable. They kept me on step one for four weeks until the penny dropped. Such is the denial that surrounds addiction that I was not alone in this sort of thought pattern. I gave no thought to payment for all this until a Yorkshire miner, also called Malcolm, complained in group that people with assisted beds were made to do more chores than others. This was not of course the case and I reassured him that I too was an assisted bed and I didn't see any justification for his grievance. After group Beechy called me aside and told me I mustn't lie even though it was for a good reason. 'I wasn't lying,' I said. But he asked, 'What about your Australian trustees?' and so it all came out. They could have thrown me out there and then but I suppose they thought the best way to get their bill paid was to allow me to continue to get well.

It was a good place, staffed by kind and thoughtful people. At one point I had a nasty shock when the head of medicine, Henk, who was a very keen cook, told us that when he had got clean and sober he found he had forgotten how to cook. I froze: if that happened to me how would I manage in a sober world? Dear Henk, realising how upset I was, invited the entire group back to his house, an old converted railway station, and let me cook dinner for them. My anxiety was relieved and everyone had second helpings!

For virtually all my life my main resentment had been against my father; my hatred for him had dominated my life and weighed like an iron bar across my shoulders. It had come up a few times in group but we had moved on with no change. Now here I was on this fine May day, when Patsy was telling us another riveting part of her life story and Malcolm was on the edge of a panic attack so I was concentrating on my two friends rather than myself and unbidden into my head sprang the thought that if I couldn't forgive my father how would I ever forgive myself. I mentioned this towards the end of group and Emma, who was my own counsellor, and Beechy decided to set up a Gestalt process. This means that the patient sits facing an empty chair and tries to picture the person they want to talk to and then has the conversation. My anger levels were so high at this time that they removed all the furniture from the room and closed the shutters as they didn't know how I would react. I sat across the room trying to picture my father and suddenly there he was in my mind's eye in his black jacket and pinstripes with his stiff collar and bow tie; the image was so clear that Emma subsequently described him to me exactly. I don't think he was a ghost, I think it was just the power of the mind. I started to speak to him and to my astonishment what emerged was not hate or expletives but a huge wave of sorrow. 'You poor stupid man, didn't you realise all we wanted to do was love you and have you love us?' Beechy and Emma were flabbergasted but no one more so than me and I burst into tears.

I cannot say that the hatred lifted there and then but a dam was breached which has gradually allowed me in the intervening years to see my father as a person and to understand him more. I cannot love him, for by the time I was old enough to know him the disease we shared had eaten away at his soul and there was nothing left to love. Certainly from that day on, if the iron bar didn't lift it shifted and eased a little. Anthony, Marah and my step-nephew Edward had visited regularly while I was at Promis and when I told them of this experience they were as surprised as everyone else. While in the treatment centre I had written to Christine saying I was afraid of what I might change into and she had replied with a very powerful letter saying it didn't matter what it was but it had to be better than what I had become and that 'the you that is you is going further and further away and I am afraid one day you just won't be there'. That was what had happened to my father; you will remember he was fifty when I was born and he had gone so far away. While I can't love him I have forgiven him. I became very like him through my drinking and I can see where he was coming from.

Curiously, the morning I knew I was going to write about this incident I was indulging in displacement activities and found a book on Chinese star signs and discovered much to my amusement that my father was also born in a year of the fire pig just like me! Also I have come to thank him for various gifts both genetic and learned that I have from him but more of that later.

At Promis we were told that only one in three of us would make it and while most of the others ranted against this I determined in my heart that I would be in the survivor category. I expected that without the drink and its accompaniments my life would be very boring, dull and glum and always grey, but knowing that I had many years ahead I assumed it would be at least manageable. A lot didn't even make it through the course: some were asked to leave because they were caught having sex with each other, some simply couldn't take it and left and some relapsed. Young Scott was sent away because he was found sniffing from someone's spray deodorant, and although he came back later and finished he was never really right. He had a horrible stepmother who had once sent his own mother a deadly poisonous tarantula wrapped up as a birthday present; luckily no one was harmed. Scott killed himself on his eighteenth birthday in a corner of the playground where he had been happy as a child. Never diminish the danger of our illness: it is a destroyer and a killer.

The third of my room-mates was an anorexic called Caroline; she had been orally sexually abused by her father who went to prison for it when she was four, and her mother, a heroin addict, remarried a kindred spirit. Caroline and her brother were chained like dogs and made to eat their meals out of bowls on the floor without using their hands, so no wonder she had problems with food. She was very small but had been taken into hospital weighing only four and a half stone, and when they had got her weight up to six and a half she came to Promis. Beechy wanted her to get in touch with her anger which is why no doubt he sent her to share with me but it was never going to work. She used to say to me, 'You're not fat, I'm fat.' Anorexics have no visual ability to see themselves as they really are, in a form of denial peculiar to them. Most of them have problems with their parent of their own sex, i.e. daughter to mother and son to father and in the case of girls do not want to grow up, become that parent. After I left Promis, Caroline left a box, which was the only thing she had from her mother, on her bed full of vomit with a note saying sorry and ran away; she died not long after when the top sphincter on her stomach blew, drowning her in digestive acids. This dreadful death is how many bulimics die.

There was a psychologist at Promis who used to give us something called Mippi tests which were designed to tell him things about us that weren't obvious; everyone else did one once while I ended up doing five. Duggie told me I had a very unusual mind and that I was very angry (both of these things I could have told him); he also told me I had an IQ of 196, which seemed unlikely and in any event had been a fat lot of use to me. The only place my brain had ever got me was one step off the Embankment.

My step four, the 'full and fearless and moral inventory' of ourselves that we make, was interspersed with melancholia, Celtic gloom and quotes from Yeats's poetry; and when in the middle of my reading I was interrupted by the little sparrow of a man who said, 'You're really a very happy person, aren't you?' I could have killed him. Years down the line I recognise that he was right and that basically I am and have a huge capacity for happiness. Then the time came to take my step five, which is where you share this inventory with another human being just prior to leaving the centre. At Promis this was heard by Robert Le Fevre's father who was an Anglican vicar.

So I left Promis ten weeks sober, and the rape that had been sprouting when I arrived was being harvested when I left on 23 June 1987. This was the day before my fortieth birthday and I remember Christine sent me one of those cards that read 'Life Begins at Forty' and had written inside it: 'May this be the only cliché of your life'.

It was also true for me. I went to the Promis halfway house in St Helen's Gardens, W10, which was actually Robert LeFevre's own house, he and his wife Meg having moved into the basement to leave the rest of the house for us. Really he is a remarkable man. Malcolm said of him that other people built castles in the air but Robert then set about turning his into bricks and mortar. Malcolm had already gone up to the halfway house and there were other people I had been in primary with including a girl called Sally Ann who had hated my 'posh' voice in the beginning but had written in my book when she left: 'Never lose the voice'. Malcolm was still having terrible panic attacks and vertigo, when the ground felt unsafe beneath his feet, buildings fell out of the sky and heads came screaming out of the television set if he watched it. The medical team at Promis couldn't understand this but in fact Malcolm's case rewrote the medical text books on benzodiazepine withdrawal: previously it had been thought that one week's detox for every year it had been taken was sufficient but he had been prescribed them for twenty years and it took him five years exactly to stop having bad withdrawal symptoms. A less robust character wouldn't have tholed it. Another patient who had come up from Promis was called Clive, who was the same age as myself and a pot-head; his addiction had almost exactly mirrored my drinking but his drug was much more harmful. He seemed to be caught in a time warp, talked strangely and in a garbled fashion and couldn't get his head round the simplest things. There was a lot of worry that Clive had suffered irreversible brain damage and would never recover but I saw him at a meeting when he was four years clean and he was perfectly normal and restored to sanity. He was one of the lucky ones. It makes me angry when people speak of marijuana as a harmless drug; addiction may lie in the addict but certain drugs affect the brain worse than others. Heroin addicts get their brains back in about two weeks, as do alcoholics, but prescribed drugs and pot can do a lot more damage and I know several victims of skunk whose brains may be gone for ever.

I had only been at the house a week when an extraordinary thing happened: a girl called Biddy with whom I shared a room announced that her sister was being released from Holloway and was coming to stay the night. She had apparently asked to go to Promis before doing her time for being involved with her boyfriend in heroin transactions. She walked into the sitting room, saw me and gasped, 'My God, it's you.' I didn't recognise her till she told me she was the junkie going to court in the Black Maria; she had taken my advice and I'm happy to say she's still clean and living a nice life at the time of writing.

I liked the halfway house; it had a kitchen in which I could teach the others more cooking skills, it wasn't far from the Portobello market, had handy food shops and allowed me freedom within a safe framework. We had group sessions every day and we were required to go to four AA or NA meetings a week but other than that we were free. I felt raw and uncertain and extremely vulnerable. I remember one day Malcolm was in bed with Valium flu and everyone else was occupied. I had no one to play with. I thought, I'll go to the Antelope and see who's there, not for a drink just for company and got on the bus. By the time I reached Marble Arch the insanity hit me and I scrambled off and went to a meeting at Hinde Street; it had just started and was very full but to my surprise I saw an empty seat and fell into it. Sitting down, I realised why it was empty. I found myself between Swiss Michael, a man with a wet brain who had been a brilliant professor, been painted by David Hockney and now had very little of his brain left and that only because of an experimental operation that had drained it, and stuttering David who had been relapsing in and out of AA for as long as anyone could remember. When David had come in he was known as Gucci David because he wore belts and shoes by that designer, drove a drop-head Bentley and had a house in W11. He still has the house but chooses to live as a tramp. If I needed any reminding as to why I was there that did it. I never went to the Antelope.

The time came for my second blood test. I was now four months sober. Robert was surprised to discover that I had very sticky blood and sent me off to a specialist, fearing my heart was affected, given my mother and Anthony. I was quite worried but it emerged my heart was in excellent condition, so one bemused specialist sent me on to a metabolist at St Mary's Paddington. After various tests he asked me if I had spent much time in the malarial belt. I had not. This was, he told me, a condition found in people who had imbibed quantities of quinine over a prolonged period. 'Tonic water,' I cried. 'My dear madam,' he said, with all the patronising arrogance of a senior hospital consultant, 'you would have to have drunk an awful lot.' Four pints a day for twelve years. Why? I was asked. Well, to go with the two pints of gin a day! This is the reason I don't lose weight, because I have damaged my adrenal gland which drip feeds constantly; it's also why I have a lot of energy. Funny old world, eh!

There was a young man in the house called Jay, who was a brilliant drummer but had walked out of a fifth-floor window while under the influence of hallucinogenic drugs, thinking it was the French doors into a garden he could see outside, and various bits of him were still in plaster. One day in group he asked me why I didn't trust the group. I replied that that was rubbish and I told them everything. Jay then said that when they told me I was good at something I dismissed it out of hand, which to his mind meant I was calling them people-pleasers and liars. I was completely taken aback. I had never seen it like that but it is true: if you dismiss positive remarks from those you care for and trust that's exactly what you are doing, and how are you ever going to learn about aspects of yourself that matter to other people? It was a good lesson.

One day Malcolm and I were walking down the Portobello Road, when suddenly he started having a panic attack and needed to sit down. There was nowhere we could see, until I spotted a billboard that read 'Annie's Restaurant at Books for Cooks' so we scurried left and came upon this cookery book shop that was newly opened. I later found out that that was the only day the billboard was out as no one brought it in that night and it was nicked. We had a cup of tea and once Malcolm had recovered went back to the house. Little did I realise I had found the place that was to change my life.

11

Life begins at forty

Among our number was Nick, son of two heroin addicts, who had burned his school down. He had been drinking two litres of codeine linctus a day at the time, and had got clean on at least two occasions but had relapsed because he had no life skills. Having read about Robert's halfway house Nick had gone to ask for admission and after a short time at Promis had moved there, but the trouble was that everyone was walking on eggs around him. Not me or Malcolm, however, and between us we taught him how to cope: I taught him cooking, ironing and other household chores while Malcolm taught him how to buy clothes and how to wear them. Nick said we were like surrogate parents to him. He went on to run the laser centre in Covent Garden, which was the first exhibition of the use of lasers for creating hologram images. Nick then went to university, got a degree, went to Poland where he helped start AA and now, a married man, still cooks happily. It is really because of Nick that I am where I am today. I wanted to buy him a cookery book as a present and remembering the shop went back to look for something suitable and that was the beginning of it all. The shop was being run that day by a woman called Mel and in conversation it emerged that her mother's best friend was Anthony's first mother-in-law.

The owner of the shop, Heidi Lascelles, was a German married to an Englishman, and had bought the building with an inheritance she had received and set up the shop in emulation of Nach Waxman's cookery book shop in New York. There was only one problem: Heidi on her own admission didn't know much about food and had realised that her theory of one copy of every cookery book wouldn't perhaps work. Heidi had been suffering a lot of stress and on doctor's orders was going to sit calmly on an alp somewhere while Mel ran the shop in the interim. I fell in love with the shop: it was a long, book-lined room with a small kitchen at the back and a bit set aside for tables and chairs, and this had recently become the domain of Annie Bell who served coffees, cooked light lunches and baked goods. Malcolm and I would often go there for lunch and in my spare time I would hang out in the shop looking at the books and talking about food.

One day in September Malcolm and I were having lunch when Heidi received a telephone call from Mel who had broken her leg quite badly and wouldn't be able to take over running the shop. Heidi had hysterics, swearing she was going to die, and good little adult child of an alcoholic that I am I felt it my duty to fix the situation. 'Don't worry,' I cried, 'I'll run your bookshop for you.' Gosh, I thought, where did that come from? I was after all barely seven months sober and still in secondary treatment. 'What a good idea,' said Malcolm and Heidi hugged me. I arranged to come back at 4 p.m. and took Malcolm back to the house. I intended to go back and tell Heidi that I couldn't do it and explain the situation but on my return she was so excited and had fetched bank mandates for me to sign as a signatory. No is a very difficult word for recovering alcoholics and I found myself agreeing to take the job. We had several weeks together for me to

grasp how things worked and then off Heidi went. I sat in the
shop feeling rather fearful, then the phone rang. I picked it up
rather gingerly and it was someone wanting a Mrs Beeton, and
even I knew where that was and we were away. Malcolm and I,
our time up at the halfway house, moved temporarily into the flat
above the shop. Annie Bell fed me my lunch and after about a
month I asked her whether it was because I ate so late that I always
got a vegetarian dish. She roared with laughter and asked me if I
hadn't realised she was a vegetarian cook; her food was so good
that I must confess I hadn't. After six months Heidi returned and
was pleased with how I had run her shop. I had even cooked on
the days Annie had off which was fun but Heidi was now fit
enough to take it over again and I had decided to go back to the
law to make money.

I had had a successful interview with a firm of solicitors to run
their litigation department, the only hurdle being when they
asked me what I had been doing in the missing years. Inspiration
struck and looking tearfully at the ground I replied, 'He died . . .'
They were most sympathetic and the job was mine. I had written
to the Bar Council asking them to lift my disbarment and they had
agreed so off I went. The job was in Blackheath and I had
acquired a small orange car which I called Famous Grouse because
I got it on 12 August, the day the grouse shooting season begins.
A woman called Glor who I knew in AA had rented me part of a
house which I shared with my co-tenant, another person in AA
called Jenny. It was not a huge success but every day I set off in the
Grouse round the South Circular Road. I have to say my time
there was not a great joy for them or me. I had one or two rather
good successes but by and large we didn't like each other's way of
doing business and now that my rationale for being a lawyer had
gone with my father's death I didn't much enjoy the whole

process anyhow. The best part about the place was that this was the area of London where most of our quota of the Vietnamese boat people had been settled and several of them had opened small, simple restaurants with excellent food. I ate in one or other of them every day that I was in the office and day-dreamed of Books for Cooks.

One main difference between barristers and solicitors is that barristers never worry about money and just get on with the week. Assuming I knew, nobody told me that I had to record every billed hour and I soon ran into problems making up the bills. I hadn't really expected to have to tackle this area of the work and tempers became frayed. If I had a day when I finished early I would ring Heidi and tell her to keep the coffee machine on and hare up to the Portobello Road. By the end of a year I had had enough; after all I owed nothing to anyone but myself, and the fact that I was a qualified lawyer didn't mean I had to be one. I remember the senior partner telling me there was neither money nor glamour in cookery as I left. Wrong!

I asked Heidi if I could have my job back and she was delighted at the thought. There was a gap of a couple of months before she could arrange for me to start and I spent the time doing painting and decorating and then on 1 May I was back at my desk. It is generally agreed that it was me who turned Books for Cooks into a household name worldwide; after all, I had nothing else to focus my attentions on, I worked very hard and it was a huge success.

During all this time I had been attending AA meetings locally and working on my recovery; within the AA framework each group is autonomous and there were some very good groups and I made friends who have lasted twenty years. Probably my best friend in the fellowship is Carin who I first met while I was still in the halfway house. She is six months longer in sobriety and I suppose at this stage it is like making friends in a new school. Carin was a successful photographer, very blonde, very sexy and living in some comfort in a flat on one of the fashionable gardens off Kensington Park Road. Her description of first seeing me was that she walked into the room under the Westway and saw this thunderstorm with a bright red face sitting at the table and thought I was wonderful. I was still incredibly angry so that my anger simmered off me like reflected heat. In 1989 the police went down All Saints Road in threes during the hours of daylight; it was a dangerous road full of black drug dealers and on one occasion a car clamper was beheaded with a martial arts axe. I used to walk back from meetings, when I should have been at my most serene, detouring down this street in the hopes that someone would try to mug me and I could kill them and get rid of my anger. The dealers knew King Kong when they saw me and would step back into their doorways and respectfully mutter, 'Good evening, mistress.' Once two youths followed me and I deliberately walked under the underpass which was dark and secluded; they shot round the corner after me and turning with delight to meet them I shouted, 'There is a god!' They fled.

The Portobello and its side roads at that time too were full of drug dealers openly trading and the police did nothing to stop them. We had two tables outside the shop and every now and again I would see dealers sit down with their clients, and greatly incensed I would grab a broom and rush out, chasing them up the street. Thankfully West Indians are used to being berated by large angry women and they duly fled. They came to hold me in great respect and when all dressed up would bring their children in to meet me, telling them I was one fine lady. One day a whole lot of youths were sitting on a car belonging to one of my customers which was parked outside the shop; they wouldn't move when she asked them and when she saw a passing policeman and complained all he did was point out that she was parked on a yellow line. I came out with my broom and before he could ask me what I was doing the youths had fled. It was and remains my impression that the police were too afraid to intervene and nearly twenty years down the line it explains the conditions we find ourselves in.

In 1989 the Notting Hill Carnival was not the travesty it has become with mechanical music instead of real steel bands and the West Indians who still lived locally could dance and party really well. The old ladies used to run the food stalls and make proper West Indian black puddings with groats, which they would bring me to sample, and proper Caribbean hot pepper sauce. The celebrities had not moved into the district and there was still an edge to it, the market was thriving and it was a great area to work in; now I find it rather sanitised as is always the case when money moves in.

One dreadful tragedy occurred. Malcolm's AA sponsor was a gentle Scotsman called Barry who used to do a lot of prison work for both AA and NA, and he made the mistake of giving one man he was helping his home address so he could write to him. The man was released, relapsed on PCP, known as angel dust, ran amok and brutally murdered him. Malcolm had to go to the flat with the police to see if anything was missing, and afterwards he came to the shop pale green; apparently the walls, floor and ceiling were soaked with blood.

I don't want to give the impression that it is dangerous being in AA; the murder was caused by Barry's mistake. There are very careful rules about twelve-stepping, bringing people to the fellowships to prevent precisely this sort of event. The twelve-

The only photo I have of me and Clive, the love of my life.
With his daughter Francesca on a ferry on the way to France.

For five years after
Clive's death my life
was all about drinking.
This snap was taken at
the first Christmas
after I got sober.

Once sober, I turned to cooking. This was taken in the
Cook's Bookshop in Edinburgh.

My cooking business
flourished. This was
taken in Asprey's
window.

Two Fat Ladies changed my life. The bike and sidecar became almost as iconic as we were.

Jennifer and I had a marvellous time but we all worked very hard for our success.

Food styling the
Caribbean way – with
a whole suckling pig.

Jennifer in relaxed mode.

Pouring Jennifer a drink as we cooked in my kitchen at home.

Opening the dancing at
my fiftieth birthday party
to 'Ra Ra Rasputin', with
Henry Crichton-Stuart.

My great friend the food writer
Henrietta Green,
and companion . . .

With the wonderful Pat Llewellyn,
the producer of *Two Fat Ladies*.

Serving the Rector's Round after my inauguration as Rector of Aberdeen University.

With Johnny Scott on the filming of *Clarissa and the Countryman*.

This extraordinary photo of Johnny and Tug was taken during the foot and mouth crisis.

Me and Johnny, exercising my right to drive a flock of sheep over London Bridge to Smithfield market.

I was proud to be a part of the fight for the countryside.

This was the first time I had been on horseback in 20 years, at the
Salters Gate Farmers' Hunt in 2001.

step fellowships are an incredibly tolerant place; when people first come in they are extremely vulnerable and often their lives are in shreds, so newcomers are encouraged to come to coffee or something to eat after meetings. Nobody rams recovery down your throat but there is a lot of good conversation on such occasions. The newcomer feels alone and often full of shame and the discovery that whatever they have done, so have others before them can provide enormous support and encouragement. I know that for me I had to go through a treatment centre but most people in recovery come straight in off the street and the simplicity of not drinking or using just for that day keeps them coming back. If anyone had told me back then that I could never drink again I would probably have relapsed but the message is, don't have a drink today, get through without it and the days and the self-confidence will build.

There is a saying that religion is for those who don't want to go to hell, spirituality is for those who have been there. Certainly no one comes to the fellowships lightly or for fun; they say it is the most expensive club in the world to join and they don't mean just in terms of money. Alcoholics are a huge mixture of low self-worth and egocentricity and the steps are all designed to reverse that balance, to overcome the insane denial and to focus on a power greater than yourself. The fellowships are not a religion; it is the only place I know that allows you to define your own higher power, whether it is God, or the power of the group, or even in the case of one person I knew *The Times* crossword puzzle: it doesn't matter just so long as it isn't you. For me steps two and three, handing things over to my higher power, were a great relief, as I had seen where my own plans and intentions had taken me and I didn't want to go back there. I enjoyed my work and there is no doubt that it was never anything I had in mind or had planned. Henry Kissinger described the twelve steps as the greatest spiritual advance since Jesus Christ and I believe he is right, but fortunately no one has managed to turn the twelve steps into a religion rather than a pattern for hope. Drinking alcoholics think they are the centre of the universe, that if they turn over too violently in bed the San Andreas fault will crumble; we need to learn that like other people we are simply part of the pattern of life. I didn't have a problem with the concept of God. I don't think that then I recognised quite as clearly as I do now that the inexorable series of events that brought me into recovery stemmed from that day in the kitchen at Wotton, when out of my despair I had called to God for help. I hadn't been kicking and screaming against them because everything fell into place so smoothly I didn't see it happening but I had no doubt that some force greater than myself had heard my cry from the heart. I remain a Catholic because that was what I was born but the God of my understanding is not the God of my Church. Like the story of the leper who came back to thank Jesus I like to have somewhere formal to go to say thank you, but the spiritual energy I find in the rooms of the fellowship is what heals my soul.

I had reached my first AA birthday while working in Blackheath, something that seemed a huge milestone. Carin had a party for me and my heart sang. Sometimes it seems that that first year was the easiest in that all the focus was on not having a drink, whereas after that the world starts to fill in the spaces. I had asked Christine to write me an account of that day at Wotton when I was taken away, lest I forget and become complacent. When she sent it to me I was surprised; surely, I asked, you didn't have to overegg the pudding quite that much. Her reply was that she had actually toned it down quite a lot in case it upset me! The fellowship advises that you do service in meetings, and I had worked my way through teamaker and literature secretary and finally was elected secretary of the Westway meeting. The secretary in English meetings is responsible for finding a person to do the chair (to tell the story of their experience, strength and hope), ensure that the room is set up and that the teamaker makes the tea and that the literature secretary and the treasurer are doing their jobs. What gave me the greatest joy was inviting the priest from Sussex to do a chair for me. I had lied to him when I was in relapse before I went to Promis and although I saw him after that this was the one way I could convince him that I really was sober.

Books for Cooks flourished and became like a club for food writers: everyone came. Adrian Gill sat on a stool beside me and talked about Brown Windsor, my heroes Anna Del Conte, Claudia Roden and Sri Owen came often to discuss books. One day the phone rang and when I answered it it was Elizabeth David. I was so stunned I dropped the phone. When Elizabeth asked me what was wrong I said for someone of my generation it was rather like answering the phone to God. She thought this very funny and when she rang in future would say, 'God calling.' We used to talk quite a lot on the phone. I didn't realise at that time that she was in the chronic stage of her alcoholism, which was why she seldom went out. She came once to the shop for a book signing but fled when someone took a picture, although not in fact of her. Elizabeth would only allow that Cecil Beaton picture of her to be used for publicity which is why there are no later images of her. Ageing and ill, she had wonderful bones and so remained beautiful. At her memorial service, after speaker after speaker had talked about the kitchen table and the little blue bowl of black olives and the wine, Margaret Visser, who was sitting next to me, asked, 'Why is there no mention of food or cooking?' Finally a very old actor who had performed with Elizabeth in

A *Midsummer Night's Dream* in Regent's Park described how when a performance had been rained off they had gone back to Elizabeth's flat and she had cooked him the most perfect omelette he had ever eaten, and then I cried for that sad, lonely, talented woman who had never found AA.

Jane Grigson came too at the beginning but soon the cancer that was to kill her took hold. Even Delia Smith came. One day a customer asked me how to make an Irish stew, and I said, 'Why not ask this lady?' She asked why, who was she? When I told her she was delighted and they spent some time exchanging recipes. I have always been an admirer of Delia's: she has, after all, given more people the confidence to cook than any other author. In my opinion the food world generally was jealous of her huge success and so dismissed her, and said that she doesn't make up all her own recipes but that is not uncommon among food writers. In fact I know of one television cook whose only series was filmed abroad, as she simply couldn't cook and so the on-screen cooking images are the director wearing her apron and being filmed from the neck down!

The 1980s was the era of New Wave British cooking and was a heady time. Marco Pierre White at Harvey's was probably the most exciting cook of the day and to my mind still holds that title, far surpassing all the present age of chefs. Marco was closely followed by Alastair Little and Sally Clarke, who had trained at Chez Panisse in California and brought Alice Waters' style to England.

In the late 1970s and early 1980s five American chefs, Alice, Jeremiah Tower, Deborah Madison, Wolfgang Puck and Mark Miller with his Mexican fusion, had changed the face of cooking by inventing New Wave American Cuisine. Before this each country's cooking followed its own mathematical equations: for instance the French put peas or orange with duck, the Moroccans used specific spices in specific tagines and never varied, we served horseradish with beef and mint with lamb – you get the idea. The American five burst this whole pattern wide open leading to some amazing combinations and techniques, and when it worked it was fantastic but when it didn't you'd be using mouthwash for a week. This is the fusion that was taken up by Australia and changed into Pacific Rim fusion but it also affected Britain in its own right. Antony Worrall Thompson, who I remember with pleasure from his days at Dan's and Ménage à Trois, was a frequent visitor and a regular customer hoovering up imported American books. I have always regarded Antony as an under-rated chef; I used to love his food and wish we hadn't lost him to television. Marco would come, usually with no shoes on and very over-excited, and Alastair lived just round the corner and was a constant presence. The chef I most admire, Shaun Hill, visited and every year I would save my pennies and make a pilgrimage to Chagford where he was cooking at Gidleigh Park. Gary Rhodes, a brilliant chef not yet lost to television, came in too. Gary had trained at Kit Chapman's the Castle at Taunton and I regard Kit as one of the three finest hoteliers in Britain. His grandfather had arranged the *fête champêtre* for Edward VII's birthday when they flooded the forecourt of the Savoy Hotel, all the guests dined in gondolas and the cake was carried out by a baby elephant. I'm sure Kit would do something just as dramatic if asked. Kit trained both Gary and Phil Vickery to television but the last time I ate at the Castle the food was just as good.

One of the people most important to me was Henrietta Green. When I came out of my bottle I was horrified to discover the grasp that supermarkets had obtained on the food world as a whole. The only person fighting the cause of the small producer was Henrietta, whose first book *British Food Finds* was just a directory, printed rather than published, listing producers throughout Britain that she had visited and found to meet her exacting standards. Delia mentioned this on her programme and I sold all the remaining 1,200 books in four or five days; sadly there was no reprint. However the BBC publishing arm then commissioned Henrietta to write *Food Lovers' Guide to Britain*, for which Henrietta and her extremely bad-tempered Yorkshire terrier Violet set out to source more producers. Violet was a rescue dog and used to be left tied to my chair in the shop when Henrietta went up to the market and my ankles still bear the scars! I once spent a day going around with Henrietta, thinking what a nice gentle experience it would be, but I have to tell you I was exhausted by the end of it and yet she did it day in day out, cross-examining the producers she visited with the ferocity of a leading barrister. The book ran to several editions and was a huge help to those who wanted to produce real food rather than dross for the supermarkets. In due course Henrietta started her Food Lovers' Fairs but I will talk about them later. It is difficult now, when so many people are interested in good produce, farmers' markets are flourishing and every chef jumps on the bandwagon, to remember how bleak it was back then and how hard Henrietta fought the system single-handed. She has never really had the acclaim she deserved but it is often thus, isn't it?

Meantime my recovery continued. People think that this is just about stopping drinking, but if you don't make use of the rest of the steps to change your persona and outlook on life you will most probably pick up your addiction again. I often feel life in recovery is like looking at the bottom left-hand corner of a picture: there is no way you can tell what the rest of the picture holds from looking at that square. It is a matter of trust that you will like at least most of the rest of the picture as it is revealed. When I left Promis they gave me a goal, which read: 'I will jump off the precipice.' I was very resentful about this but now I see that it meant jump out and trust that something will catch you and it certainly worked for me. Carin and I would go to meetings on most evenings and meet up with other friends. In early recovery it is good to go to as many meetings as possible, laying up treasure for the days ahead when the world speeds up and there isn't so much time. I never had a problem with going to the pub every day and I have to tell you that meetings are much better than staying home watching TV. Laughter wells through the pain and is the best healing medicine, while no writer could ever dream up the real life stories that one hears or if they tried they probably wouldn't be believed. One's own problems are quickly whittled down to size and the simple fact of sharing them out loud with others reduces the hurt.

I moved many times during those first few years. For a while I was in a bedsit in St Helen's Gardens, where the bed collapsed every few nights because the cups for the slats were too worn and I was too scared to go and complain. Seems unlikely now, doesn't it, but I was very raw and, as any adult child of an alcoholic knows, on a bad day even the dustman is an authority figure. I spent one day off wondering how I could afford to move and scanning the evening paper, until finally I threw it down and snarled at God, 'Okay, so you're so clever you fix it,' and went off to a meeting. There I met someone I used to drink with who was newly in AA and arranged for me to take over a Housing Association flat in Battersea, with a sitting room, bedroom, bathroom, good sized kitchen and small garden and all for what I was paying for the bedsit! Scoff if you will.

It is very important for those who are newly clean and sober to realise that it is fine to go to parties or dinner parties but it is best to start these excursions in a safe environment so Carin had parties, and now I was in the Battersea flat I had parties too. I also grew forty pounds of Jerusalem artichokes in my tiny flowerbed.

By now I was three to four years sober and had acquired sponsees of my own. The system of sponsorship in the twelve-step fellowships requires a person to approach someone whose recovery they like and ask them to be their sponsor. From the latter's point of view it requires the sponsor to help the other person with their step work, to encourage them to go to meetings and to listen, within reason, to their woes and their life problems. It should be a supportive rather than a controlling relationship, which is not intended to be permanent and either party is free to opt out. In my years in recovery I have had quite a few sponsees: four of them have died, three of natural causes and one in a car crash brought about by relapse, a couple have drifted away, and some have become among my dearest friends. I feel it is a great privilege to be asked to sponsor, although the three I have had as my sponsors in twenty years might not agree!

One of my sponsees was a quirky Irish man, who we called White Rabbit John because he had prominent front teeth and he rushed about like the *Alice in Wonderland* character; he was the sweetest and dearest of men and I am telling you about him because when he was dying of cancer he asked me if I ever wrote my autobiography to give him a mention. He was a terrible insomniac in the beginning and would ring me up at all hours; I would tell him that no one died of lack of sleep and he should go and clean the silver. He worked as a carer for an old man with Alzheimer's and they were very happy with each other's company but I think the silver was almost rubbed away. John was very camp and used to say that his parents wanted him to be a priest but he wanted to be a nun! He died much loved and sober and I still miss our early breakfasts together in Mick's café on the Portobello Road. In choosing a sponsor you usually choose someone of your own sex to avoid any emotional complications but if you are gay obviously this is reversed, so I have had two gay male sponsees. The second was a lawyer called Jonathan, a New Zealander who worked for David Morris, who had heard me extolling the virtues of sobriety and out of the blue rang me and asked me to take him to a meeting. Jonathan had had fully blown Aids for seven years and his doctor had told him he could either die of Aids or cirrhosis of the liver and he recommended the former so Jonathan had decided to stop drinking.

My brother Anthony's health had been deteriorating over these years, and I was desolate that I couldn't persuade him sobriety was a better option. He was delighted that I had got my life back together although he kept insisting that I wasn't an alcoholic, that alkies were men in dirty macs sleeping rough. I pointed out that while I wasn't a man and didn't have a dirty mac I had actually slept rough, but to no avail. I had persuaded him to come to one AA meeting and although there was a man there who had been in the same physical condition as him but who had stopped drinking and climbed a mountain Ant didn't want to know. He had had a large number of strokes and heart attacks brought on by his drinking and smoking and now having reamed his veins out as many times as possible they cut his legs off. He had had such beautiful legs and they had twinkled so well on rugby pitches up and down the country. I couldn't bear it and wondered how Marah managed.

When you get sober you get quite obsessive and my obsession was with the cardoon: for some unknown reason I decided it was my duty to restore this vegetable, the largest edible thistle, to the

British nation, a nation I should add that had never been devoted to it. Cardoons look like giant celery and taste like artichoke heart and the iridescence of their seed head is what is used for vegetarian rennet. The French, Spanish and Italians love them and they are an especial must at Christmas, the Moroccans have special tajine recipes for them and they are much eaten around the anchovy belt of the Mediterranean; they also grow wild on the pampas of Argentina but not, you will observe, in the UK. Antonio Tarrucio at the Yew Tree in Abergavenny loved them and so did a woman called Patricia Heggarty who lived in Elizabeth Barrett Browning's family home but that was it. As you have probably never heard of them, dear reader, you will see that I failed in my endeavour but I owe this giant vegetable a great deal. I bought my first one with Marah at a garden opening in Surrey but that one was never eaten. However a friend of mine who owned the last field in Chapel St Leonard's decided he wanted to grow them for me. Chapel St Leonard's is an extension of Skegness and if you looked over the hedge round the field you would see such delights as the Friar Tuck Fish and Chip Bar or the Maid Marian Bingo Hall. The soil was sandy loam and good for cardoons, which don't like getting wet feet, nor, I should add, do they want to dry out as they then panic and run to seed which makes them inedible. Come the autumn you need to wrap them up to blanch them and keep wrapping them as they will grow quite a lot when wrapped, so you see they are fairly labour-intensive. Stefan grew other specialist vegetables for local restaurants and grew beautiful cardoons. I banged on so much about cardoons that long before I was even slightly well known the *Independent* in its New Year's column on what don't we want to hear about in the coming year put 'Cardoons from Clarissa' high on their list!

It was at this period that I first met Patricia Llewellyn, who was working on Sophie Grigson's *Eat Your Greens* and used to come to the shop to ask my advice on suitable vegetable growers. Someone said to her, 'Have you seen Clarissa's cardoons?' We went down to have a look and she was delighted with the whole set-up and wanted to film them and me for both the growing and the cooking section of the programme. We filmed the cooking bit in the kitchen at the back of the shop, making three recipes with what Sophie later described in one of her books as 'the mighty cardoon' and my TV debut was a vision of me emerging from my tent on the edge of the beach at Stefan's. Pat was very pleased and declared, 'You're really good at this, we must do something else,' but in the event it was a while before we did.

Books for Cooks, despite the recession of the late eighties and early nineties, maintained its popularity and every year our turnover rose by 25 per cent. We attended various outside events and one of these I loved was the Oxford Food Symposium, which took place every year in an Oxford college. The person I associate it with was Alan Davidson, the most learned man on food I ever met. Alan had been an ambassador and rather foreshortened his career when he chose Ulan Bator in Mongolia over a Washington appointment because he wanted to study a particular type of freshwater shrimp found only there. He wrote three great books on seafood, covering North Atlantic, Mediterranean and S.E. Asian, which remain the definitive works. He also with his wife Jane owned a company called Prospect Books which published really recherché titles on Tibetan food or his own on Laotian food, not the world's best known cuisine. Not long before his death he published his life's work, the massive and wonderful *Oxford Companion to Food*. The symposium attracted food writers from all over the world and was a deeply serious event. The papers I remember best were Dr Asti Ridstom on salt fish and lute fish in the Scandinavian tradition, a terrifyingly dry paper on the herring as the staple food of the Baltic, Margaret Visser on eating traditions and Camellia Punjabi on the myth of Mogul food. I had met Margaret Visser when she came over to England to receive the Glenfiddich Award for her first book, *Much Depends on Dinner*, which was the first to address the effects of GM and corporate lies on the food we eat. Margaret was very charismatic and wowed the symposium.

Camellia Punjabi was the chief executive of Taj Hotels, who had come into the shop demanding to know why there was no decent book on Indian cookery. I told her to go and write one herself, but she cried, 'I am a very busy woman,' to which I simply raised an eyebrow. Some time later we met at Euston Station on our way to record the pilot for a radio programme called *Curious Cooks*, and she told me it was all my fault but her book, *50 Great Curries of India*, had just sold its millionth copy. It is a source of great delight to me that there are a great many food writers who I encouraged and even introduced to their publishers but none more than Annie Bell. Annie was leaving Books for Cooks to open her own restaurant when she became pregnant, but sadly the child was born with severe epilepsy and couldn't be left. I told Annie she must write and introduced her to Georgina Morley, then of Transworld; they hit it off and Annie wrote several books and went on to be the columnist for *Vogue* and the *Independent*. I am also happy to say she now eats meat!

So my life at Books for Cooks was running enjoyably and smoothly, I was building a reputation and a reasonable income when my worst nightmare happened. I was at the Earl's Court Restaurant Show selling books on my own when they brought me news of Anthony's death. It was an obscene black joke of a death. He had been reaching into the fridge without putting on his wheelchair brakes, the chair had shot backwards and he had fallen into the fridge and broken his neck. Poor Marah came home and found him lying there. I went to the loo and sobbed my eyes out then went back to my stand. Ant and I had used to joke with black alcoholic humour that with my grandmother dying on the thousandth anniversary of the Battle of Hastings and my mother on Derby Day what dramatic exit was left for us?

I had never envisaged something as horrible as this but given his other options at least it was quick; he was only fifty-seven when he died. I sat there all day with the image in my head, the tragedy of it making me feel quite sick. The only displacement activity I had was to sell books. Someone in an AA meeting once said that recovery was like having ten pots and nine lids so that one was forever having to change the lids around. Secondary addictions are quite commonplace and one needs always to keep a weather eye. Mine is without doubt work; fortunately I love all the things I do but I am aware that I can drive myself to the edge of exhaustion, where there is the danger that I might push myself back to the first addiction. I sold an awful lot of books that day. There was no phone to call for someone to take my place and strangely I never thought of packing up and going home. I worked till the show closed then rushed off to an AA meeting to unburden my pain, then on to Ant's house to be with Marah. Much to everyone's surprise Ant, who had been an affirmed atheist for years, had been back in touch with Downside, his old school, during his illness and had directed he be buried under the rites and obsequies of the Catholic Church. The funeral was packed and I spent my time carving the ham I had cooked the day before. Poor Anthony, his life, like that of any alcoholic, had been a rollercoaster of highs and lows but at least in Marah he had found a loving helpmeet.

From the time I left Promis it had always been my greatest fear that I would not be able to avoid drinking at my brother's funeral. I was now five years sober and the nature of Anthony's death was not likely to encourage me to drink. His death affected me deeply; as with my mother, I felt that I had failed to save him and over the years ahead this led me into actions that common sense would probably have dissuaded me from and I repeated this pattern of trying to save people. I had started going to Al-Anon, the fellowship for relatives and connections of alcoholics, in an attempt to deal with my pain around Anthony but didn't at this point really see where my adult child and co-dependency issues were taking me.

I would have spent the rest of my days happily running Books for Cooks, where I had been working for seven years. I had the luxury of an assistant in Rosy Kindersley who loved the shop too, which was a great help, but it was not to be. Heidi, who was having problems with the taxman and in any event had been spending more and more time in her villa in Tuscany, decided she wanted to sell the shop and offered it to me. Shortly before this I had met Henry, scion of an aristocratic Scots family, descendant of Robert the Bruce and member of my club, who had come to London to find Nicotine Anonymous, or Nicos, with the intention of stopping smoking. The nicotine had held him back and when I met him he was almost grey with it, having tried everything from Allen Carr to hypnotherapy and this was his last resort. Nicos is a small fellowship, its members are mostly people who have been in recovery for some time in other fellowships, and everyone agrees that nicotine is one of the hardest drugs to give up. Although I had given up by accident in Promis, being under the illusion that I had already stopped when I was in my twenties and having no recollection of having started again, I still wanted a cigarette. My friend Henrietta had taken me to a meeting and I realised that I probably needed to spend some time in Nicos or I might very well smoke again. Henry had asked the secretary of an AA meeting I was at where he could find Nicos, which had only just started in London, and the secretary who happened to be Jonathan had sent him over to speak to me.

Henry was not that much younger than my brother and I suppose somewhere in my subconscious I decided that if I had failed to save my brother I could at least try to save Henry. I arranged for him to have a room at Mel's next door to Books for Cooks and to do some part-time work in the shop. When I told him I was trying to put together a package to buy the shop he suggested he might come in with me. We got every sort of valuation you could think of and agreed the value of the building, the stock, the equipment, and several valuers all came up with the same amount. We fell down on the valuation of the good will, which was ironically largely mine anyway. Also Heidi wanted to build in a value for the ground floor of the upstairs flat to be used as a commercial cookery school despite the fact that the council had made it plain they would never allow such change of use. It is impossible to get people to lend or invest money on an illegal premise so we were at an impasse. It all became rather unpleasant and all my character defects that I thought I had thrown out of the pram when I worked steps six and seven seemed to be creeping back like so many gremlins.

I decided to have a short holiday and took myself off to Topsham for part of a week. There is a house in that Devonshire town called Reeka Dom (River House) built by a Russian sea captain in the eighteenth century, whose wife had insisted on a light tower looking down the estuary of the Exe where she could keep a lantern burning for his return. I had been there on holiday with Marah in my second year in sobriety and loved the peace of it. The tower had a bedroom, kitchen and bathroom and the tower room above, which had a 360-degree view, two-thirds of it over the estuary and the remainder over the hills behind. And nearby Exeter has an excellent selection of meetings. I don't go there since I moved to Scotland as it is rather far to travel but I still think fondly of it.

Back in London I felt much more serene, and still had some days before I was due to go back to work. I rang Henrietta Green to catch up on all the gossip, as there is a saying in the food world that you hear everything first from Henrietta and in this case, as in so many others, it was true. 'Clarissa, I'm so sorry,' were her opening words. 'What?' I asked and she said she had been into the shop that morning and Heidi had told her she had sacked me. It was the first I knew of it. I rang David Morris who had been trying to reach me because he had received a letter from Heidi telling him I had been sacked and was not to go back to the shop.

A friend of Henry's in PR, Martin Hunt, had been suggesting a link-up with a big Scottish kitchen equipment supplier to sell cookery books in their store after we had bought the shop. I was due to fly up to Edinburgh on the Monday to discuss this. Henry was already in Scotland but I couldn't get hold of him. I met him at Edinburgh Airport and we decided to go and see the company anyway. I had heard of a Scottish book distributor called Book-speed so I rang them from the airport as I needed to know if I would be able to source books in Scotland. I spoke to Kingsley Dawson who together with his now wife Annie Rhodes ran the business. I have dealt with them ever since and but for their early kindness and in the early days eternally extended credit I would never have remained as a bookseller. They are good friends but I believe they still think I'm mad. Henry and I went to our business meeting and decided to go ahead with the link-up project even though we didn't have the shop.

I returned to London and to hospital. The only thing wrong with me after years of self-abuse was an umbilical hernia; they hadn't tied the knot properly when I was born and now it had begun to grow. The doctor had sent me to St Mary's when it was quite small but nothing was done. I was on some imaginary waiting list and as it got bigger had to wear a hideously un-comfortable leather truss. Finally I rang the senior surgeon, explained who I was and demanded they did something about it; they set a date and in I went. It had all the elements of a farce: the anaesthetist was determined I must have a bad heart due to my size and was, I think, mortified when he had to admit it was the healthiest heart he had seen in ten years; and the operation was performed, unsuccessfully as it transpired, by an Indian doctor with very average English. I was in the Dickson Wright ward and we had a ridiculous debate because he couldn't grasp that my name was the same as the ward's and thought I was mocking him. Later on the day of the operation someone actually came and served a summons on me in my hospital bed for unpaid parking tickets and, to add insult to injury, after waiting half an hour for a bedpan it was a choice of either wetting myself or getting out of bed and taking myself and my drain to the loo. Although I was supposed to be on liquids only they brought me dinner so I ate it and after forty-eight hours (I was supposed to be in for a week) I happily agreed to be discharged and went to Carin's house.

I lay there in some discomfort for a week and then got up and went to the André Simon Awards of which I was the assessor that year. There were two major food awards at that time, the Glenfiddich, which carries the most money, and the André Simon named after the founder of the Wine and Food Society, which carries the most prestige. I remember André Simon from when I was about eleven and I was amazed that he could tell his champagne glass had been washed with soap because the bubbles were fizzing downwards. His daughter, a nun of the Sacred Heart, told me that on his deathbed she asked, '*Un peu d'eau, Papa?*' at which he shook his head; she then asked, '*Un peu de champagne, Papa?*' at which he smiled and nodded and died with the taste on his lips. It was the year that Delia Smith's *Summer Food* had been published and I had suggested to the organisers that they should give her a special award, and they had agreed provided she was there to receive it. I had rung Delia and reluctantly she agreed, if only to hear my speech so I was duty bound to be there. It was Delia's first award within the food writing industry, possibly because there had been too much jealousy and resentment of her success, and we presented her with an unusual bookcase made from the fork of a tree with which she seemed delighted. I think she enjoyed my speech, although, woozy from the anaesthetic, I was not at my best.

The next day I set off to drive to Scotland in an old Volvo with a bullet hole in the windscreen. I had bought it for £500 off All Saints Road where it had previously belonged to a dealer. I spent the first night in Birmingham with Christine and then left early the next morning without listening to the weather reports. It was February, there was snow lying and it started to snow again just as I got on to the M6 and it was soon falling quite hard. There were no other cars on the motorway which seemed rather strange, the only other vehicle being a snowplough which I tucked in behind. The radio suddenly started to work and I discovered that drivers had been told to avoid the M6 because of heavy snow; moreover I couldn't turn off the road because all the side roads were blocked. Any sensible person would have stopped at a service station and spent the night but on I plugged behind the snow-plough. Finally I got to the top of Shap, the highest point of the road, and as if by magic I came through the curtain of snow into bright sunshine and a green landscape. Two miles further on my exhaust pipe fell off and I roared my way into Scotland and into the village of Inveresk where I have lived for the last thirteen years.

12

A geographical north of the border

I was to stay with Harry and Marianne More-Gordon until I worked out what was going to happen, but it wasn't at that point my intention to stay in Scotland; after all, apart from Henry and the M-Gs I knew no one and all my offers of work were down in England. I think I was determined to come to save Henry from relapsing into his nicotine addiction; he was so obviously going to die if he reverted to smoking and my brother's memory was still fresh in my mind. One cannot of course stop any addict if they want to keep using and intellectually I knew that but I felt driven to try and nowadays, smoke-free for years, Henry kindly says he couldn't have done it without my help, which may even be true. The M-Gs were very kind and made me most welcome. I opened an account with Bookspeed, and Henry and I rented an office off the Meadows and bought a company which we called Global Gourmets, through which we supplied cookery books to the trade and at various events. We started dealing with Scobie and Mackintosh but they didn't really want what I had in mind, especially as they had given up the retail shop they had had at the West End of Princes Street and only had their retail outlet at the Gyle.

The withdrawals from heavy nicotine addiction can be very unpleasant and debilitating, with cramps in the stomach and in the limbs, constipation, indigestion and a constant feeling of flu and Henry suffered them more than most. I was still feeling the after-effects of my operation and particularly of the anaesthetic. I was seven years sober, my carefully built world was in ruins and I was horribly miserable.

I was filled with rage, fury that everything I had worked so hard to achieve at Books for Cooks was all turned to dust; it was as well that I was in Scotland for had I been in London I don't know what I might have done to Heidi or her shop. I would wake up with Kalashnikovs and flame throwers in my head. I had books on my shelves signed by Heidi 'to the saviour' and now here I was cast aside like an old shoe. Heidi had even told one customer who asked that I was very ill, possibly fatally. Fortunately, of course, the papers took it up and after an article in the *Daily Telegraph*'s Peterborough column it became quite clear that I was not ill. I took Heidi to the industrial tribunal and with the help of David Morris and ACAS obtained a settlement but it seemed such a long climb back. It is of course when the twelve steps come in to their own: it is quite easy to be serene when everything is going well and smoothly but when your back's to the wall that's when you really need them. Some days the first part of step one was all there was when I got to bed at night and yet I hadn't had a drink so that had to be enough. Scottish meetings were different from London ones and in the beginning I didn't like them as much, but I remembered my first sponsor saying, if you share in a meeting what you don't like then at least there are a few minutes you can't object to and I soon realised it wasn't so much the meetings that were out of step but me. I went back to the steps and reworked them all again, pestering my sponsor and howling down the phone to my friends in the fellowship. My former customers from Books for Cooks were terrific; they tracked me down and ordered books from me rather than Heidi, and even the Oxford Symposium asked me to handle the bookstall. I lived hand to mouth, people lent me money unsolicited and somehow I got by. I had written bits and pieces before but now I got a letter from the editor of *Decanter* magazine suggesting I might like to do a monthly food column for them, which I accepted with alacrity.

My greatest benefactor however was James Thompson, who now has an Edinburgh restaurant empire encompassing the Witchery by the Castle, the Tower at the National Museum of Scotland and Prestonfield House Hotel as well as luxury elegant catered flats around the Castle area. Back then he co-owned the Witchery and was the working partner. I had met James with Henry when we had had dinner the summer before I came north. He was a brilliant restaurateur and we got on at once. When I started living in Scotland he offered me a consultancy, which exactly paid my rent. I spoke at his twentieth anniversary of the Witchery and said that each of us there had a reason in our hearts to be grateful to James: we each knew what it was and that was enough. Every single person at that party came up and told me I was so right.

I decided to go on a pilgrimage: the foremost shrine in Scotland had been that of St Margaret at Dunfermline Abbey. She was Edward the Confessor's niece and following the Norman invasion she was fleeing the country back to her native Hungary where she intended to become an abbess, and en route the ship had to put in to Berwick-upon-Tweed which at that period belonged to Scotland and she fell in with Malcolm Canmore, King of Scotland. They had met when he was a hostage at Edward's court and he must have taken a shine to her for he proposed marriage. It is said that her chaplain convinced her that she would do more good for the Catholic Church as Queen of

Scotland, which at that time adhered to the Celtic not the Roman Church. Margaret was a huge success in Scotland, brought the country to Rome, and moved the capital to Edinburgh. To this day only Scots women called Margaret tend her chapel in Edinburgh Castle and she is generally regarded as a good thing. Canmore means black-tempered, so I thought I might go and ask her how she coped in a strange land; make no bones about it, Scotland is a foreign country. Off I set in Hasdrubal, the old Volvo. I always give my cars names and I had already worked my way through Hannibal, named by the friend I had bought it from because it was grey and had been over the Alps, and Hamilcar, the blue Vauxhall seen in my TV debut.

When I reached Dunfermline the car park by the abbey was closed for resurfacing, so, cursing, I drove off and in my head I heard a well-bred voice say, 'I thought you came on a pilgrimage; you walk on pilgrimages.' I found another car park and walked to the abbey, and as I made my way through the town I thought I might have some lunch first. Again I heard the voice: 'I thought you came to see me.' On arrival at the abbey I found it all locked up, as was the visitor centre in the grounds. Stomping about, I found a gardener, who confirmed the abbey was shut but when I said I'd come to see St Margaret's tomb he pointed me round the back. The lavish chapel that once surrounded the tomb was demolished by the Presbyterian Scots, Mary Stuart took the silver gilt reliquary containing St Margaret's head to France as a wedding gift to the Dauphin and all that remains is a plain tomb with a simple inscription. I stood in the chill February drizzle and talked to her, asking for some guidance as to what I should do. After a while I heard the same voice: 'Stay put, do nothing and it will all be all right,' she said and that was it. I waited a while longer then wandered away and found some lunch. All I have to say is that she was perfectly right.

When I got back to Inveresk I found that Jonathan had been taken into the Middlesex Hospital with meningitis and was asking for me so I travelled south on the train. When I got to the ward the consultant was with him so I went to look at the chapel, which is High Victorian and much regarded by experts. As I walked in the first thing to catch my eye was a splendid bronze and ivory statue of a woman, and when I went over to look more closely I discovered it was of St Margaret of Scotland, which I found very emotional and rather wonderful. I went to see Jonathan for what I assumed was the last time, and the next day I headed north again. There is a spot just by the Scots border at Berwick-upon-Tweed where the train passes a stretch of the sea coast. Looking out of the window I felt, Oh, it's so lovely to be home, and if it's home, I thought, I'd better stay and I have been here ever since.

One more person who was kind to me was Delia Smith; she had recently started the *Sainsbury's Magazine* and asked me if I would provide a list of books for their readers, with a review, each month. The added bonus of this was that we were able to use the Sainsbury's postal account for all mailings which meant we could send out books far more cheaply than before. A further source of income came from Henrietta Green who had now started her Food Lovers' Fairs, which took place in huge tented villages on an estate or a show field. Henrietta would invite producers who featured in her book to come and sell their wares and I handled the book sales for the chefs who demonstrated and brought other suitable books to sell. Like the producers I used to camp on the show sites and in the company of people involved in the best food production the atmosphere was wonderful.

It was here that I met two of my dearest friends in the food world, Peter Gott of Sillfield Farm in Cumbria whose quirky bowler hats and moleskin breeches with red socks hide a man totally dedicated to producing the finest pork and wild boar. Peter was given a breeding pair of wild boar by his brother Walter and now has a large herd which run wild in his woods, and his wild boar prosciutto and pancetta are better than any I have eaten anywhere, while his pork is second to none. Peter has never sold out, even refusing to sell to Waitrose, and his success has matured as slowly as his hams but he is now recognised as one of the finest producers in the country and even travels with his cured meats to Slow Food Fairs in France and Italy to take on those nations at their own game. My other great friend is Jan McCourt of Northfield Farm at Cold Overton on the Rutland/Leicestershire borders, who, while still a young man, left a career in banking to raise and finish rare breed animals. It is agreed that the best way to stop a breed being rare is to eat it. That may sound strange but if customers clamour to eat it more people will take the trouble to raise the beast. Most rare breeds in domestic creatures have fallen from favour because they are slow to finish or the purpose for which they were intended such as pulling a plough or a wagon has become redundant. The passion among farmers for fast-growing hybrids is easily explained in terms of money: for instance foreign breeds of cattle that put on condition and reach the butcher's carcase weight very quickly, breeds of sheep like Texels that acquire carcase weight easily, and pigs with numbers not names originally intended for the bacon market that have no fat and less flavour. Even Aberdeen Angus can be so called if the father is of that breed while the mother can be any scrubby foreign breed. One of the nastiest joints I ever cooked was an Angus Limousin cross which was impossible to carve because of the flap of muscle running through it. But I digress.

The best part of these fairs was the evening when we used to have huge barbecues with all the traders contributing something good to eat or drink. One year Peter had had to shoot a wild boar that had escaped which meant he could not sell it for food. When the Victorians introduced their game laws wild boar had already died out in Britain so wild boar is not counted as game and has to be slaughtered in an abattoir. Not a lot of fun for the slaughter-men, as boar are dangerous and unpredictable creatures. Anyway, Peter donated this boar to the barbecue, we cooked it whole with the bristles still on it, and it was quite delicious. I got the first slice and Peter says he wishes he had taken a photo because I looked so happy.

I had come late to camping, as my childhood didn't include family holidays, and anyway we did 'lavish' rather than tents by the time I was born. I was in early recovery when Christine decided it was time that I stopped whingeing that I had never been camping. She, with another friend and her daughter and David, my honorary godson, were off to Bala in the Welsh mountains, and Christine decided I should come too. We all set off in glorious sunshine and pitched our tents beside Lake Bala, then went to eat excellent fish and chips at the Golden Aur. During the war this restaurant could not get sea fish and the poachers used to bring the salmon up from the Dee, so to this day the Aur serves battered salmon and very good it is too. After a drink in the pub, lemonade for me and the children, we shuffled off to bed. I had never slept in a tent as an adult, and indeed not since pony club camp and I curled up in my one-man tent very comfortably. In the morning I woke up feeling very blank. I looked out and it was raining, the grey steady mizzly rain of a Welsh mountain summer and I fell in love with the whole process. There was a great deal of laughter and bad verse: 'grey were the clouds over Cader Idris, grey as the cloth Annette had to wipe the floor with when she had forgotten to take her boots off.' When we got back to Birmingham I went straight out and bought a three-man ridge tent (you never know who you might meet!) with two bell ends so I could cook when it was raining. It was this tent that I took to the shows and Henrietta, Valentina Harris and I cooked lovely breakfasts over my two-ring Calor gas stove and fell about laughing.

Back in Edinburgh I was now living in the granny flat of a house across the road from the M-Gs. Philip Mackenzie Ross whose house it was had lost his wife a year earlier and just wanted to hear noises of someone else around the place. Staying at Philip's I made a new friend, June from Wallyford. She would come to house-sit when Philip was away and would invite me into the kitchen for tea and to listen to her daughter Lee sing. Her brother Charlie was the brilliant gardener who everyone in the village kept trying to poach and who had trained under the famous Mr Scarlett, the man who established the Musselburgh leek as the definitive strain and bred the standard ornamental thistle. They were two of eight children whose coalminer father had died down the pit at forty. Their mother raised them and they would earn extra money by going to the tattie howking (potato harvesting) and berry picking and making rag rugs in the winter. We would sit round the kitchen table discussing Shakespeare and Burns, historical incidents or music, and it brought home to me as nothing else the superiority of the Scots educational system in my generation. June tried to teach me to speak proper Scots, to say 'I'm away the messages' for 'I'm going shopping' or to ask for gigot chops for lamb leg steaks; notice the French influence: message and gigot, and even stovies come from *estuver* – the Auld Alliance lives on in the language.

It was clear to me that I needed a shop if Henry and I were to succeed but we could not afford even to rent one. I was interviewed for the *Scotsman* and as a result of the interview a woman called Moira Elias rang me up to tell me about her shop at the bottom of Victoria Street on the Grassmarket, which was quite small and was believed to be the oldest retail premises in Edinburgh. Moira had amazing and eclectic taste and the little place had umber walls and dark green columns. I agreed to draft some affidavits for her to cover the rent for the first year and the Cooks Book Shop opened.

Another delight of coming to Scotland was to discover an old friend. Henry gave me a number and when I rang it Johnny Scott was on the other end. He had married and moved to Scotland where he was raising Blackface Hill sheep in the Lammermuirs. I had lost touch with so many people in the maelstrom of my drinking and it was wonderful to see him again, more weatherbeaten but as laconic as ever and with a merry pretty wife Mary and two children, Rosie and Sam. Suddenly Scotland seemed less empty. And I got to know Scottish food writers who had been but acquaintances in London by reason of distance. Sue Lawrence the columnist and food writer became a great chum and although we are both incredibly peripatetic we still manage to meet at least for breakfast on a monthly basis. Claire Macdonald and her husband Gog who own Kinloch Lodge on the Isle of Skye also became friends. I had always hated Christmas, because as you will remember my father had gone to great lengths to make us miserable, till I spent it with them and discovered what a splendid occasion it can be. When Godfrey, who is only a few years younger than me, converted to Catholicism I stood as his god-mother, and since he is Lord of the Isles imagine what an important role that would have been historically. I made new friends too in Philip and Mary Contini who own the wonderful delicatessen Valvona and Crolla on Elm Row at the top of Leith Walk. Elizabeth David described this as the best Italian deli outside Italy, although I rather think I might include Italy in this. When I was first in Edinburgh and broke I used to spend quite long periods of time simply standing in the shop to smell and take in the lovely sights. I mentioned this to Mary and she told me they used to watch me, not knowing what I was doing and trying to work out if I was shop-lifting. Fortunately Henrietta Green came up for a visit and introduced us.

However life was still tough with very little money coming in, and then some six months later I received a phone call from Pat Llewellyn. 'Do you know Jennifer Paterson?' she asked. Now I had met Jennifer precisely once when I was staying with Heidi in Tuscany, when Heidi had organised a big house-warming party but the cooker hadn't arrived so we had scrubbed out the old bread oven and lit a fire in it, and by the time the guests arrived it was hot enough for me to be cooking pizzas. Jennifer, ever curious about food, had come over to enquire what I was doing and stayed for about ten minutes. I knew who she was from her food articles in the *Spectator* and her book, *Feast Days*, but that was it. I told Pat this. 'Do you like her?' she asked. 'I don't know her, I don't dislike her,' was my reply. 'Well,' said Pat, 'come to London. I've had an idea.' It emerged that Pat had had lunch with Jennifer and afterwards Jennifer had ridden away on her own motorbike and Pat had had a vision. Embarrassed, I had to ask her to send me a return ticket, because I didn't have the price of it. In London, Pat, Jennifer, Simon Andrae, at that time a partner in Optomen TV, and myself all had lunch in Nico's restaurant in Victoria. When Pat told us her idea, that we should go round the country cooking from a motorbike and sidecar, Jennifer and I fell about laughing. We both said we were certain the BBC would never commission it, but Pat asked if she could put it forward and we both agreed, then went our separate ways expecting to hear no more.

Some months passed and I received another phone call. It appeared that BBC2 had commissioned a pilot. We again forgathered on a wet day at the Holland and Holland shooting school in north London. Jennifer and I spent the morning having rather facetious conversations under umbrellas and then shooting at clays from the different towers and the clays that ran along the ground simulating rabbits. Lunchtime came, the weather cleared and it was time for the shots with the motorbike and sidecar. Although Jennifer had ridden a motorbike for thirty-five years she had never had one with a sidecar, a very different technique. The bike on the pilot was not of course our own dear Triumph but an old BSA with a sidecar that resembled nothing more than a converted coffin into which I had to wedge myself. I felt I might never get out again. Jennifer, who was well refreshed after lunch, managed the first three takes perfectly; on number four we did stop with one wheel of the sidecar in the ditch but as we set off on the fifth take I heard Jennifer's cut-glass vowels very clearly: 'Oh my God, it's gone mad, I can't stop it,' and the bike roared at what seemed like 100 mph towards the brick wall in front of which stood the camera, the camera crew and of course Pat Llewellyn. Only Rex the sound man had heard what was happening and he was the other side of us so could do nothing. I felt we were all going to die, but Jennifer didn't lose her head and managed to wrench the head of the bike round at the last minute, side-swiping the camera and wrecking its carbon-fibre stand which was the price of a small yacht. Off we went again, heading for three flagpoles and beyond them the shooting grounds where young men were having shooting lessons: it was a daunting prospect. All I can remember thinking was, Dear God, don't let me die under the American flag! Jennifer managed to steer the bike between two of the poles where it wedged and came to a halt without any damage. We were wheeled back into position, Jennifer was fortified with a shot of brandy while I had to make do with a cup of tea and we did our piece to camera with me sitting firmly in the sidecar.

We were to be filmed cooking together at Pat's godmother's house but when we arrived we discovered that heavy overnight rain had set off the burglar alarm and we had to wait for the technician before we could start. Jennifer and I were sent to the drawing room with a cup of coffee where we waited for the next hour. This was the first time we had been alone together and able to talk about things.

We had much in common: both Catholics, both born of expatriate Scottish lineage, Jennifer's grandfather being a Dundee Paterson of the jute trading family who had sold up and retired to Helensburgh where she was born. Had my grandfather lived he would probably have delivered her. Jennifer's father, like mine, had served through and survived the First World War, he with the Seaforth Highlanders. She had spent time in China and I in the Far East and we had both travelled extensively. Then obviously there was food. Jennifer had started cooking because during the Second World War her parents had had no servants, her mother couldn't and wouldn't cook and Jennifer had been driven to cook by, as she put it, sheer greed. Jennifer had adored her father, who it seemed had had a bad war and emerged fairly damaged, only wanting to sit and play his piano, and had hated her mother so we were reverse coins if you like. We were also of course both alcoholic though we seldom discussed it and Jennifer, twenty years older than me, had no desire to stop drinking; she was, however, very protective and supportive of me. Once when someone offered me a glass of champagne Jennifer flew at him, and I had to explain that I was quite capable of refusing on my own but I was very touched.

As to differences, Jennifer was an old-fashioned pre-Vatican II Catholic. The Second Vatican Council had done away with Latin as the language of the Church and introduced the vernacular, the priest now faced the congregation during Mass and all the strange things that would send you straight to hell such as eating meat on Friday or on a day of abstinence, or attending a service in a Protestant church had gone. Jennifer was deeply disapproving of all these changes and during Mass when we were told to offer each other a sign of peace she would stare fixedly ahead and if anyone put out their hand she would glare fiercely and nod! As a result of this, although she lived just behind Westminster Cathedral where the uncle she lived with was gentilhommo, or steward, to the cardinal and another uncle had been a monseigneur she would get on her bike and ride fifteen minutes through the busy streets to attend Mass in Latin with, as she put it, all the bells, smells and glamour that make it fun. Another difference was that Jennifer was deeply musical, and left to her own devices she would sit quietly, or not so quietly if there were people about, singing or humming tunes. She and her uncle when in the flat spent their time changing radio channels as soon as the other moved away from the machine: he liked Radio 4 and Jennifer loved music. One of her greatest delights during our time together was to find a tune that she could lodge in my head and then sing it every time I got rid of it. 'All Day Through I Think of You' and Noël Coward's 'The Baby in the West Wing' are two I am still plagued with.

Finally the burglar alarm was silenced and off we went to the kitchen to cook. I have always believed, but never asked, that the intention was that we should fight with each other, that that would be the source of the energy and the viewers would laugh at us rather than with us – after all, the Chinese symbol for war is two women under the same roof. Of course things worked out very differently. I don't know in what previous life we were best friends but what you saw was what you got: the minute they turned on the camera we bonded. Pat was very pleased with the outcome of the two days and went off to edit it and we returned to our separate homes.

Back in Scotland it was clear that Henry was not cut out to spend his days running a shop but help was at hand. I had met Isabel Rutherford at a demonstration I had done in the George Hotel to raise money for aid convoys to Bosnia and she had sometimes looked into the shop for a cup of coffee. She had just endured a horrible break-up of her marriage and was part of the Lloyds disaster of the nineties, after which the Hardship Committee had bought a flat for her and her two children in the Edinburgh New Town but she was very miserable and pined for the Scottish Borders. I had been impressed with her knowledge of food and wine, particularly when one customer asked what wine it was that smelled of elderflower and without hesitation she had replied Frontinac. One day when she was in the shop I had to go off to record a radio interview. I asked her if she would like to stay and run the shop while I was away and rather nervously she agreed. On my return she had sold £150 worth of books and was looking happier than I had seen her, so she now came in two days a week to help with the shop and learn the ropes.

We also organised demonstrations for authors and held signings in the shop, which Johnny Scott used to organise, finding venues and invitation lists, as I felt he needed time away from his sheep. I was also commissioned to write my first book. *The Haggis: A Little History* is to date the only serious book on the haggis although I have to tell you it fits perfectly into a sporran and I gather Jo McSween is writing a larger tome, but I expect people will still be eating haggis and talking about it long after I am forgotten.

My home is not actually in Edinburgh but in the village of Inveresk, nine miles to the east of the city. Let me tell you a little about it. Inveresk stands on a ridge between the Esk and the Firth of Forth; it has been inhabited as a fortified site and was once occupied by a Roman cavalry fort so that every time you dig you find something and there is a Mithraic altar in the park. The core of the village is a street of Georgian manor houses running along either side of the ridge, all built between 1748 and 1780 for rich merchants who had moved out of Edinburgh rather than endure the mess that accompanied the building of the New Town. The original house, Halkerston is sixteenth century and the coach house in which I live was built in the seventeenth century for Halkerston rather than for the manor house in whose grounds it now stands. The church at the end of the village is known as 'The visible church' because it can be seen from many miles around. It was originally built to take 2,000 people and to attract to it the famous Scottish preacher Jupiter Carlyle; during his time as minister he filled it week in week out. It is now much reduced in size but is still very impressive and from the churchyard you can see the fireworks when they are held in the port of Leith. There are Victorian houses at the end of the village nearest the hills and since I have lived here some rather hideous modern houses beyond them; the splendid Victorian house where they developed thalidomide was still the Research Centre when I came but now houses a gated community of nasty but very expensive modern homes which have ruined the walk along the river bank. They are built on a flood plain so if we have a particularly wet winter I expect they will get their feet wet.

Down the hill is the town of Musselburgh, the honest toun, so called because when Regent Arran lay wounded after the Battle of Pinkie, with all his servants fled, no one stole from him and he gave them a charter and their name. It is the most northern town to have a Border riding during which many horsemen ride a flag up to Fa'side Castle on a hill above the town. The Border ridings are a type of beating the bounds where the inhabitants of the Border towns celebrate their freedom from the English and a young man and woman are elected to lead the procession, in Musselburgh known as the 'Honest Lad and Lass'. Musselburgh, so named for its great mussel bed now sadly gone due to the pollution in the Forth, was once a great fishing port. It still boasts one of the best fishmongers in the British Isles in Clarke Brothers: the family have been in the trade for a long time and have inshore boats and fantastic connections among the fishermen.

13

The magic of television

One day just when I had given up even thinking of television I was down in London running my bookstall at a Christmas Food Lovers' Fair in St Christopher Place: it was a chill day and the Traquair Ale crowd were dishing out hot spiced ale just across from us, Johnny Noble was opening oysters like they were going out of fashion, Henrietta was buzzing about trying to prevent Violet from savaging people and we were all having a great time, and my mobile rang, which, in 1995, was the size of a house brick. It was Pat to tell me that Michael Jackson, the head of BBC2 at the time, had commissioned us to make a series. The world stood still around me, and I found it very hard to believe. At that time we were all in love with the idea and thought perhaps it might be a cult series with a moderate but good audience. We had no idea.

We had lots of meetings and read lots of contracts, for the series of six, for the accompanying book, and we discussed clothes or rather I did. Jennifer had a set style which she had no intention of varying. I hate clothes shopping but next door to the bookshop was a shop for people of my size called Big Ideas, and I bought every outfit I wore on every programme of all three series from Rosemary and she never let me down. Now Pat raised the question of the title, rather nervously. She wanted to call it *Two*

Fat Ladies and rang each of us, saying the other had agreed, and was slightly surprised that neither of us had a problem with it. It refers of course to the bingo call '88 two fat ladies'; the Lottery was just starting and she felt it was apposite. If you look at the number plate of the motorbike you will see it is 88TFL; and of course neither of us was thin!

The first programme was to be filmed in March 1995 in Mevagissy in Cornwall based on the theme of fish and shellfish. The BBC bought a Triumph Thunderbird, a replica of the one Marlon Brando rode in *The Wild Ones*, only he had had a 650cc engine while ours had one of 900cc. A Watsonian Jubilee sidecar was fitted, and I came to love that wide roomy sidecar in which I could take refuge with bottles of water, bags of bitter lemons and books. A production team was put together. Lisa, later to marry Simon Andrae, was our chief researcher, and her golden smile and endlessly long legs could persuade any re-calcitrant contributor or churlish police officer to do her bidding. Leslie Gardiner was our production manager and Pat of course was directing, with Luke Cardiff, who I had last seen as a very young man painting a friend's drawing room as a holiday job, and Rex Phillips, the best in the business, on sound. Rex was a vegetarian who started his day when at home by swimming between the two piers at Brighton, and he was such a perfectionist that I ruined many pans so that he could record the extra sizzle. Jennifer and I went down on the train with a picnic and we were all raring to go. We booked into the Sharksfin Hotel where, in televisual terms, we were supposed to be running the restaurant so that John and Audrey Goodhew who owned it could have a break. John was the brother of Duncan Goodhew the swimmer and unlike him sported a lush head of curls. The bike was under the care of a young man called Steve Scourby for whom Jennifer took a passion and declared him Essex to her Elizabeth.

The first day was a wasted one as we woke to thick fog; one can film in almost any weather conditions, and we did, but not fog. After an aborted attempt at driving around trying to record soundtrack we gave up, and nor could we film in the kitchen as we didn't have access to it or any ingredients, as our specific day for the cooking sequence was not yet due. Jennifer and I spent the afternoon visiting the Lost Gardens of Heligan, which at that stage were still very lost with not much to see so that Jennifer, who had decided to have a kip in the car, had the best of it. That evening Pat produced the last thing we expected: a script. Neither Jennifer nor I was keen. In fact we were quite horrid to her. I remember it contained the line, 'Now I'm going to make some toothsome recipes,' which we squabbled over like spoilt children, each demanding that we wanted to say it. The next day dawned bright and clear and Pat produced the script once more and off we went again; in the end she threw it down, exclaiming, 'All right, you're so clever, do it yourselves,' and we did. I have always felt it's what made the programme so unique.

We had both made relatively little TV before, me with Sophie Grigson and Jennifer with a few appearances on *Food and Drink*, so it was fascinating to see how it worked. Watching the first programme it is interesting to see how in the course of it the relationship between us developed; at the beginning it is a little slow and we are feeling our way but by the end everything that made it so successful had slotted into place and we are falling about with laughter like a couple of old friends. We picked mussels on a beach for the cameras and later got into conversation with an elderly couple who lived in a small cottage by the shore, who, to our surprise, despite having lived there for most of their lives, had never eaten mussels until they saw Delia cooking them on TV. There were whelks on the beach too, which they said they did eat, but only on Good Friday, although they weren't sure why other than that it was an old tradition dating back to when everyone was a Catholic. Another scene involved going out on a crab boat, when the sea was very rough and it was pouring with rain. Fortunately both of us were good sailors, but poor Pat, who wasn't, crouched in the cockpit out of line of the camera, was rendered very ill indeed by the smell of hot oil mixed with smelly bait and the bilges; to make matters worse the mate would come and shake slimy bits of fish at her during breaks in the filming just to be bloody-minded. I must say when we got back to the hotel I seldom remember a bath feeling quite so good except after a day's hunting.

The most unusual experience was the cooking days. The first thing I ever cooked on *Two Fat Ladies* was gigot of monkfish larded with anchovies, cooked on rosemary and with a hot tomato vinaigrette, followed by crab and sweetcorn fritters. Jennifer cooked fish pie with prawns for treats and scallops (which had to come down on the overnight train from Scotland) with leeks and white vermouth, which, in her words, she liked to have in the kitchen because she wasn't tempted to drink it. We had to do everything three times: once in the wide from which they took most of the banter between us; then 'teeth and tits' where the shot was cut off at breast height and we didn't actually cook anything but mimed the actions, and from this was taken our descriptions of what we were cooking and how we were cooking it with reference to various techniques. The third run was for close-up just focusing on our hands and the pans on the stove with no conversation. Over the years this proved something of a nightmare as we were both ambidextrous and while I could usually remember which hand I had used Jennifer was a free spirit. In the end after various continuity disputes they brought in a TV set and showed the first tape to the researchers so that they could make copious notes. In the whole of the three and a half series there is only one error. Pat was a total perfectionist, and the finest director I have ever worked with; she played Jennifer and me on a very loose rein but she got the best out of us. While all the programmes are good the first series which Pat directed in its entirety stands out as the best. Her attention to atmospheric detail was infinite, as seen in the fifth programme, with the shot of a small plump scout running out of the loo tent pulling up his shorts.

I went back to Scotland to write my half of the book, *Two Fat Ladies: Gastronomic Adventures (with Motorbike and Sidecar)*. The first book is, I think, probably the easiest for a cook to write: you have a store of recipes you have built up over the years, you know which are your favourites and they are tried and tested and ready to go. Jennifer and I compiled a recipe list for the book and gave it to Optomen so that they could pick suitable recipes for each scene (they had by then chosen locations for each programme), and build the scene around the recipes. So, for instance, they picked my monkfish recipe because they knew there were monknetters at Megavissey, which had already been selected as a location. The one recipe of Jennifer's that I envy and wish I had invented was her tomato summer pudding – such a simple and delicious idea.

Isabel was doing well with the Cooks Book Shop and I had the opportunity to move into a house of my own. The American woman who had rented the M–Gs' lodge had fallen and broken her knees. East Lothian Council, her employers, had offered her a bungalow and she had taken it, so I was across the road like a shot proposing myself as a tenant and was accepted. It was hard telling Philip because we had become good friends but I was delighted to move into the coach house.

Filming usually ran from late March to September, one week a month, but on a few occasions we filmed back to back. We spent five working days on one half-hour programme: two of those days were dedicated to cooking and the rest to visiting places, biking and location shots. The process of making television is very tiring; perhaps the camera does steal your soul or maybe it is just the days of intense concentration interspersed with periods of hanging about. After the week is finished you just want to sit and stare at the wall for days and even that is a bit over-stimulating.

Over the series we discovered just how poorly England was served for hotels and restaurants: we stayed at the Wheatsheaf, an old coaching inn, which was probably very comfortable in the days of Jane Austen but not in 1996. Jennifer was yearning for Italian food – she was a great fan of things Italian – so we went to the town's only Italian restaurant which was unable even to produce a pasta simplice, much to Jennifer's disgust. As we were leaving the owner was standing by the door with a tray of Ferrero Rocher. ''Ave a chocolat,' he cooed, and with a heavy attempt at humour, 'I 'ave made them myself.' 'In that case,' retorted Jennifer, 'they're bound to be disgusting,' and swept out. A similar occasion first made me aware of how withering Jennifer could be. We were dining in a restaurant, both eating the scallops which were quite revolting and I asked her what she thought the sauce was made with. There was a long pause, as the entire restaurant held their breath waiting for her reply, and finally it came in a booming voice: 'Copydex!'

To my mind one of the missed golden opportunities of the series came in the second programme when we were to cook for the lacrosse team at Pat's old school, Westonbirt. In one scene I fall into a daydream as to how I used to be good at lacrosse, then the goalie is knocked out and a girl rushes up and tells me I must step in, the school mustn't lose. I put on a set of pads, stride into the goal and save the day! Curiously, I found I hadn't lost the knack as the sixth form tried their best to hurl balls past me, though of course it is easier when you are blocking rather more of the goal than when I was eight and a half stone. Adam Kemp, our commissioning editor, felt the nation wasn't ready for a cookery programme with dream sequences, although he promised me a six-part series on lacrosse instead; I know he was joking but I'm still waiting!

One of our most famous stunts appeared in that same programme. Jennifer came to me and said she had learned a new trick and should we try it. When I suspiciously asked her what it was she told me to shout that I had forgotten something and hold on tight. We didn't tell Pat but told the cameraman to follow us closely as we came out of the gates. The 180-degree turn Jennifer executed perfectly was shown on every political show from *Have I Got News for You* to *Question Time* and even on political programmes around the world in due course. Jennifer casually told me the next day that had she done it on the gravel rather than the tarmac we would have flipped the machine! Our second stunt came in the second series where we changed places with each other while the machine was moving. The Automobile Association and the Ministry of Transport both suffered a sense of humour failure and hit the roof, accusing us of encouraging dangerous practices.

We filmed at the Prince of Wales's estate at Highgrove, which was magical, breathing wholesomeness and health, and was quite the most wonderful organic farm I have ever visited. It seems to me that whatever Prince Charles turns his hand to he does well and don't carp and say it's the money: I have seen plenty of attempts by those with more spending money than he has that have fallen far short. The ultimate test is in the meat itself, and that piece of fillet was in and out of the oven more times than I care to remember and at the end it was still perfect and delicious. I asked one of the aides how much of a loss Highgrove ran at and was surprised to discover that even back then it washed its face and was beginning to show a profit.

Jennifer's hedgehog meat loaf where she plunges her beringed hands with their exquisitely painted nails into a bowl of minced meats roused the ire of the health and hygiene people who felt that it was detrimental to their message, despite the fact that twice in the first two programmes Jennifer alludes to hygiene practices, saying of her hands, 'which are of course spotless before you start', and of a sieve she had put on her head when singing the tin man song from *The Wizard of Oz*, 'This will have to be sterilised.' After much toing and froing I rang them up and discovered it wasn't the painted nails, which we agreed if a piece chipped off would show up like the blue sticking plaster they recommend, but the rings. Jennifer, who had inherited most of her jewellery from a former Duchess of Westminster, snorted and enquired whether they would trust them on the sink with television people about! It also had a life-changing effect on a four-year-old. Louis, son of Annie and Kingsley of Bookspeed fame, watched it with his vegetarian mother and cried in delight, 'Mummy, I can't wait to eat meat.' I am happy to report that now the whole family are carnivores.

Neither of us particularly enjoyed cooking puddings although I, bearing in mind that men love puddings, was more practised in this course. I remember watching Jennifer knocking up the sides of the pastry of a galette de roi with great proficiency and saying admiringly, 'You've done that before,' to which she replied that she had never done it at all! It was Jennifer's idea that we should cook for the priests at Westminster Cathedral, and she was very keen that they should include the late Cardinal Hume of whom she was a great admirer. Sadly, he was a man of retiring disposition and she had to content herself with inventing a recipe for him: Peaches Cardinal Hume which is essentially peach Melba with icing sugar on top to represent his magnificent head of white hair. Our scene at the end of the programme – you know, the one with the drinks, lemonade for me, and vodka, whisky or wine for Jennifer with her Woodbine cigarette – could sometimes be a little more dangerous than intended. At Westminster Cathedral we shot it on the roof and, probably because of the proximity to her home, Jennifer had been hitting the drink quite hard on that last day and was quite whistled when we got up there. I was worried that she might not get through the scene as she seemed to drift off into long daydreams, we were not far from the edge and when she rose to her feet to drink the toast we nearly lost her!

Back in Scotland I was booked to demonstrate at the Highland Show, not in the big Demo tent but in the Food Hall kitchen. As I tottered through the Hall I saw a beautiful sight: a glass cabinet lined with dark red velvet and on it stood the most perfect rib of beef, the fat like good clotted cream and the meat the colour of garnets or dark pigeon blood rubies. I stopped and stared, feeling refreshed by every moment I stood there. I take great pleasure in looking at good quality, well-hung meat, just as other women do when looking at clothes or shoes. I was jolted out of my reverie by an Essex voice saying, 'You all right? You've been staring at that for ten minutes,' and that was how I first met Colin Taylor. Colin had left school at fifteen to work at Smithfield and had been in the meat industry ever since. During the BSE scare the Duke of Buccleuch had formed a co-operative to sell his meat directly into the restaurant market, focusing on London. It was a bold and brilliant idea and he had hired a man named Roger More as well as Colin to run it. At its height every London restaurant was clamouring for Buccleuch beef, but sadly, in my view, the brand lost its way somewhat. None the less the Duke remains one of my few heroes, a man of great ideals and imagination. So too is Colin; although no longer with Buccleuch he still deals in the best meat and has become a dear friend.

Mention of good meat reminds me of Jessie Smith's wonderful butcher's shop in Cirencester, where I believe Jennifer secured our place as gay icons with her remark about the produce: 'Haven't met a good faggot in ages.'

I have never believed Professor Pennington's theory that variant CJD (which is now better known by its popular name BSE) had varied so that it could now be transferred to humans who have eaten infected meat, and I will tell you later why I am even more convinced now. Pennington was at that time Professor of Bacteriology at Aberdeen University, and funded by the government. The link remains a theory that has never actually been proved. One of the patients suspected of having it was Anthony's first wife Angela who had fallen into a coma and been taken to St Charles Hospital. No tests can be done for this supposed disease until the patient is dead, but Angela didn't die at that point and when she finally did it was found that the holes in her brain were caused by Korsokov's syndrome, an alcohol-related condition that leads to a wet brain. The medical profession consequently lost interest. Many butchers and a lot of farmers believe that BSE is another modern name for the age-old disease of staggers which has been around for many centuries. The government without any proof almost ruined the beef industry and it has taken many years to haul itself back. In Scotland there was not a single outbreak of BSE in a beef herd but very little attention was paid to this. I am also somewhat mystified by the killing under twenty-four months rule, whereby cattle had to be killed by the age of twenty-four months, so as to be free from any possible infection. Creutzvelt Jacob identified the disease in Austrian cattle, which are invariably eaten as veal. I ran about East Lothian buying up ribs of beef on the bone and storing them in people's freezers, only to discover that it was not so difficult to continue buying them if you had a dog, no proof needed, or a catering company. I remember writing that it was easier to buy heroin on the streets of Musselburgh than beef on the bone.

Filming once more, we were soon confronted by an Aga; now people either love or hate this method of cooking and Jennifer and I were in the latter bracket. The Aga was invented by a Swede whose wife had lost her sight and he wanted a method of cooking in which she could take the food to the heat rather than the other way around, and also there are no naked flames on an Aga. I acknowledge that Agas are good for slow stews and fruitcakes, baked beans and baked hams, drying Wellington boots, baby lambs or chicks and perhaps if you have your own so that you are used to its foibles it will prove okay but for us over the coming years we were presented with ovens of all sorts of temperatures that proved horribly hot, especially with the arc light needed for indoor filming adding to the heat. One kitchen had an incredibly hot Aga in front of which we stood to cook. I was making Christmas pudding ice-cream bombe, which I could see melting before my eyes; at the point when I had to clamp the two halves of the bombe together had I missed I would probably have soaked the camera. Neither of us had any cause to love the Aga that people so identified us with.

When we were filming it was often impossible to get to Mass, as the Catholic churches were either too far away or the services were at times when we were working. Hallaton had a charming medieval church and as we were hanging about while a service was going on I told Jennifer I was going inside to meditate. She became very agitated telling me I was risking my immortal soul and that she would pray for me. It was very peaceful at the back of the church and I had done many things more likely to endanger my soul. I particularly remember filming at Hallaton when, sitting between takes on the lawn of a house with a group of Leicester-shire ladies in the heart of the hunting shires, conversation turned to Michael Foster's proposed Private Members Bill to ban hunting with hounds, a subject on which the ladies were very heated, as of course was I. This was the beginning of nine years of legislating which finally led to the 2005 Act banning hunting. The Optomen team were extremely surprised, especially at the threat that half the magistrates in the county would retire if it was passed and the other half would refuse to sit on any hunting prosecu-tions. Surely, they asked me afterwards, no one could feel that strongly and this must be a tiny minority. Well, as the old Scots expression goes, I expect they ken the noo.

When occasion demanded we were not too proud to stoop to sleight of hand, as happened in the fifth programme with the Boy Scouts at Kielder Forest. As a piece of frivolity I was to dig a hole and cook trout in it with the aid of hot stones, which was partly to show off the Scouts' ability to make and light a fire with a single match. The stylist had got hold of some nice brown trout but someone nicked them and when we came to film Jennifer and me fishing for and catching them all the replacements we had been able to find were some frozen rainbows which had already been gutted. In order to disguise this fact, when Jennifer pulls the trout to the pontoon from which we were fishing I dive to my knees and grasping the trout in both hands lift it from the water and bash it on the head. A more unlikely way of landing a trout is difficult to imagine but it was felt that any other method would reveal the awful truth. We are also seen searching for mushrooms in a wood where they are arranged like some Disney scene with species that would never grow there seen side by side including a fly agaric. I recall a further instance when we were supposed to be cooking in a lighthouse at which we were seen arriving, although the actual kitchen was thirty miles away in the country. Every so often one or other of us had to look out on to what was in fact a baked hillside and comment on gulls diving or how cool and blue the sea looked. It was very surreal. Anyway, the Boy Scouts had a lovely time and covered our delicious food in tomato ketchup. Lake Kielder is one of the worst places in the British Isles for midges so the dusk shot was something of a problem, not because of any discomfort to us but because the midges, drawn by the warmth of the camera, kept clogging up the camera lens. In the end Steve had to lie beneath the camera with a cigarette blowing smoke in front of the lens to keep them away!

I must tell you about our food stylist: by this time we had acquired Pete Smith, the doyen of stylists, a six foot four Aussie who looked rather like a handsomer version of Desperate Dan with a wonderfully rugged and cleft chin. He had been born in the outback and had begun his adult life as a horse-breaker before moving into food. He was wonderfully camp, which delighted Jennifer, who was a dedicated 'fruit-fly', and a fantastic stylist.

The last programme in this first series was on game and was largely filmed at Lennoxlove, the seat of the Duke of Hamilton, the world's only triple duke. The first dukedom is the French one of Chatelherault given to Regent Arran for arranging the marriage between Mary Queen of Scots and the Dauphin; the second is an English one, Brandon, given to another who married Henry VII's sister after her husband James IV had died at Flodden, thus making their children Plantagenet heirs to the English throne; and the third, Hamilton, was a Scots one given for support to Charles I in the Civil War. Both the Hamilton brothers died in his service and their sister, the redoubtable Duchess Anne, persuaded Cromwell to vest the title in her. I have never worked out why but I can only say that from her portrait she had a magnificent bosom. A passionate lot were those Hamiltons, usually with multiple wives, dying in battle, dying in duel, and the tenth Duke, *el Magnifico*, when shown Versailles remarked, 'I have something rather similar for my dogs at home.' When Hamilton Palace fell down as a result of subsidence from the mine workings beneath, the fourteenth Duke bought Lennoxlove from the Bairds and another property at Archerfield and the family moved to East Lothian. He was a national hero, the first man to fly an aeroplane over Mount Everest and the man who Hess was flying to see when he was captured in Scotland in 1941.

Johnny's sister Sally had married Angus, the fifteenth Duke, a marriage that ended in headlines and sorrow due to both parties' alcoholism, but their four children were very fond of Johnny who had been a good uncle to them. Since moving to Scotland I had met Angus at dinner at the Scotts', a handsome but withdrawn man with a splendid quirky brain. When his marriage to Sally was dissolved he had married an Australian but that too had ended in tears, rather expensive ones at that. Lennoxlove is a beautiful fifteenth-century Scots tower house just outside the town of Haddington, built by Mary Queen of Scots' treasurer. Its charming name comes from the fact that Frances Stuart, Duchess of Lennox, the model for Britannia on the coinage and one of the very few women who said no to Charles II, owned it. She left it to her nephew Lord Blantyre and its correct name is 'From Lennox love to Blantyre'. Angus did not take part in the programme, as he was flying aeroplanes in Le Touquet with King Hussein of Jordan, but his eldest son Alexander and Johnny's daughter Rosie were filmed roaring past us on a quad bike, although sadly they ended on the cutting room floor. Only after the edit did Pat notice how like the Earl of Arran, Mary Stuart's regent, Alex looked or he might have made his television debut.

We filmed scenes on the grouse moor at Glenturret, the first place they ever shot driven grouse, where there is a whisky distillery and I recommend the food at the visitor centre. I never minded sitting in the sidecar when Jennifer drove, even if I knew she was on her second bottle of vodka – after all I had driven drunk many times – but I was very scared indeed being with her on a grouse moor with a loaded shotgun, especially as she thought it a great joke to fire from the hip. For some reason I cooked three dishes to Jennifer's two in this programme and invited various friends to the dinner party sequence, none of whom you get to see. Henry, who is addicted to grouse, started to eat his every time they put one in front of him and ended up having three!

So that was it: the filming was finished, the book completed and we sat back to wait. The programme went out, and its only good review was from A.A. Gill. I yearn to speak on a platform with Roy Hattersley, who wrote, 'These two hideous women will never succeed,' or maybe I should simply send him a mirror. However the great British public took us to their hearts, the viewing figures doubled by the second week and kept on rising and it was a huge success. At the age of forty-eight and Jennifer sixty-eight we were famous; it was all very surreal.

Fame is a curious thing: suddenly overnight everyone wants a piece of you, they clamour for your attention, want your time and your image. I remember going to the BBC autumn launch and finding ourselves in a room with over fifty photographers, all calling to us to look at them, and there were so many flashbulbs that had we been epileptic it would no doubt have brought on a seizure. *Two Fat Ladies* went on to be the most successful cookery series ever, at its height watched by 70 million people worldwide, and it was dubbed into eleven languages including Japanese. In this instance they recorded it with men's voices as Japanese women have little breathy voices, and this still causes a lot of problems for me when I meet Japanese! It was subtitled into other languages including Inuit though what the Eskimos made of it I dread to think. Butter and cream sales rose by 19 per cent in the UK, a fact of which I am very proud. It was loved by people of all ages and all backgrounds. During the first series we received a letter from an elderly lady in an old people's home, who had, she told us, turned her face to the wall intending to die. Someone had made her watch *TFL* (our shorthand name for the programme) and she was asking us to assure her that there would be another series so that she would have a reason to live. Another woman wrote to us and told us that her mother, who had been severely depressed at the thought of her imminent death from cancer, had died roaring with laughter while watching us. Children drew pictures and sent them to us. The Two Ronnies swept on to stage to huge cheers at the Royal Variety Performance in a motorbike and sidecar pretending to be us. Over the next three years *TFL* mania swept the nation and even the world.

Alcoholics in recovery find it very hard to say No. I remember a man who after twenty-five years sober and on the edge of a nervous breakdown had been admitted to treatment where the first question they asked him was, 'Just what part of No don't you understand?' I had to learn fast as I was wearing myself out accepting too many things. Fortunately, living in Scotland I could decline those awful celebratory parties. Jennifer went to them with gusto, as, in her own words, she would 'go to the opening of an envelope'! I was grateful for this as these sorts of parties have never been my bag and without the benefit of alcohol seem even more pointless and dull. The advantage of becoming famous in middle age is that you know who you are and are unlikely to be overwhelmed; moreover my friends made no bones about telling me not to believe publicity good or bad. Christine remarked, 'Well, you always thought everyone knew who you were when you walked into a room; now reality has just caught up with you.'

Due to my filming and media commitments I had very little available time to spend in the bookshop and was probably only there five or six days a month, but I happened to be there one evening when a dark-haired young man bounced through the door, introduced himself as Aaron Hinklin, editor of the *Scotland on Sunday* magazine and asked if he could take me for a drink. I shut the shop – no easy task as it had huge wooden shutters to cover its arched window – and we went across the road to a truly soulless sports bar which had the advantage of no customers. He wanted to persuade me to write a weekly diary with a recipe for *Scotland on Sunday*, but I was not that keen as I was very busy with *TFL*. I had become increasingly anxious that Johnny, with only a few events to organise as a break from looking after his sheep, was not using his talents to the full – remember I'm still trying to save people since my brother's death – and was mindful of his daughter Rosie's opinion that he wrote beautifully and it was a pity all he ever wrote was letters. I told Aaron that I would agree if he gave Johnny a column too and he said that while he was prepared to take my word for his talent he really needed to see some example before he could commission him. I then had the task of persuading Johnny, which I had tried before but to no avail. Claiming exhaustion from *TFL* I asked him if he would write my November piece for *Decanter* and he agreed to write something on the great tripe extravaganza his father had once organised. Aaron was delighted with the result and I then had the rather delicate task of explaining to Johnny what I had been up to and arranging for him to meet Aaron.

Scotland on Sunday was then owned by the Barclay brothers, those mysterious twins who having made a fortune in the building industry retired to live a reclusive life in a castle in the Channel Islands. They bought the paper because their Scottish mother had liked its sister paper the *Scotsman* in the same way as they bought the Ritz because she had taken tea there. At that time it was edited by John McGurk, known as shopping trolley McGurk because the twins allowed him everything he wanted in the way of contributors. The editor-in-chief was Andrew Neil. Both Johnny and I wrote for them for six years, until they took the writing in house. I was interviewed by Aaron who then turned it into a three-part life story which tripled their turnover for those issues and I did an advertising campaign for which they paid me handsomely. It was a lot of fun writing for them, and sadly now their readership has sunk well below the *Sunday Herald*'s.

14

Fame

The first series had proved a massive success. If either of us went out and about we were greeted by cries of 'Love the series' from cabbies, lorry drivers and the great and good alike. We were quite sanguine going into the second series that we could repeat the product because of course we were both being ourselves and were neither acting nor scripted. Series two opened at Hesket Newmarket in Cumbria, where we cooked lunch for a vintage motorcycle rally and a lot of men watched the programme because of the bikes. We knew this because they wrote in and also because later, driving with Christine near Lake Windermere, my car had got a wheel stuck in a rut in a ditch and we were unable to get it out. Round the bend had swept a group of bikers who had stopped and lifted the car out with many quips about sticking to motorcycles and where was the sidecar! Also I had been made an honorary life member of the sidecar club. The rally was fantastic and included among other rigs a Burrows with a silver tube that wrapped round the sidecar and looped in an arch over the top. When I enquired whether this was merely a decorative feature I discovered it was the extended petrol tank.

I had a lovely surprise when we were filming a cocktail party at the Brazilian Embassy and shot a sequence at the piano bar of the Dorchester Hotel where Jennifer was to make a Caipirinha, a very strong cocktail native to Brazil. We arrived at 9 a.m. and I discovered the bar manager was none other than lovely Gino who had been the charming young barman at Dukes Hotel when I was at Wilde's Club. We greeted each other fondly and he told me he had been so glad when *TFL* started because he had genuinely believed I was dead. Jennifer was supposed to take a slug of the cocktail and burst into a Carmen Miranda number but was refusing to co-operate. She sang at the drop of a hat but not when she was supposed to. I think it reminded her of her mother making her perform. I told Pat to tell her to actually drink the Caipirinha even though it was only 10 a.m. Jennifer took a hefty swig and immediately burst into 'Aye aye aye, I like it very much' with great verve.

The bike rally had been Jennifer's programme and now my turn came when we made teas for a cricket match. Wallington and Oxford Cricket Club was selected out of eighty-four possible cricket grounds, as Pat said she was looking for John Major's England with women on sit-up-and-beg bicycles riding home from Vespers against an English twilight. I had been an accredited cricket umpire at village league level since my days umpiring at Chalvington and was glad to don my white coat and take to the wicket again. One of the dishes I made was a luscious Hungarian cake named for a Hungarian violinist who caused a sexual scandal in Budapest and shook the Austro-Hungarian Empire. The club adopted Rigo Jancsi chocolate cake as their club cake, and the unlikeliness of that occurrence often fills me with delight.

By now I was finding it a strain staying with the others, as there was a lot of drinking and smoking after filming as a way of relaxation, and while I didn't want a drink I found the conversation dreary after they had had more drink than they were accustomed to, and I used to yearn for a cigarette, especially when everyone but me and Rex would troop out between courses for a fag. Jennifer, brought up in a household of brothers, felt it her duty to entertain the party but as so often with drink would repeat her stories. Also I have a strong solitary streak in my nature and needed a quiet evening with my own company or a chance to go to a meeting. I asked Leslie if I could stay separately and this was arranged and often I fared rather better. This was particularly so in the fourth programme where we were cooking a picnic for a Welsh male voice choir on the Great Orme at Llandudno. I stayed at the St Tudno Hotel where the crab risotto was so good I ate it three nights out of five.

We went up the Orme in the funicular railway with the choir singing all the way: it was enchanting. I was reminded of a young man who was at Gray's Inn with me, who was also Welsh and had a voice like an angel, rather at odds with his face which showed his other passion for rugby. After dining in Hall he would walk home singing quietly to himself but as his voice would have filled the Albert Hall without a microphone he was often arrested for being drunk and disorderly. One day I was in Marlborough Street Magistrates' Court waiting for my case to come up when my friend was brought up. The beak, in order to teach him a lesson, happened to fine him more money than he had on him. Looking about, my friend saw me. 'Hang on a minute, sir,' he cried with delight, and looking across to counsel's benches shouted, 'Hey, Clarrie, lend us a tenner.' Greatly embarrassed I did and off he went. He's a judge now and a pillar of the community but he knows who he is and I hope he's still singing. I don't know why the Welsh sing so much better than anyone else but they do. They certainly did that day on the Orme looking over the Menai Strait and it reduced me to tears, sobbing like a baby I was at the thought that Edward I had gone, the Castle was in ruins but the

Welsh were still singing. And do you know what? That rotten Pat Llewellyn kept the camera running pointed straight at my tears!

This was 1997, the year you elected Miranda with a landslide, but curiously I find so few people who own up to voting for him, even in Sedgefield. I remember writing in *Scotland on Sunday* that this would prove a disaster. I was never conned by our Tone, not even a little, and I think anyone who remembered him from when he was younger knew what a slippery customer he was. The previous year Jennifer and I had been presenting prizes at the Comedy Awards and oddly enough so was the Leader of the Opposition as he then was. No one was talking to him in the green room and he was roving about rather like those people at cocktail parties who don't know anyone and so are for ever hailing some illusionary friend at the other end of the room and striding purposefully through the crowd, only to repeat the performance a few minutes later. I took the opportunity to speak to him. I doubt he remembered me although he said he did, and it was like talking to a psychopath, where nothing moved behind the eyes and there was this constant attempt to work out what the other person was going to say and allude to it first, as if scoring brownie points to prove his cleverness. I am not easily frightened and yet I found him a very frightening man.

I have never had any inclinations to socialism, and my visit to Russia in the late 1960s would have put paid to any I might have had. Mollypop once addressed a trade union group having engaged in debate with a garage mechanic who turned out to be a shop steward. They both thought the other wonderful and she went off in her mink jacket with poacher's pockets to speak and told them it should be for everyone to drink champagne rather than for nobody, that they had got it the wrong way round. They cheered her to the rafters and she came home happily smelling of mild and bitter. I believe that unions can do a splendid job. I marched with the miners to show solidarity even though I was rather surprised to discover that Arthur Scargill stayed opposite my friend Olga on Eaton Place and he used to come in to the Lyons Arms, the pub at the end of Eaton Place where one went to escape one's friends. However I do see the need for a real socialist party to counterbalance a conservative one but of course Blair's lot aren't socialists or rather those that are Old Labour won't stand up for their principles lest they should fall out of government. Throughout my life people have always been pushing me to stand for various parliaments: George Brown with whom I got drunk on a train once offered me a safe seat as an MEP even though I told him I wasn't a socialist. I can think of nothing worse than spending my days among such a bunch of time-servers and hypocrites.

That summer saw my fiftieth birthday. I hadn't had the chance to have a big party since I was twenty-one, as either I had been too drunk or I had no money or both but now here was the opportunity and I was also ten years sober that year so I had a lot to celebrate. Where to have it? I had become quite friendly with Angus Hamilton and Kay, and we had been to dinner in each other's houses. I loved Lennoxlove and so asked Angus if I could hold it there. Leith's catered it and seemed to liberate every lobster in Scotland for the buffet. Henry was in charge of the music and due to my love of things West Indian suggested a steel band as well as a discotheque and had also had rosettes made like prizes at a gymkhana saying Happy Birthday. Supper and drinks were to be in the house with the buffet in the Great Hall and puddings in the dining room, and then we would all migrate to a marquee for dancing. Claire Macdonald made my birthday cake and Gog the speech toasting me. Everyone I cared about was there, the weather in a wet summer was perfect and it was altogether a magic evening. Henry and I opened the dancing to 'Ra Ra Rasputin'. I glowed in a wonderful piece of sari material my sister-in-law Marah had made into a dress, and if I tire of it and burn it I will be left with an ounce of silver. The whole evening was a huge success and come 3 a.m. the disco finished the musical side of the evening with another rendition of 'Ra Ra Rasputin'. There I was whirling on the dance floor with great joy and energy when I felt a terrible pain in my left breast. I thought I was having a heart attack it was so acute, but I kept on dancing and the pain got worse. Well, I thought, what a perfect time to go. When the music stopped and I staggered to a chair, I discovered – heart attack my foot – I had broken my underwired bra!

Let me tell you a bit about Kay; she is the sort of woman you find in the history books. Born in the slum area of Torry round the Aberdeen docks, she had pulled herself up by her own wits, until now she is the wife of a Scottish duke. The glory of the dukedom had somewhat faded by the time Kay met Angus, originally as his nurse, but it was still a far cry from Torry.

I was still intent on rescuing people from themselves and Angus, like Johnny, was one I thought I could help. His drinking career, well recorded in the national press, had been a disaster for everyone but more especially for him; he had stopped drinking but was clearly white-knuckling it with the aid of pills. It is a curious thing recovery: one cannot simply put down the substance and leave it at that. Until I got sober I never understood the story in the New Testament of the house from which the devil had been expelled, the house swept clean and then seven other devils invaded it. If you don't put something in the place of the addiction, madness and other addictions move in. I have watched over the last twenty years people try all sorts of answers but the only thing I have seen work are the twelve-step fellowships and this potentially charming man really needed to join the fellowship.

In 1997 the Countryside Alliance organised the first pro-hunting rally in Hyde Park. I travelled down on the train with the Scotts and Isabel. On the train I saw a giant of a man, a real Viking throwback, striding down the carriage in a Newcastle United shirt. I asked him if I could stand next to him on the barricade. It emerged that he was a shepherd from Wooler whose alarm had failed due to a power cut and he had missed the bus that was going from his town. He had driven across the Borders in the fog to catch the train from Berwick-upon-Tweed. He had never been south of Newcastle before and had spent all his money on his train ticket. We all had a whip-round so that he would at least have some money for food and drink until he found his friends in the park. I asked why the football shirt and he said that he had thought in case there was any trouble and he was arrested he could just say he was a football hooligan.

We found the park packed with balloons identifying the different counties. Marchers had come from all over the United Kingdom and I remember seeing the only protestor, a drunk who was shouting, 'Get out of my town,' heckling the Scottish marchers, who inflated their pipes and started to play at him and he simply shrank and slunk away. I was reminded that the bagpipe is a weapon of war.

It was a fantastic rally. I saw people sober that day I had never seen sober before and I stood and cried as my old friend and president of the Countryside Alliance Annie Mallalieu made her beautiful speech. I stood there wishing there was something I could do to help and pledged in my heart that day that I would do whatever I could in the years ahead. Willy Poole wrote a brilliant article in the *Telegraph* where he said that we left the park tidier than we found it and he was surprised we hadn't closed the Queen Mother's Gates behind us. The police always said they liked our marches because we were never any trouble, and later we saw the police horses and their riders snoozing under the trees in Birdcage Walk. Most people just went straight home after the rally but the Scotts and I went to Simpson's so that Johnny's son Sam, still young, could tip the carver and see the place where Johnny and I had had so much fun in the years before.

Meanwhile we were still filming, and next on our agenda was breakfast for the workers of the Black Sheep Brewery in Masham. When Scottish and Newcastle had bought Theakstons one of the family, Paul Theakston, reluctant to see the end of a centuries-old family tradition, had set up on his own with the payout from S & N, bought the pubs that they didn't want and has thrived. Although I have brewed beer I have never seen it brewed on a large scale and found the whole procedure fascinating, and appreciated the great sense of purpose and camaraderie among the workers and the sense of humour in production. Their very strong beer was called Rigwelter, after a rigwelted sheep, which in Yorkshire is one whose fleece has become too heavy and so he falls over on his back and can't get up on his own! What the workers made of Jennifer's kedgeree or my Mexican eggs I was never quite sure but a good pint washes most tastes away. It was in this programme that I made my comment about Anglican vicars no longer needing substantial vicarages for their large family as now so many of them were gay. This caused much mirth and many letters of appreciation, not least from the gay community. I love North Yorkshire and it was a happy programme for me, especially when I found the antiques yard where I added to my kitchenalia collection with several rarities including a butter table and a lark spit. I also discovered the most fantastic Indian restaurant in Harrogate called the Raj Put where an elegant Indian woman lithe as a nautch dancer cooked fantastic food. I recommend it to you.

I was staying in London with Carin waiting to film programme five when Princess Diana died. Carin woke me to tell me and I muttered, 'Well, that will save the monarchy,' and went back to sleep again. Poor unhappy Diana, who had all that charisma and yet was such a lost soul. I met her once at a Business Against Drugs Dance Premiere and she was completely stunning with the perfect skin of a bulimic and her charm as a barrier against the world. There was no hope of recovery really once she became Princess of Wales; hers was an early death waiting to happen especially once she took up with Dodi – that expensive world of drink and drugs is no safe place for the likes of us.

We were about to film with the Ghurkhas and Pat was worried that with the funeral pending we would be cancelled but we were not. It was a fascinating time: the colonel was the first Ghurkha Colonel of Infantry in the regiment and it was like being in the room with Shere Khan, the tiger in *The Jungle Book*, as he had all the power, energy and menace of a tiger. Rex shouted, 'Quiet please,' as he always did before a take and the colonel reared up in his chair off shot; he was not used to being shouted at in his own territory and didn't like it. I had to calm him down, explaining it always happened like that. The Ghurkhas themselves were delightful laughing little men full of smiles who regarded the filming with delight so it was difficult to believe they were the most deadly killers in the whole British armed forces. For one scene they dropped to the ground in camouflage rig and Jennifer and I, who knew where they were, simply couldn't see them. Pat yelled, 'Cut!' and up they popped, laughing as if the ground had swallowed them.

We cooked on an army field kitchen not much changed since the Crimea except for the introduction of gas but still usable with solid fuel. Jennifer cooked coq au vin, and this was the famous sequence where she remarks, 'I'm using an old cock,' and I reply, 'I always say there's a lot of good in an old cock,' and we ramble on with all the innuendos going straight over Jennifer's head. (In similar vein I once managed to elicit from a nun the remark that she 'had a man once a week'!) We gave the Ghurkhas beef from Buccleuch and turbot with pickled walnut, quail and coq au vin and the setting was dinner in the officers' mess. Curiously the Ghurkhas have always had British officers. I asked one of them about his troops; his father had been a Ghurkha officer too and he told me that while for regulation equipment they have a dress Kukuhri, the large curved knife peculiar to the Ghurkhas, and one they use for everything from cutting wood to chopping off the head of an ox, they all have a killing one, inherited from a parent or relative, hidden away for battle and that they never draw that without shedding blood even if just from their own thumb if they are only cleaning and sharpening it. The Ghurkha troops fed us delicious curry and their army rations, which were rather less delicious but still palatable. I said to the colonel that I was glad we had been able to film and he replied that the Queen would not have asked them to march at the funeral; clearly they took a dim view of the Princess's behaviour. Ghurkhas, rather like the Cossacks of the Tsar, take their oath of loyalty to the Queen not the country.

Such was the programme's success that the BBC commissioned a Christmas special that year which we filmed with the choirboys of Winchester Cathedral at Pilgrims' School, where I made the mistake of playing snooker with one of them and was well and truly thrashed by this angelic-looking ten-year-old. We were also rather held up because the bishop's dog peed on the alternator and fused it, and got a nasty shock and I doubt became a father for some time after.

And in a personal compliment, we were bidden to cook dinner for John Birt and the governors of the BBC. We were sworn to secrecy as it was a very lavish meal with the finest food and wine and included among other delights goose, with which Jennifer had a particular talent, stuffed with foie gras. I can see why we weren't allowed to tell, since the licence-fee payers might have objected, to say nothing of the fluffy bunny brigade, and in my eyes was a total waste of foie gras.

In 1997 Jane Root was appointed the Commissioner for the Independent Commissioning Group. Pat was nervous as when she had worked for Jane at Wall to Wall on *Eat Your Greens* Jane had been unable to understand Pat's fascination for stout middle-aged ladies and had told her to find some younger presenters. However Jane liked nothing better than a success and all was well. I mention Jane Root here to set the scene, for you will hear a lot more of her later.

That autumn of 1997 I discovered coursing, a sport that has given me great delight and pleasure over the last ten years. Johnny Scott had a great friend from childhood, Guy Ross-Low who, after various vicissitudes with Lloyds, ran a splendid pub called the Cholmondeley Arms in a converted school on the A49 in Cheshire, which is always winning awards. Guy had at some time been Master of the Cheshire Fox-Hounds and his huntsman had been the legendary Johnnie O'Shea, a whippety, witty Irishman who had hunted hounds with the Cheshires for twenty-five years and was known for his skill with hounds and his ability to find a fox and keep the hounds on the scent. Johnnie's hips had taken him out of hunting slightly early and he was miserable with it. Both Guy and Johnnie lived on the Cholmondeley Estate and Lavinia, the Dowager Marchioness, consulted Guy as to what Johnnie might do. On being asked, it emerged that Johnnie had always wanted to train coursing greyhounds; he hails from Tipperary, which is a great centre for the sport. A syndicate was formed and two puppies brought from Ireland to be trained, Malpas Mick and Malpas Pat.

Johnny Scott approached me about becoming a member and I said I had never been to a coursing meeting, so I went with him and Mary to one held by the Coquetdale Club in Northumberland. Legal coursing (let us not confuse it with the rough boys who trespass on people's fields and whose aim is to gamble on how quickly a dog kills a hare) is run under very strict rules set down by the National Coursing Club. It is a sport as old as time, and has been since Alexander of Macedon took his greyhounds over the Himalayas. You will find coursing depicted on early Greek pottery – no doubt it entertained the troops besieging Troy – and the Romans introduced the brown hare into England for the purpose of coursing. The aim is not to kill the hare but to test the respective abilities of two greyhounds in pursuit of it. The hare is given a law or start of 80–100 yards then the greyhounds are slipped by a man with a specially designed leash which fits round the slipper's wrist, with two leads, one to each greyhound; the skill in slipping comes in balancing two 100-pound dogs until the moment of releasing the catch on each lead, which frees the dogs simultaneously and they pull away together 100 yards or more behind the hare. Points are given for the first dog to pull ahead of the other, for getting close enough to make the hare turn and for various other skills, but no points are awarded for a kill.

The hare's method of flight is to twist and turn; a hare is lithe, much smaller than the dogs and in its own habitat so that the chances of it being caught are very slight. Opponents of the sport say the hare is terrified but I have seen hares almost thumbing a metaphysical finger at the dogs, slowing for them to catch up then darting off again in a different direction, and I have seen hares peacefully grazing on the coursing field a few hours after the event is over. Greyhounds are sight hounds so that as soon as the hare goes out of their line of vision they stop. What, you may ask, is the benefit to the hare? Well, I suppose the answer is a free lunch, as farmers will tolerate hares who can eat up to 40 pounds of vegetation a week for the sake of coursing but will shoot them when not allowed to course and thereby sell them for £8 a beast to a butcher. Statistics show very clearly that the brown hare flourishes in areas where it is coursed or hunted with beagles and harriers.

Anyway, it was my first sight of coursing and I fell in love with it as do most who see and understand it. I joined the syndicate with pleasure. I remember I was sitting in the Cardoma coffee house in Swansea, the last left in the British Isles, when Johnny Scott rang me on my mobile to tell me Mick had won the Altvar puppy stakes. I gave a loud cheer but thought that perhaps the journalist interviewing me at the time didn't need to know what for. Coursing is a sport harassed by the media and decried by those who vehemently oppose field sport supporters known as antis, banded into three major groups, who spend a lot of money on hostile publicity. One such example was a poster depicting two greyhounds tearing at a hare; it was however obviously a set-up picture by the antis as both dogs were wearing red collars, while competing greyhounds wear a red or a white collar for identification by the judge.

Back in Scotland, Angus had discovered a fish sauce recipe in an old recipe book, a handwritten household book that had belonged to the wife of the tenth Duke although it had clearly been started earlier and contained recipes that were traceable in her father's diaries, where he refers to dishes he ate. I made up some of this fish sauce, which was quite delicious, and Angus was very impressed and keen that I should make it and we should market it. We therefore formed a company and K17, the title referring to a marking on the cover of the book, was registered and we had frequent meetings.

Angus and Callum Bannerman, the CEO at Lennoxlove, were keen that I should take over the catering, which was rather lacklustre, and the café at the house since, as Angus phrased it, 'I would like to see Lennoxlove a centre of culinary excellence for East Lothian.' He could be very pompous, but it made sense. I took the hook, found a chef in the person of Sam Governo, a half-Scots half-Portuguese girl with a great deal of enthusiasm and we set off. I was frenetically busy with *TFL* and so really just paid the bills.

15

The fight for the countryside

As our fame as Two Fat Ladies grew so did the demand for our appearances, endless interviews both jointly and severally, and book signings all over the country. The most memorable was in Harrogate where the queue stretched round the block despite the cold rain; we started at 6 p.m. and didn't finish till 10.30, signing solidly the whole time, and the shop, which had expected to shut at 6.30 kept open with delight. James Thompson asked us to open the Edinburgh Christmas Fair and attend a charity Gala and I was happy to be able to repay his kindness in some small way. Picture the scene: Princes Street in Edinburgh on a clear crisp December day, a white open stretch Cadillac with pink oxhide seats; seated in the front seat was Father Christmas, and the car loudspeakers were blaring 'Baby Love' by the Supremes into the cold air. Marching in front of the car in full regalia including the feather bonnet, a Scots piper was playing in direct competition, 'There was a soldier, a Scottish soldier'. It was the day of the South African v Scots Rugby International, but *TFL* hadn't reached South Africa yet so their rugby supporters doing their morning shopping couldn't understand why the polite little children were pointing and shouting, 'Look, Two Fat Ladies.' Jennifer and I were sitting not in the back but on the back, i.e. on the top of the back seat and as we passed the New Club, that home of

Edinburgh propriety, Jennifer turned and whispered to me, 'Just like Dallas, darling'!

Jennifer and I made our first promotional trip to America at the beginning of 1998. *TFL* was a huge hit in the States and our first cookbook was the fourth bestselling title (not cookery title, please note) in Los Angeles, where, as the population lives on a diet of lettuce with low-fat mayo for treats, they must have read it for pornography. Jennifer, Pat and I flew to New York where we appeared on *Good Morning America* twice and at our signing at the Rockefeller Center the queue was again round the block and only Colin Powell had been in more demand. The programme had been bought by the Food Network, who extracted their pound of flesh from our visit not just with the obvious interviews and signings but endless lunches and dinners with their sponsors. Jennifer and Pat had great fun sampling the American cocktails especially something called a Cosmopolitan; not realising the strength of American measures, Pat discovered the headache a cocktail can bring.

We flew to Los Angeles to be interviewed on the *Tonight Show with Jay Leno* and stayed at the Chateau Marmont, which is a wonderful place where some British pop singer once drove his Rolls-Royce into the swimming pool. Sitting by that same pool, now *sans* RR, I fell into conversation with a sweet handsome young man. We talked about the beauty of trees and the history of the hotel and then he went on his way, passing Pat who was coming to look for me; she was in a state of great excitement and when I asked her why she pointed to the receding young man and told me that was Keanu Reeves, the film star. She became even more excited when I told her we had been talking together for the best part of half an hour. Remembering the High Court judge who had once asked, 'What are Diana Dors?' I felt maybe I had missed my vocation on the Bench.

I outdid that lapse when the three of us went to Nobu for dinner, where the Food Network had in error booked us seats at the sushi bar rather than at a table in the restaurant. Asking Pat and Jennifer to have a cigarette outside, I went in to bat with a splendid tantrum in my best English vowels. A rather ordinary-looking man with stubble on his chin and unkempt hair came up and said we could have his table. On being seated Pat asked how we had got the table and I pointed out the man; again her jaw dropped, since the man was none other than Robert de Niro, the owner of the restaurant. We thanked him profusely but to Pat's disappointment he wouldn't join us. De Niro had discovered and backed chef Matsuhisa, the creator of his new wave Japanese cuisine. There are now Nobu restaurants in New York, Paris, London, Aspen and even very bravely Tokyo. I find his food incredibly exciting and whenever Pat offers to take me out to dinner in London I ask to go to Nobu.

While in Los Angeles we also recorded a rap video for advertising purposes, and dressed in suitable street boy chains we danced about, singing, 'We're two fat ladies, two fat ladies in da house,' and other suitable lines. I think the makers of this were rather surprised at how easy we were with the concept and how well we performed.

In Los Angeles I was taken to a farmers' market, the first I had visited and I was enchanted by the whole concept. I knew that Alice Waters of Chez Panisse had persuaded local farmers to grow vegetables especially for her and to sell off any surplus they had, which started farmers' markets. I was entranced. I had now found something to rave about on both American and British chat shows, and suddenly here in the land that gave us junk food was a real movement for good produce and proper eating. When I got back to England, Henrietta Green, who had asked me to help with her Borough Market Project, also started a discussion about farmers' markets in Britain. Jennifer and I opened Borough, which we all felt would probably only last the couple of years that the council promised, by milking a goat. Borough now has a footfall of 55,000 a month outside the Christmas period and my heart swells with joy every time I visit it. Thanks to Henrietta I am now Patron of the National Farmers' Retail and Markets Association (since 2002 co-President with Hugh Fearnley-Whittingstall) and President of the Scottish Association of Farmers' Markets. Farmers' markets have proved a godsend to farmers and customers alike and the movement grows and grows, one of the few arenas where the countryside actually gets to talk to the town and the town has a chance to taste proper food and learn not to buy fresh foods in supermarkets. I am proud to have been part of it and proud for all who love good food to watch it grow.

While Section 36 of the Trade Descriptions Act (the only piece of legislation to cover food labelling as to origin) remains unchanged and says, 'a product may be labelled as being of the country where something was last done to it' we will continue to get Third World chicken (now proved to be the main cause of MRSA) labelled as British, Polish pork full of growth promoters being cured and labelled as British bacon, and Chilean salmon smoked in Italy sliced and packed in Scotland and so labelled Scottish. Fight, dear readers, for the truth about your food and don't shop in supermarkets for fresh food. Their attitude to food is exemplified by the following. I was once rung by a journalist whose father was an Ayrshire potato farmer, who told me that one of the major chains was selling Ayrshire earlies when it had been so wet that not a single potato had been put in the ground. The supermarket eventually admitted that these were the previous season's salad potatoes, which had been chilled and irradiated over the winter. The supermarkets are so hand and glove with the government who want to keep the public quiet with cheap nasty food, just as the Roman Caesars ensured that the mob had free bread and circuses to keep them quiet. Jennifer and I had the chance to show our dislike for supermarkets in one programme by jumping on a Tesco bag full of cream crackers to make cracker crumbs for my clam chowder while shouting, 'Supermarkets!'

February took me to my first Waterloo Cup, which is the Blue Riband of the coursing events, started by the Earl of Sefton in 1837 and at one time as important as the Derby. It is a fact that the Grand National was started to entertain the crowds who had gathered for the cup, and in Buchan's *Thirty-nine Steps* when Mr Mystery is asked who won the cup he asks, Waterloo, FA or Wimbledon in that order. Black and White whisky originally bore a label of a black and a white greyhound coursing a hare, and baskets of pigeons were released to carry the name of the winner to the London Stock Exchange and to all the regions. Eleven special trains carried spectators to Altcar, where the cup is held, from all over the country.

Attendance was not on that scale in 1998 but was still good. I went over with the Scotts and Guy Ross-Low. Malpas Mick had hit a bookies box when winning a course and a cup at Bryn-y-Pys in Wales earlier in the year and had a bruised shoulder so we had no dog in the race. Pat had proved not to be a contender and had retired from coursing early to the sofa of a syndicate member's daughter. There was a huge press presence, as with a Labour government there was always a threat of it being the last cup; indeed for the last forty years the antis had been promising that it would be the final one. The antis had caused trouble at the cup for years and in the 1970s there had been fights between them and us which had resulted in a large police presence; this time the police marched the antis in at the lunch interval where they stood on the footpath and screamed abuse at us for about an hour, thus breaching the law twice at least, since it is illegal to stand still on a public footpath, which is for passing and repassing, and shouting 'paedophiles, perverts' and coarser expletives is without doubt 'Words and Behaviour Likely to Occasion a Breach of the Peace'. Having never seen this before I was rather taken aback and more than a little angry. Still, it was a compromise and we endured it. The police were very agreeable to us and would come round afterwards and share a sandwich or a soft drink. I was of course famous and so the press honed in on me with radio mikes, TV cameras and notebooks. Lord Leverhulme, who now owned the Altcar Estate, had once said to me, 'If you're ashamed of something don't do it and if you're not you must stand up for it.' As I was not ashamed of following coursing I stood up to be counted. There were some positive interviews and articles on the back of my efforts so that was no bad thing but it did spoil my enjoyment of coursing.

The first great countryside march took place on 1 March 1998. It had become clear that the carrot Blair was dangling in front of the Old Labour backbenchers on whom the façade of New Labour had been uneasily plastered was a promise to outlaw hunting and coursing. After all, Keir Hardy's two major tenets were banning fox hunting and abolishing the House of Lords, so what price New Labour? Here we had a supposedly socialist government who would happily prostitute themselves on health, education, pensions and welfare but were fixated with fox hunting. I flew down to London with Isabel to go to the invitation-only power breakfast at the Savoy. It was full of politicians in new country clothes, the labels almost still on them, talking politics. I heard Paddy Pantsdown holding forth on how they had socked it to the Tories last week, and when I asked him who he hunted with he responded with a bemused look. Sickened by the atmosphere, I went upstairs to join Isabel and Jo McSween and ate a very bad breakfast in the River Room looking out on the crowds gathering on the Embankment. We then went down to the entrance to the tube to meet the Scotts and other friends from Scotland. Due to the crowds we had a long wait; very pleasant though as we saw lots of friends arriving. I remember two old boys coming out in their moleskins and battered wax jackets, who looked at the similarly dressed crowd and remarked, 'I reckon we're going to set some fashion statements.' The man in the newsagent's remarked to Jo, who had gone in to buy a bottle of water that the Countryside Alliance were so well organised that they even had one of the Fat Ladies. I waited, greeting people as they came out of the tube! Eventually the Scotts arrived and we all set off to march along the Embankment, then along Whitehall, the hunting horns echoing off the empty weekend buildings. We were always so law-abiding we countryside supporters that there was no traffic for us to stop on a Sunday in March. The march ebbed and flowed round my rather slow pace, while I marched with farriers, saddlers, hunters with coursers and those who simply cared about freedom of choice, democracy and the rule of law. It was a heady day. The figures vary but everyone agrees we were over 260,000 passing White's Club where we were hailed by friends who dragged us in for a drink. White's is firmly closed to women so Mary Scott and I achieved a first. Then we all went home, no mess, no trouble, nothing to show we had ever been. I am an anarchist at heart, and I suppose I just wish that having gone all that way we might have left some sign of our passing, perhaps a cairn of stones stuck with superglue outside the gates to Number 10.

Other countryside marches took place around the country during the year. I went to several but was asked to speak at the Newcastle march, where 20,000 people marched through the town and I hobbled over the cobbles with them feeling very lame from my metal instep, a result of a riding accident when I was young. (I had snapped my instep when I fell from a horse and my foot got trapped in the saddle. I was dragged and it was all rather terrifying. My instep wouldn't heal and a metal plate had to be inserted.) All sorts of people spoke, talking of rural post offices, rural bus routes and the like. When I went on to the platform all I could see was a sea of placards supporting hunting, coursing and other field sports and I said so to hearty cheering. I had Isabel's banner, made specially for the countryside marches, which bore a picture of Hitler with the words: 'First he banned fox hunting' which is of course true; he did it with the chilling words in Nazi Germany of the 1930s: 'Henceforth all the killing in this country will be done by professional butchers'! I told the crowd this and went on to say that we must not allow ourselves to be destroyed by 'that mimsy psychopath in Downing Street' which took the roof off with cheering.

It was while I was filming at Smithfield that we opened the café at Lennoxlove and I remember sitting in my sidecar ringing Sam on my mobile at 3.30, and she could barely speak to me as they were still being mobbed. It had been meant to be a quiet opening ahead of a publicised one but the *Telegraph* and the *Scotsman* had both got hold of the date and announced it. Still, they coped without me and the project thrived from there on. We filmed an air race at the Museum of Flight in East Lothian and Angus was to be a pilot, but he didn't show up and later rang me from a car park to tell me he and Kay had been secretly married that day. Kay and I had never got on, in large part due to her vociferous support for anti-hunting measures, and it was the beginning of the end of my catering at Lennoxlove which two years later was on the road to bankruptcy.

Flying in an open Tiger Moth over the Bass Rock at 100 miles an hour was very exhilarating, better than sex possibly, and the filming was a great success. I was into open machines that year: Saab had offered me a celebratory package and I had chosen a convertible. Angus, watching the roof fold on and off, said it looked like the illustrations in the *Kama Sutra* so I called it Kama and loved driving around with the roof down even in the coldest weather. I had one every year for several years: there was Kama 2, Soutra for the Border hill of that name of course and Scud for the clouds I kept pace with!

Jennifer and I were very tired at the end of the third series: we had done many things over and above filming *TFL* including a Lottery advert for the bingo cards as of course 88 Two Fat Ladies but there was more to come.

Shortly after this I appeared on my first *Question Time*, the political discussion programme on TV, to speak for hunting. Interesting, a live audience, in this case mostly against me, who cheered as an unthinking Pavlov-type reaction when I slapped the table and said, 'Remember a fox is not a sweet cuddly animal it is a vicious cruel killer.' On *Question Time* you get asked about lots of different subjects and in this instance the question of tuition fees came up. I was surprised at how angry it made me. I hadn't had a maintenance grant as a student, as we had had too much money, so that was right, but most of my friends did. I am not a believer in rights really, and there are only two I feel strongly about: education and healthcare and with those you are set fair for life. In the event I spoke forcefully against tuition fees and two young men sitting in Aberdeen saw me and wrote asking me to stand as

Rector. The rectorships of the ancient Scottish universities (Edinburgh, Glasgow, Aberdeen and St Andrews) are an amazing institution. The Rector is elected for a term of three years by the students for the students, is the voice of the students to the world and to the faculty and chairs the University Court, which means they can ensure that student issues get a fair share of the discussion. Rectors date back to the sixteenth century and are unique. Jennifer and I had already turned down a joint candidacy for Dundee and I had been approached by students from Edinburgh and refused, but my grandmother had been an Aberdonian and I rather liked the thought of the connection, so I accepted.

The two young men were Hamish, reading Land Management, and Paul, reading Law, and they were clever lads who when the time came both took firsts. This was the year when I had no time for anything and very little time to canvas but I am a cook so I used the weapons to hand and went to the refectory to meet the students with two very large delicious chocolate cakes. Paul and Hamish ran a great campaign, and used my favourite picture of me lying on my back with my hat over one eye as a poster under the slogan: 'She's fat but she's effective: vote for the heavyweight Rector'. They organised a question and answer session at which one young man, Rami Okasha, a name to watch for the future, asked me if I was a Tory. I answered that if an upmarket accent denoted that to him he must be very troubled listening to his leader Mr Blair, and we glared at each other. As far as I was concerned, I said, in the same way that a barrister was the mouthpiece for his client so I would be the mouthpiece for the students and it was not my views that mattered.

I went back once more for the Rectorial debate with the three other candidates: Magnus Linklater, former editor of the *Scotsman* whose father Eric had been Rector; a Scottish Nationalist candidate, the previous three Rectors, the last one dying in office, having been Scot Nats; and a man who ran a ski and sports centre in the Cairngorms. I am a good debater and enjoyed the evening. I couldn't make the election because I was on a London and Home Counties book signing tour with Jennifer and in the evening I had been to an AA meeting. As I turned on my phone afterwards it rang and Paul's voice said, 'Good evening, Rector.' I had won. My inauguration would be the following year.

Jennifer and I embarked on an Australian tour. *TFL* was a huge hit in Australia too and this time ABC allowed us to meet our public. We flew Quantas with beds; lying flat on aeroplanes was a welcome innovation and one that allowed us to arrive in Sydney in some way fit to meet people. We spoke at lunches and dinners in Sydney, Melbourne, Noosa and Brisbane, each event hosting about 800 guests, and I'm told the tickets sold out within minutes of the lines opening. We would speak and sign books afterwards. The first time we walked into an event and a huge cheer went up and everyone waved their napkins, Jennifer said she felt like a cross between the Queen Mother and the Beatles. We did press interviews and photocalls, and were entertained by Ronald Macdonald, head of ABC and his Aberdonian wife. In Melbourne we were introduced to Mr Howard the Prime Minister, who spent a flattering amount of time with us, and we ate mud crab which despite its name is totally delicious. The food in Australia was superlative, much better than in America; the torch had passed. We were filmed on stage at the Sydney Opera House with Jennifer giving a trill, had lunch with the legendary Joan Campbell, food director of Australian *Vogue* which despite its name is possibly the best food magazine any-where in the world. I met old friends: Andy Harris, last seen in Greece, and Philippa Gregory who had managed my friend Sally

Clarke's deli in London and now had her own in Melbourne. We were, as Pat said, 'a triumph'. Jennifer unusually had told me she felt all this had changed her and she felt much older and more tired than ever in her life before. She was a creature of routine and she missed it.

Five days after the Australian tour we were due to start filming our second Christmas special in Jamaica. Pat and Jennifer went back to England but I had taken the decision to rent my own villa in Jamaica and fly straight there thus giving me four days to flop. I invited Isabel, Carin and Sam Governo to join me. I had to change at Heathrow and sadly there had been no flat beds on the BA flight back, and carried straight on; halfway through the flight from Heathrow to Jamaica I got an attack of itching which happens when I am exhausted and fell into such a deep sleep that I remembered nothing more till they woke me on the landing approach. I had loved the West Indies in my yachting days, and Moira Elias had lent Henry and me her plantation house on Barbados on two previous occasions which had been wonderful. My villa on Discovery Bay was just perfect. Sadly much of the north coast consists of miles of holiday hotels, soulless and to me unappealing, but ironically Discovery Bay where Columbus first landed has been preserved by the presence of the bauxite smelter and dock on one side of it. The other side has some private villas owned by rich Jamaicans, and it is all very beautiful still. Isabel went off to do an advanced diving course diving on wrecks and diving by night and painted the trees and plants in the garden. The rest of us swam and went to market for delicious things for the cook, who came included, to prepare.

The Jamaican Tourist Board had their own agenda: they were trying to develop a different part of the island and told us it wasn't safe to film at the market I shopped at every day. They dragged us off about an hour's drive to another market and as we arrived with two large policemen who promptly arrested someone for smoking ganja (marijuana) it was hard going. Market people the world over stick together and are often related, so they were not best pleased and in an area of joking, friendly stallholders, largely women, we were greeted with total silence. It took all our charm to get them going. Everyone else was staying at a hotel in the hills which must have been splendid in Noël Coward's day but now the bush had been allowed too near the hotel and the mossies were dreadful, whereas on the coast we had none and it was sheer bliss to finish filming and fall into the sea or the pool if it was already dark.

The following year, 1999, was the year of my inauguration as Rector. After the actual robing ceremony the Rector is mounted on a stuffed Highland bull called Angus and carried from Marischal Hall, the largest granite building in Europe where the inauguration takes place, to a nearby pub. The rugby team and Paul and Hamish picked up the traces and off we set. Not the most comfortable ride of my life but one of the most fun. At the bar the Rector buys the Rector's round for any student who chooses to attend. Being flush in those days I left my credit card behind the bar and picked up a tab for about £500 – quite modest I thought. In my speech I castigated the officers of the student union for not protesting against the proposed tuition fees, saying that they were more interested in a future as Labour politicians than in their duties. In the bar afterwards Rami came and asked me if I meant what I had said, and if they built the protest would I come. I told him of course I would and a year later found Rami and myself, by now friends, dancing down Burns Terrace with delight at the eleven coaches and the street drum band that Aberdeen had sent to the student protest. It was the largest single contingent from any of the Scottish universities. And we won. There are no tuition fees at any Scottish university. I had invited all my dear friends – the Macdonalds, various M-Gs, Christine, Carin and many others – to stay at the Marcliffe at Pitfodels for my inauguration. David came a day early and drank Château Pétrus to toast my success and it was a happy time. The university gave a big dinner and Bishop Mario Conti (now the Cardinal Archbishop) had composed a special grace. I was not only the first woman Rector of Aberdeen but I was the first Catholic since the Reformation.

I enjoyed the role of Rector although it was a lot of work to do the job properly. Once a term I set up surgeries for the students, and at first only the whingers came, then the people with real problems, then finally the people with real projects. One of my policies for election was cheap transport, and we managed to coerce First Bus to give reduced and in some cases even free travel between Forest Gate, the medical campus, which was on the edge of town, and the main campus. I spent a lot of time getting permission for first-year students in halls who were working to have early supper, which until then they could only obtain if they had a class. I was appalled how many students were working to make ends meet although they still faced huge debts at the end of their four years (in Scotland an honours degree course is four years). Aberdeen, because of its science and medical excellence, hosts a lot of overseas students but doesn't attract the rich glitterati from England who flock to Edinburgh and St Andrews. The bulk of its students are Scots and it has a strong bond with the Orkneys. There is a union of universities going across the northern countries of the world, through Canada, Scandinavia, Russia and on to China and Japan called the Light of the North. The Principal of the University was C. Duncan Rice, a historian brought back from New York University to take over. His great gift was fundraising and the Five Hundredth Year Fund was set up to raise huge amounts of money. Aberdeenshire has always been a well-to-do county with its fortunes moving from farming to fishing to oil and always with the docks and the trade with the Baltic and the Russian ports. I came to admire Duncan enormously and he joined my list of heroes.

When the Scottish Educational Trust threatened that if the university didn't dumb down academic standards they would not give Rice money for the building of MRS2 and the cleaning centre for MRS1 (these were important centres of scientific and medical research in Britain) he told them he would raise the money independently which he did so that SET had to plead to donate to ensure that their name would appear on the sponsors board. As you may imagine one of my special loves was the Rugby Club. We secured permission to play again on the pitch in front of King's College and set about collecting for a tour to Australia the following year. I like to think that I helped press forward the cause of all the sports clubs by pointing out the importance of facilities for attracting overseas students. Foreign students or their governments had to pay up front so they were much sought after.

In March that year I received a surprise phone call from a stranger called Bob Long, the head of Community Programming within the BBC, who told me that Jane Root had a proposal for me but refused to tell me what it was until he met me. I invited him to lunch and took him to Lennoxlove. I firmly expected that he wanted to talk to me about alcoholism, about which the BBC are always so coy, but that proved not to be the case. Imagine my surprise when it emerged that Jane, noticing that several hundred thousand people had marched in support of countryside issues, especially field sports without a voice, had decided to ask me if I wanted to present a countryside programme. Johnny Scott and I had often discussed this and Johnny had even gone as far as devising an outline for a programme for him to present and sending it to Pat. She had binned it for no better reason than that she didn't think Johnny would make a presenter. She now admits she was wrong. I told Bob that while I would love to present such a programme I was a townie but I knew a man who could help. I went into the kitchen and rang Johnny. I think my exact words were, 'Stay put, I think a miracle has happened.' I dragged Bob to my car and drove him up into the Lammermuirs. As we drove I remembered that day at the rally in Hyde Park and the vow I had made. The Labour Party had said it would do to the countryside what the Conservatives had done to the miners; this not only seemed negative logic but I remembered how the miners had held the country to ransom, and the lack of power caused by the three-day week had ruined many businesses including my brother's, but no one could accuse the farmers of doing the same. I knew that if we did this countryside programme properly I would very likely ruin my television career but if we helped get the truth across it would be worth it. We were just about to start filming a fourth *TFL* and I wondered how I would ever make two series in a year without dying of exhaustion, but I would try.

We arrived at the Darned House where Johnny was on great form holding forth about hefted sheep, on which subject he is endlessly fascinating. Bob was entranced. He went away and came back with a small camera to do a screen test some time later. The ewes and their lambs were just being turned loose on the hill so we filmed them skipping away, with Johnny and me holding open the gate, and also a dead badger pup which Johnny had found. Bob was delighted and the thing moved forward. He proved to be a strong supporter. I suspect at the time that Jane Root had intended to throw me as a sop to the Countryside Alliance, thinking me a fat urban cook who would probably make *Carry On in the Countryside*. I am a fat urban cook but I have spent most of my life trying to learn about the countryside ever since that morning on Firle Beacon.

Meanwhile Jennifer and I went to Jersey to film the Jersey Royal harvest. I had always loved the little early potatoes grown under seaweed on the steep hill slopes of the island. A bad gale at the start of the year could blow the crop into the sea and they had a unique flavour all their own. Now sadly the supermarkets have picked them up and greedy growers are producing them in polytunnels on the flat land and they taste of very little unless you go to the island and find one of the producers who have not been corrupted. The potato picking community changes with whatever nation is providing cheap labour at the time; they have had Scots, Irish and even Poles on Jersey but when we were there they were Portuguese, much to Jennifer's delight as, somewhat to my surprise, she spoke that fiendishly difficult language with aplomb. We cooked among other things a fish stew in the Portuguese style. In one scene I had to push the plough up a very steep hill and I really felt for the workers; it was horrendously hard work.

We also went picking ormers, which are only exposed by the spring tides. The name is a corruption of *oreille de mer* or ear of the sea and is the only western abalone, and they live in the deep water between the Channel Islands. I was to be seen pulling them out of rock pools very near the land, but don't be inspired to follow suit as you won't find any so close in. When the ormer is removed from the shell it is beaten, historically on a flat rock, to soften and flatten it. I remember I was in a furious temper with

Leslie about a striped windbreaker I didn't want us to use that I splatted my ormer with such force that I flattened it with one blow. I have something of a flash temper and my nickname on set was Krakatoa. I don't think ormers fried in butter are particularly tasty. It needs the Chinese to take them away, dry them, marinate them, resuscitate them and produce something delicious. I remember eating some with my friend, the Chinese food writer Yan-Kit So, and they were fantastic.

On the Ardnamurchan peninsula we cooked for the lumber-jacks clearing the conifers to make space for the regeneration of the old Scottish forest. It was all midges and rain. Jennifer got a very bad reaction to the bites, and then we noticed that all the lumberjacks had a pink bottle in their back pockets. We asked what it was and were told Avon Skin So Soft, which is indeed the only thing that works on the Scottish midge. The workers had taken to it when the commercial midge repellent they were issued with actually melted the plastic on their helmets.

Knowsley Safari Park I think must have been Jennifer's favourite programme, as she loved anything that she associated with the circuses of her childhood – lions, tigers, elephants – and they were all here. In the shot where we feed the elephants we couldn't get her away, she just wanted to give them one more cabbage like a small child. Jennifer had told us that as a child she had always wanted to be the lady on the Rosenback in the pink tutu with all the spotlights upon her. Knowsley, once the medieval menagerie of the Earls of Derby, breeds lions like rabbits, since the prides there have been established and accli-matised for forty years or so and they get more cubs than they really want and have to give them to other zoos and safari parks. They also have a magnificent collection of Bengal tigers. Jennifer loved them all. Carin, who had come to take photographs for a

Swedish magazine, said she had never seen Jennifer in better form. The dusk sequence was filmed with us sitting peacefully by the elephants; it was charming and it was also to be our last.

We went our separate ways and a week before we were supposed to start filming again in late June 1999 Jennifer rang me, and as she hated telephones this was unusual. 'I don't feel well, darling, I'm going to the hospital for tests,' she said. I told her on no account must we allow ourselves to be pushed into filming if she wasn't up to it, to which she replied that she didn't think she could. At that I knew something was badly wrong as Jennifer was the finest trouper I ever knew and the show always had to go on. The tests discovered she was riddled with cancer, although apparently she had felt nothing. They took her in and within twenty-four hours she nearly died but on receiving extreme unction, which she called extra luncheon, she revived. After that, dying was something she knew she could do and do very bravely. May it be given to all of us to die with such fortitude and courage. She announced that she didn't want flowers but that visitors were to bring caviar and champagne and she would have a party. Every time I rang over her few weeks in hospital there were friends there. She told me she was incognito under the name Lady Vita Circumference!

Rex went to the hospital to film Jennifer's voiceovers, and I was due to go down on the Wednesday to see her and to record mine, but on the Tuesday Peter Gilbey rang me, to say that Jennifer had died in her sleep. She had always said she would pray to St Joseph for a quick and happy death and he didn't disappoint her. Within the next forty-eight hours I did 187 interviews for TV, radio and press around the world. The following week found Pat and me weeping on each other's shoulders in the middle of Soho outside the recording studio with me repeating, 'But you gave her her Rosenback.' It was hard to do the voiceovers. Jennifer and I weren't friends in any conventional sense, we were working companions and the friendship rested on that, but we had had amazing adventures and many laughs together. So much success, us against the world really. No one laughed at us or mocked us, they all laughed with us and it was a great achievement for two old bats whom the press labelled eccentric. These last four programmes were shown on TV that autumn and were a huge success.

Jennifer had had no time for her family except the uncle she shared a flat with. She once told me a tragic story: Jennifer had loved her father very much but had not got on with her mother who she said preferred her brothers. Her father had died in Venice and Jennifer had said wistfully how wonderful the funeral must have looked with the gondola with black plumes. I queried the 'must have' and she told me that her mother had not told her of her father's death until after the funeral. In any event Jennifer left all her money to the Brompton Oratory Choir and they sang their heart out when we laid her to rest. Her favourite helmet was placed on the coffin like some medieval knight and carried out in front of her. The vast church was packed with friends, fans, colleagues and the rest. Father Roland gave the eulogy in which he referred to Jennifer's endless childlike enthusiasm for life and reminded us that Christ said, 'Unless we are as little children we shall not enter the kingdom of Heaven.' Jennifer believed so firmly that it would be a churlish God who wouldn't give her such a heaven. We had a good party afterwards as a send-off and then our lives were all that bit poorer. As for me, I had a war to go and fight for the countryside.

16

The Countryman years

Before this could happen I decided to take a holiday, and booked a villa in the hills between Fuengirola and Mijas and invited Carin and Henrietta to join me. It was late November but still very pleasant. We had been there for four days when we packed up our card game and went to our beds, and suddenly as I was undressing there was a noise like cloth tearing and an excruciating pain. I yelled for help and they both came running. The hernia operation I had had in 1994 had never healed properly and now it had ripped right across. They called an ambulance, but there was fog on the mountain, and when it came I had to walk 100 yards down a very steep slope to it. I thought my guts would come out. Henrietta drove the car ahead of the ambulance to guide the way, while Carin came in it with me. The pain was dreadful and it didn't help remembering that Great-Uncle Kenneth had died of a strangulated hernia. I tried to make a joke about *Alien 3* but most of the time I just prayed, and tried not to think of Manolete, the nation's hero and greatest matador, dying in Linares of infections, not because I didn't want to die particularly but not at that time. I had work to do. I was four hours on the operating table, and woke in intensive care. Be ill if you must in Spain, where the cleanliness, the care, even the edible food in the small town of Benalmadena are such a great contrast to English hospitals today.

There are very few hospitals here from which I would have emerged without some horrid infection. The Spanish surgeon told me, because his father and mine had been colleagues, that the English scar would never have held because the stitches were too close together, too small and some of them were on necrotic tissue. He asked why no webbing had been inserted and when I told him it was because of hospital cuts, he looked appalled. My heart rate was very fast and my Spanish was not good enough to tell them about my adrenalin problem, and they said they were going to stop and restart my heart, something I really didn't want. The day before this was due to happen the Thomson Holiday vicar arrived to see another patient and with him was his wife, six foot of solid Yorkshire and former matron of the Leeds Royal Infirmary. She recognised me from television and came to talk to me. I told her my communication problem and she marched off to fix it. With true Yorkshire pragmatism she told them to take me out of intensive care and if my heart didn't re-regulate they could take me back and stop it. I was moved to a two-bed room that day, where I was on my own, and as I lay there I felt as if a light had come on inside me: I knew I was going to live and to everyone's surprise but my own my heart rate had gone back to normal.

I was afraid that if the London press got hold of my plight they would have a field day; after all, I had nearly died in the same year as Jennifer so we had a conspiracy of silence lest the BBC got spooked and pulled the countryside programme. After ten days the hospital reluctantly allowed me to go home, and Carin, who had stayed on, escorted me. I stayed with her for two nights in London and then like a wounded animal crawled home. When I heard a Scottish accent on the train I burst into tears of joy.

We had been due to start filming before Christmas but due to the staples not being removed till January it had to be postponed. The staples came out on 3 January 2000 and on the Epiphany we set off to begin our filming. We had asked for and obtained editorial control of the series. Our producer was a man called Steve Sclair, a descendant of Russian Jewish immigrants, now living in Brixton with a Nicaraguan wife. Anyone more firmly removed from Johnny or indeed from the countryside it would have been hard to find. On meeting him Johnny had dragged me into the kitchen and snarled, 'Asking that man to make a programme on the countryside would be like asking someone who'd been deaf from birth to make a programme on Mozart.' Steve and Johnny walked round each other like a couple of terriers, stiff-legged with raised lips showing teeth. I pointed out that we had to convince the townies with this series and to educate him would be the best possible start. In the event the countryside tells its own story if only people will look and listen and Steve became among its greatest supporters.

Our first filming was with the Wells wildfowlers on the Norfolk coast to whom we were introduced by William Heal of the British Association for Shooting and Conservation (BASC). Wildfowlers, through their organisation WAGBE, were the first wildlife conservationists, and are a tight-knit lot who don't welcome media attention. We could not have made the eight programmes in this series without the help of BASC and we were most grateful to them. The BBC had been desperate for some quirky series vehicle like the bike in *TFL* and despite the robust battle we had fought against the more cockamamie ideas they turned up with an Argocat. This is a six-wheeled semi-amphibious vehicle much used by stalkers on deer hills and keepers on grouse moors but not on marshes. The wildfowlers dismissed it out of hand. For a start it would disturb the geese on their night roosts in the marshes and we wouldn't get any of the shots we wanted. This of course left me with a challenge: I would have to walk and on top of my right instep breaking down, I had a very new, tender and fragile 22-inch scar from one side of my stomach to the other. We went across in a boat in the dark and then the walk began. I had asked Tim, who on this occasion proved a rather useless researcher, how far I would have to walk and he said three-quarters of a mile. Sadly what he had looked at said 3/4 miles and it was a good four miles. Mark Trett's nine-year-old son lit every step of the way for me with a pencil torch, and how could I let him down, so we went our laborious way across the marsh in the pitch dark. When we got to the spot, Mark found me a box to sit on so that I presented no silhouette above the line of scrubby bushes. He gave me my gun, a Greener 8-bore, and I sat and waited with him for the dawn to come up. He gave me tips for goose shooting, information about lead, range and so forth. Eventually came the dawn, the most beautiful Michelangelo sky, marbled pink and blue with little streaks of clouds. I turned to the boy and whispered, 'It's a beautiful morning.' Wildfowlers are born not made, and he whispered back, 'We could do with more wind and a touch of snow to bring them down lower,' and he all of nine. He shot his first Canada goose at ten.

In the event he was right: with the dawn came the geese and the sight of 30,000 pink-footed geese streaming over my head was not something I had ever expected or hoped to see in my life. We fired a few shots for the camera and the nation saw that I didn't know the safety catch on a Greener is on the side! But they were far out of range. Wildfowling is rather like fishing: you have to know the flight patterns of the birds, where they will cross the marsh to their feeding grounds inland and really only very bad weather brings them low enough to shoot. The wildfowlers, with their knowledge of the marsh and their tightly limited bags, have conserved the birds more than any other conservationist group. The pink-footed geese had been poached off the marsh during the war and had virtually left it. A fortuitous combination of the wildfowlers patrolling the marshes, thus combating poachers, and the closure of the Siberian gulags where the birds nest had brought them back. Their numbers were decreasing alarmingly in Siberia as goose eggs were the only protein the Siberian prisoners really got.

We also filmed the sugar beet fields where the geese feed inland. The beet farmers are happy to leave the beet tops for the geese to eat and they in turn manure the fields. Sadly the government allows more and more sugar beet to be brought in from central Europe and if the farmers plant winter wheat, the alternative crop, they are not so keen for the birds to eat that. I don't know why government agencies won't allow nature to work hand in hand with farmers but has to interfere. The conservation groups in Britain pay others to pierce the Canada geese, gulls, or other eggs to limit numbers but will not acknowledge this practice or be in any way honest about it. However, I had the fun of driving a beet harvester at a very brave cameraman who expected me to stop in time, and happily I didn't disappoint. The Wells wildfowlers were well chosen: Kevin Thatcher, the president, was an eminent radiologist; another member was a long-haul pilot; and Mark was a countryman whose grandfather had helped to carry George V's coffin. The King was a very keen shot and uniquely was borne in state by his Sandringham keepers. There was also a wonderful old ex-keeper called Bob Battersby who in his youth had eaten every bird from bittern to curlew, and

I had great fun talking to him because I always want to know what things taste like. We filmed our goose dinner at a most excellent pub called the Three Horseshoes at Wareham, which I can strongly recommend to you.

Whenever you see hunting on TV you see a lawn meet outside a grand house somewhere in the south-east, usually with added actors in smart hunting clothes, so no wonder people think it is all for toffs. We wanted to show a different side: the fox is a vile predator and none more so than in areas where sheep are kept on the hills. Foxes take lambs, make no mistake about it, newly born so that the ewe is in no position to defend its baby. The Border Hunt is a Northumbrian hunt whose country runs right along the Scottish border and over the other side into Scotland. It has been hunted by three families throughout the 300 years or more of its existence and the current Master is a hill farmer called Michael Headley. Michael's hound control is legendary and this is just as well for hill hounds have to hunt free, drifting up the hillside like driven leaves. It is said of the Border that they kill anything that doesn't fly and then it must fly high which is romantic as what they kill is foxes and they do it very well. Such a waste that now they have to chase a duster! Sometimes in inclement weather Michael has to wait for the hounds to come home or to go to a summer farm for shelter but home they come. His father lost all but eight of the pack when the ice broke on the North Tyne and painstakingly reconstructed the pack from what he had left, not taking in any draft hounds. They are a great tribute to a great hound man.

I was to ride a quad bike and Johnny a horse, which presented their own challenges. Johnny, while one of the most beautiful horsemen I have ever come across, hadn't hunted for quite a number of years and I had my new scar to worry about and the fact that Johnny's fifteen-year-old son Sam had given me all of fifteen minutes' tuition on a quad, the most useful bits of which were never take your thumb off the accelerator going uphill and always go down a steep hill on the gears. In the event no one got killed and we had a brilliant day's hunting, having to remember quite hard that we had to slow down for the camera. We even shot a wonderful scene of a fox bending in and out of the fence poles to distract the hounds and then going back the other way. Fox hounds are scent hounds who follow a line of scent and so they all duly weaved in and out of the fence posts. What hounds follow for miles is not the fox itself but its scent and it is usually only within the last hundred yards that they chase the fox itself. When the lead hound springs on to the fox and breaks its neck, killing it instantly (hounds are pack animals with a strict pecking order), the carcase is then retrieved from the hounds and the brush removed (formerly masks and paws were taken as well and adorned the houses of previous fox-hunting generations). The fox, dead as a leg of mutton, is then thrown back to the hounds for them to eat. It was just as well that we had editorial control when it came to this programme, because ignorance and pre-judice nearly ruined it and a scene of hounds in full cry had been overlaid with terriers' voices!

Johnny was very keen that we should film the hind cull on Mull rather than wait for stags in the summer. A hill stalker is very like a hill farmer, who watches his herd carefully and culls out the weaker or older stock that may not survive the winter. The watchword for hinds is 'old, bloody, yeld, or damned', i.e. old, injured, barren, or too weak for reasons such as age, or loss of teeth to survive the winter. Wolves were the only natural predators of deer in the UK and with their extinction man has had to fill the gap. Our director was a young woman called Esme

Anderson, who had never worked outside a studio. She was moreover a vegetarian. The BBC had given their production staff money to buy outdoor clothes but alas they hadn't consulted us and had all rushed off and bought snowboarding anoraks which not only rustled but were white or light blue and showed up on the hill. Also when wool, tweeds or loden get wet they become warmer, which is not something you can say of synthetic fibres. On Mull we got the worst weather in thirty years, and could only film when there were windows of light; the rain didn't matter but the sky glowered in that January week. Here the Argocat came into its own, bearing me into a river to muse about the out-of-season salmon and carry all the crew up the hill. Happily I was not expected to go stalking. The stalker took them all up and spotting a herd of hinds they set off. Sadly the hinds could see the BBC types a mile away and they had a long stalk with all the equipment. Finally a brief snowstorm hid them from sight and they were able to film Johnny's killing shot. Esme deserves a lot of praise, since not only did she determinedly keep up the stalk but even filmed the gralloch. I went off to a fish farm ostensibly to buy fish I was supposed to have caught. The final sequence was Johnny and myself in the pouring rain round a bonfire cooking our goodies. You can't see rain on TV so our clothes just got blacker and blacker and we got warmer while the production crew just got soaked and colder.

It was sitting in a café by the pier in Mull that we discussed the possibility of filming the Waterloo Cup. As you may imagine the BBC were not keen on the idea, until Johnny cast a clever fly. 'A lot of Pakistanis go to the cup,' he remarked. The BBC bit: ethnics, wow, televisual, and we kicked on. Johnny had a lot of trouble finding them however. Muslims don't drink so they were not to be found in bars at sporting events or even at the back of people's car boots. Eventually however he managed to contact a lovely man called Tariq. The cup was always run around 24 February, Johnny's birthday, so we didn't have much time to set it up. The Waterloo Cup Committee were very helpful, promising us we could actually put a small fixed camera in the Slipper's Shy, and Garry Kelly, the legendary cup slipper, agreed to be interviewed as did Bob Burden, the judge. We found a racing pigeon contributor as an allusion to the pigeons that used to be sent out to announce the result and also to remind the viewer that coursing, like pigeon racing, is a sport that has its English roots across the communities. Andy Capp to the Queen are pigeon fanciers all. They used to say of Lancashire that it was the land of pigeon dung and greyhound shit! We filmed our own greyhounds training with a lure with Johnnie O'Shea slipping and his assistant winding the handles.

In the Muslim religion dogs are regarded as dirty and not kept as pets, the exceptions to this rule being the coursing dogs, the greyhound and the Saluki, which for some reason are not regarded as dogs and are kept in great comfort in the tents of princes and nomads alike. Coursing is the single largest sport in Pakistan, with tens of thousands attending meetings. Tariq's family trained their dogs in the public park, which was a mile in circumference, and the young lads walked the dogs round it four times in different directions. No juvenile obesity here – they were all as fit as the dogs. They showed us a video of coursing in Pakistan and also the huge array of cups the family's dogs had won. We had filmed meeting Tariq in a Sparkbrook balti house and if you ever doubted that fields sports are the great leveller you should have seen Johnny and Tariq, the one a scion of centuries of Northumbrian squires and the other a baker, poring over the form book like two school chums while waiting for the cameras to set up for us.

Came the day, the huge crowd for the bank arrived, which is where you go if you like the cheap seats and 30,000 or more poured out from Southport and Liverpool to enjoy the day. Steve fell in love with the beauty of coursing and he personally filmed miles of footage over the meeting because he found it so fascinating. We filmed the antis screaming hate and on seeing me they broke into 'One dead Fat Lady, one to go.' The Beeb were horrified but I insisted they filmed it and showed it. At night in Southport the antis roam the streets in balaclavas looking for lone supporters to beat up, while the police on their own admission are afraid of them. One Irishman asked a policeman why he didn't arrest some who were chanting abuse. The policeman said rather primly, 'They're exercising their right to protest,' to which the Irishman replied, 'In 1916 you shot my grandfather for exercising his right to protest.' The thing you have to remember about the antis is that most of them, the really nasty ones, are paid; money is at the back of all terrorism and these are no exception. The year we filmed only nine hares died, and since the ban there are very few hares left at Altcar. The farmers aren't encouraged to grow specialist crops to attract hares, and shoot them, and without the income from the cup there are far fewer keepers on the estate so the poachers run amok in their absence. It is a sad place.

The pigeon fancier flew his bird for us in a mocked-up race showing how the clock worked and so forth. Came the time when the bird was due to return, there was no sign of it. The RSPB's ridiculous attitude to birds of prey, preserving birds of prey whatever their increase in numbers, has badly damaged the sport of pigeon racing as it has the fate of game and wild birds everywhere. The capercaillie at Abernethy, their last stronghold in this country, has almost become extinct as a result of this policy.

The Duke of Buccleuch lent the RSPB his Border estate at Langholm, a thriving grouse moor, to prove the point that hawks take grouse; in a very short space of time there were no grouse left on the moor and the falcons died anyway because there was not enough food for them. We were packing up feeling very sad for our contributor when a shout from his friend announced the return of his bird. It had been attacked by a hawk but was okay and we were greatly relieved.

In early March we headed north to film Johnny's lambing, the programme that would go out first as it set the scene for our friendship and who Johnny was. Hill ewes lamb alone on the hill, they don't like disturbance and Johnny's Blackface were no exception. Our intention was to highlight again the damage foxes do to lambs and were fortunate, I suppose, to find a dead lamb that had had its head ripped off by one, the carcase just left for the hooded crows. We explained that the hoodies take the eye from sheep when they are giving birth, and wanted to get across to the townies the need for Larsen traps to catch the hoodies and magpies so that they can be killed. Our scene of heather burning turned the editor of the Scottish *Sun* to our side when it was shown because he was so appalled by his own ignorance in not knowing that a heather moor had to be managed. Without the farmers' sheep and the grouse shoots it would all go back to white heath and scrub again. It was after this programme that Esme became pregnant and gave up location work, no doubt inspired by all those sweet little lambs with their curly coats.

I had a particular thrill in this millennium year: thanks to the efforts of my friend Colin Taylor, at that time of Buccleuch Beef, I was asked to become a member of the Worshipful Company of Butchers. This was a huge honour as it is a working livery company with the bulk of its members being butchers or otherwise involved in the meat trade. At the time the only women who were livery men who were not so involved were myself and the Queen Mother. In order to become a member you have to appear before the court to be vetted, then go to the Guildhall to apply to become a freeman. On the morning of my admission, 2 February 2000, I arrived very early at the Guildhall full of excitement. Looking for somewhere to wait I saw a church and went inside. I could see no sign of the name of the church, as it was being painted. On arriving at the Guildhall I asked which church it was, and the clerk told me to look at the weathervane, as all City churches bear weathervanes indicating their saint. I looked and saw a gridiron symbolising St Lawrence who is of course the patron saint of cooks, because when being roasted to death on a gridiron he is supposed to have quipped, 'Turn me over, I'm done on this side.' An apt beginning to a lovely day. It got better: the Queen's Remembrancer came in person to admit me to my freedom, for he was none other than Adrian Barnes, a friend from Gray's Inn days who I hadn't seen for many years. Colin Taylor came with me and then carried me off to Butchers' Hall to be robed and admitted into the livery. The Master that year was Graham Jackman, a butcher of high-class poultry for the Savoy, Simpson's in the Strand and suchlike customers. A tall man, well over six foot, with wickedly twinkling eyes, we became very good friends and remain so.

Being a freeman carries a number of privileges including the right to drive sheep over London Bridge without paying the toll, which would have been a huge financial boon in the days when live animals were driven to Smithfield. I was very keen that we should do this for the programme and Colin, who was Festival Chairman of the Butchers and Drovers Charitable Institution, agreed to help set this up, as he had always had a desire to restart St

Bartholomew's Fair. This huge fair, which started in the early Middle Ages under the auspices of St Bartholomew's Hospital and of the Smithfield Market, had run until the Victorians closed it down to prevent lewd and drunken behaviour. With the help of Graham, the City police, the Corporation of the City of London and many others it was arranged that we might drive our sheep, rush to the church of St Bartholomew the Great where the Livery Chaplain Dudley would bless them and then I would process with the butchers to open the fair, which was a huge success and continued to be so, until in 2004 it was sadly allowed to die.

A good friend of Colin's provided the sheep. Johnny, on whose shoulders the drive really fell, had hoped for nice biddable little South Downs but what we got was large independent Black-faced mules. He had brought his little sheepdog bitch Nell to work the drive, who had never been off the hill before but was as game as could be. Obviously we had to shoot several drives for the cameras but both Johnny and Nell were magnificent with the bridge traffic (slight but real at that early hour) on one side and what Graham called the 'biggest sheep dip in Europe' (i.e. the River Thames) on the other. I must really contact the *Guinness Book of Records* as we remain and I imagine always will be the last proper sheep drive across London Bridge. These were heady days for me.

We came across a wonderful example of how to get an impersonal quango to see sense when we were filming in Wales on the ruination of grouse moors by blocks of coniferous forests. At one point the Forestry Commission in Wales was going to ban hunting on their land and held a large meeting to inform the farmers and huntsmen of their decision. At this announcement the room fell silent and all that could be heard was the rattling of a single matchbox. The Forestry Commission changed their mind the next day! We had a night out with the keeper's gun pack, which showed that shooting foxes is not an easy option. Finally at 3 a.m. we went home, having tried for eight different foxes and shot none. One of the highlights of the Devon and Cornwall programme was Mark Prout's mink hounds, with fantastic shots of these old English pre-Roman hounds, formerly used as otter hounds, swimming up the river after mink followed by young women with babies in papooses and elderly grandmothers with paper-thin skin in old-fashioned tennis shorts. The mink hound puppy show was followed by a series of games with egg throwing and flour hurling which must have had every child in Britain wanting to join the mink hounds.

Johnny and I were having a lovely time, and as we drove around the country in Kama 2 there were times when we were laughing so much we had to stop the car; we had a great sense of fighting for the cause we were both so passionate about and this kept us going during the tough times. The book to accompany the series had to be delivered by 26 June and we stuck it in the post the night before with a great sense of achievement and Johnny, Mary and I went off to Greywalls, a very smart hotel with excellent food, for dinner to celebrate.

Now all we had to do was wait. Back home, Lennoxlove was going wrong on me, because they had closed the house for improvements as a result of the increase in visitors thanks to our café and catering, so we had six months with no trade at all. I had taken on the catering at the Museum of Flight to keep my staff in work but the company was bleeding money. Felicity who had run the vegetable gardens so well, which I had restored and were under my care, had quit for personal reasons and the young man who had replaced her was proving idle and unproductive. The bookshop in Edinburgh was doing well and I kept working on my recovery but other things were fraying: the fish sauce company had died without going into production and I had virtually no access to Angus without Kay intervening.

After what seemed an age, *Clarissa and the Countryman* was screened, to large viewing figures, and we had letters from people all over the country asking questions, saying they hadn't known the countryside was like this and where could they find more information. I had letters from elderly ladies saying they weren't going to contribute to the International Fund for Animal Welfare (IFAW) or the RSPCA any more as they had thought their money was going to help domestic animals. The RSPCA's £5 million advertising campaign against hunting did them few favours and wouldn't save the life of a single fox, deer or hare. The antis went on *Points of View* claiming I hadn't declared I was a Member of the Countryside Alliance. I wasn't: as Bob Long told them, I was a member of AA; Amnesty International; the Mebyon Kernow; the National Trust and BASC. In those days the Alliance and I were worlds apart, and I did not find them nearly robust enough.

Book signing tours are part of the celebrity lifestyle. Some authors hate them but personally I enjoy going out and talking to the people who enthuse about what I do. Perhaps I am fortunate because people have always turned up. Nothing can be more disheartening for an author than to sit forlornly waiting for a buyer. In Derbyshire people came through the floods to meet Johnny and myself in large numbers. The public bring you gifts and ideas and are quite frankly part of your power base. Johnny and I went on a book signing tour while the series was being shown, and we watched nearly every programme in some strange hotel or other, dancing round the room with delight at what we had achieved. That first series went on to be quoted as an authority on country matters twice in the Scottish Parliament during the debate on the Watson Bill. The Watson Bill led of course to the Scottish hunting ban which came into force a year before the English one. However in this instance the Scottish Executive showed more common sense and left a loophole which allowed the mounted pursuit of a fox with hounds provided the creature was driven towards a man with a gun, thus preserving all the industries and employment that are involved in hunting. The series was similarly quoted three times in the House of Commons during the hunting debate; and twice in the House of Lords during the same debate. I don't know of that ever happening before or since, and Johnny had every reason to rejoice in his perfectionism.

The antis became more and more incensed. They disrupted signing sessions with bomb scares or by waving placards and shouting filth as customers entered the bookshop. I was placed as number three on the Animal Liberation Front death list after Annie Mallalieu and Prince Charles, and as a result was appointed a Special Branch Liaison Officer, had to look under my car every morning for bombs and came home each time to large amounts of hate mail. Johnny's wife Mary got silent phone calls and it was all rather unpleasant. For the following book the antis redoubled their efforts, and things got quite dangerous with the police proving a feeble ally. In one ticketed event in Cirencester the antis came and banged their knees against the bookshop windows, which were unbreakable, till we could scarcely hear ourselves and the police wouldn't even stand between them and the windows. At two events in East Anglia our publicist got badly knocked about and jostled, and at another we had red paint thrown over us while we sat signing. I have to say the only injury I received was from the policeman who stood on my foot!

17

Today

Such was the series' success that we embarked on a second in 2001. At a meeting to discuss this, Patrick said that we didn't need to film hunting again as we had done it already. To everyone's surprise including my own I remarked, 'So you don't want to film me getting back on a horse to go hunting after twenty years?' They couldn't resist that. Johnny told me I was mad and who was I to disagree? We wanted to film terrier work, but obviously they threw out foxing and weren't interested by ratting, so then Johnny threw in glatting. This was a sport practised on the Bristol Channel where during the huge lunar tide drops the locals would poke conger eels out from their holes and pursue them with terriers as they raced for the sea. Televisual, they cried, and now all we had to do was find the last living glatter, which Johnny did.

The glatting was a great success, with Tug, who had never seen a conger eel, grabbing it by its tail, whipping it out of its hole and killing it like a rat. We then went on to film ratting sequences with a man called Lee Haslam who had written to me about the Merseyside Working Terrier and Lurcher Club which he had set up to teach the young lads of the rough area of Huyton in Liverpool about countryside ways using terriers for ratting. Not only is ratting huge fun but it does a great service, killing rats, which spread something like 179 different diseases, without using dangerous poisons. This is of course particularly important around the food chain. The boys were great ambassadors: in areas where most youths ended up jobless in crime and/or drugs they had learned responsibility for the terriers, respect for other people's property and went out and about in the countryside learning useful skills. We see them growing apace as they are now at various shows, many of them going into keeping or forestry and the whole scheme has proved a huge success. The BBC girls were amazed to discover how much they enjoyed the experience and many people judge this their favourite programme. It was also Tug's finest hour; flushed with triumph from the conger he showed what a brilliant ratter he is.

The last great London march took place in 2001 when just under 500,000 people flocked from all over the country to protest. Johnny and I had been made co-presidents of the Union of Country Sports Workers and so were to march with them in the livelihood division of the procession; the other branch, liberty, began in Hyde Park but we went in at London Bridge. When Johnny and I arrived the policeman on London Bridge was causing problems, saying he had no instructions, so I set off to confront him. It was most bizarre: as I reached the crown of the bridge the marchers below saw me and set up the most amazing cheers, the hollers and cries of 'Clarissa!' bouncing off the buildings and being taken up by those on either side. By the time I reached the policeman he was a cowering wreck with the noise booming over him. 'Is there a problem?' I asked and he could only shake his head weakly. I waved to the others and off we went.

It was an amazing march, all seven miles of it; we had six pipers with us who played all the way; the hunting horns echoed off the buildings; and there were banners from every hunt and coursing club; there were fishermen with their rods; shooters; stalkers; keepers hot in their tweeds. Banners read everything from 'Eat British Lamb: 50,000 foxes can't be wrong' to instructions to Blair to back off and to keep his bullshit in the town. There were farmers, rural Post Office workers; every aspect of the countryside was represented. One banner from the Basworth and Braham Moor Hunt read: 'It Isn't Over Till Clarissa Sings'! Sally Merison, chairman of the National Coursing Club, had cleverly suggested that we were silent as we made our way past the Cenotaph which was not only impressive but prevented anyone being arrested for misbehaviour as we passed Downing Street. Our pipers paused and played 'Nimrod'. When we got to Parliament Square there was a huge arch where the numbers changed as we entered, the Alliance having brought in all the livestock talliers from the auction houses to count us. Zadok the Priest boomed out on the loudspeakers and I was very grateful to sit down. People thought Johnny and I sat on that wall in Parliament Square all day specifically to greet the marchers but my foot had seized solid and I literally could walk no further. At the end of the day when the crowds had gone I literally dragged myself to a taxi. Don, our director, had insisted that he film the march with a view to using it at the head of the programme but the BBC wouldn't allow us to show it.

When foot and mouth broke out this had a direct bearing on what we could film due to restrictions imposed on movement within the countryside and so we angled the series more to urban jobs that supply goods for the countryside. We had been worried that we wouldn't be able to film the hunting sequence in Britain but luckily we just had time. Johnny had found a liveryman in Scremerston called Dicky Jefferey who provided a nice quiet cob named Killarney (I renamed him Nemesis) and had found a Yorkshire moorland hunt in the Saltergate. They were particularly interesting because they kept the hounds in the Master's farmyard and as he reared beef cattle, under government directions which precluded the feeding of dead animals around live ones, he fed the hounds on dead trout from a local trout farm. The BBC were anxious as I had shown no signs of getting back on a horse; the truth was that I had been so drunk when I ceased hunting that I couldn't remember whether I had lost my nerve or not and didn't want to find out before the day. They kept asking Johnny if I would go through with it and each time he reassured them that I didn't funk my challenges. A chance visit to Walsall with Christine took us to the Leather Museum where we discovered it is still the centre of saddlery and harness-making in the UK. My return to the saddle took us to visit all the suppliers who make such a trip possible: the boot makers, sporting tailors, boot tree makers, whip makers, the mills of Huddersfield that make the tweeds and melton cloth, button makers, bowler and riding hat makers. Came the day and there I was in my Frank Hall coat, my breeches from Mr Hutchinson in Westow, my boots specially made by Horace Batten in Northamptonshire and my bowler from Patey's. When we had filmed with Patey's the camera just filmed the hands of the workers and they were all black and inner city London at that. The years rolled back as I tied my stock that day, all those happy days with the Garth and South Berks, the Southdown and Erridge and anyone else who would have me. Was I scared? No, only that I should fail or make a fool of myself which would hurt the programme. Fortunately all went well; Johnny hoisted me into the saddle with not too much effort and I slid out of it gratefully after several hours with the followers around the Hole of Horcum, the only ill effects being that I couldn't walk again the next day. Walk! I could barely get out of bed I was so stiff.

The antis had been barraging the BBC with complaints and the politicos in the Beeb had willingly joined ranks with them, so that we had to fight very hard to get the hunting programme shown but shown it was along with the fundraising singing in the pub afterwards, once again illustrating hunting as a great rural social resource. A young man I met outside the chippy in Musselburgh after the programme spoke to me about it. He came from one of the ex-mining villages around me. 'I didnae ken there were so many jobs involved. Why ever should they ban hunting then, I cannae get a job for love nor money.' We had made our point.

Back at home, I had lost the catering at Lennoxlove: first it had been closed and then the Trustees had given me notice. Sam had married a New Zealander and gone to live there and my friend Sue MacCracken had taken her place running Lennoxlove and the Museum of Flight, but with Lennoxlove gone it was hard for me to make ends meet. The bookshop, though, was going from strength to strength. Up in Aberdeen we had a new Vice-Chancellor, Lord Sewell, the Minister of Agriculture in the Lords who had allocated the money to Professor Pennington. Now he was back in his day job as Pennington's boss. Sadly, as Vice-Chancellor he was in charge of the project to restyle the university's food. I had offered to make up a panel of food and nutrition experts and head it up, but I was never interviewed or once asked for my opinion. I was elected for a second term as Rector at Aberdeen in 2002, although with hindsight perhaps I shouldn't have done this but I allowed myself to be persuaded. I was not as effective, I think, as I had been in my first term. As I have said I never took my principles to Aberdeen but despite my refusing to debate on hunting we won unopposed and had the largest field sports society of any university in the UK.

We were filming on Johnny's hill planting trees when the photographer's assistant had a message about 9/11. We told him it wasn't even remotely a funny joke but then Mary came up to tell us it was on the television news. Johnny and I were due to go to New York to speak to PBS, an independent US TV channel, with a view to their showing the *Countryman* series. Sadly, of course, 9/11 turned America inwards like any wounded beast licking its wounds and so while we had a great time and were filled with admiration for the courage of the Americans we achieved nothing. We stayed at the Waldorf Astoria and were interested to see among the plaques at the base of the clock representing various sports particular to New York one of coursing in Central Park in the last years of the nineteenth century. We also went to the Bar Alba on the Avenue of the Americas where they serve oysters from all around the States and ate our way through thirty-two different varieties; we felt rather sick but wouldn't admit it!

Jane Root was panicked by now; the antis had really rattled the BBC and they didn't want another *Countryman*, but instead commissioned us to make a series on estates and castles. The BBC wanted Art and Aristocracy and we gave it to them: sporting art, and the North Lonsdale Hounds; productive estates supporting the countryside as at Holker with Hugh and Grania Cavendish, and here we even managed to film the beacons the countryside lit as a protest against the proposed hunting ban. What we ended up with of course was another *Clarissa and the Countryman*. The antis flooded the BBC phone lines every time the programme went out. One wonderful week the BBC replaced the hound pro-gramme with the one on Tresco where the most bloodthirsty thing we did was cook a lobster in a saucepan over a driftwood fire on the beach. During screening the BBC got 148 phone calls complaining of terrible scenes of animals being torn to pieces, clearly an organised protest that didn't bother with the reality. As I said to Jane, thank God I gave up cooking on TV! The following week there were only three, although all the hunt showed was young hounds failing to catch young foxes. The antis finally managed to complain all the way to the Governors, which is why now you never see any repeats of our three series, nor have we obtained permission to make them into videos. However we had done it and the positive effect on morale at the time was huge.

By then I knew in my heart that my television career was over. Since then I have made no more series, just bits and pieces of television, one of the most memorable being the *Question Time* on the war in Iraq where the audience hijacked the programme and I agreed with them. It was a war that should never have happened and it makes it even worse to think that the quid pro quo for it was, in my opinion, Blair finally giving his backbenchers permission to use the Parliament Act on the hunting community and bring in the ban on fox hunting.

Following the lack of commissions in 2003, I had various hard decisions to make. I could no longer afford the catering at the Museum of Flight, handing over the kitchen and equipment as a gift to the museum. Sue MacCracken moved on and now runs the catering for the National Trust for Scotland. I gave up the bookshop where we had once kept all the banners for the hunting protests outside the Scottish Parliament. Isabel, who had run it for me, still a dear friend, is now learning to paint. Then I went bankrupt after discussing it with my accountant Andrew Hamilton, the only man in Scotland to have spent time in the cells for hunting, being arrested when he was conducting the singing of the rural rebels outside Bute House, official home of First Minister Jack McConnell, a man so stupid he thought the rebels were wearing orange jumpsuits to mock him for his Catholic upbringing. Hadn't he heard of Guantánamo Bay! Lest you worry that I left ordinary people in the lurch by my bankruptcy, the only creditors were the Revenue and the bank, and the latter was very nice about it.

Johnny and I have written three more books together since, *The Game Cookbook*; *Sunday Roast*; and *A Greener Life*, the last designed to recapture the Green arguments from the fluffy bunny brigade. After all, as the Green energy spokesman, Carrots's brilliant son Tom, said at their conference, 'Isn't killing foxes with hounds the most ecological method of doing so?' Johnny and I have spent a lot of time at Game Fairs and BASC road shows signing books and encouraging people in these dark days for the countryside.

I also earn my living by after dinner speaking and consultancies. I helped Holker set up their brilliant Food Hall. I do radio and odd bits of television. I talk to the hunts, usually with Johnny, to encourage the fight against the ban and to keep us all together until it can be repealed. I go with my friend Sally Merison to Ireland to watch the coursing and dream of another Waterloo Cup.

In 2004 I cooked breakfast for the Women's Vigil in Parliament Square where 600 of us slept in the rain, and had to do it on a charcoal barbecue because the police wouldn't allow gas bottles. Pants to Prejudice was our theme and we hung our knickers round the square and decorated the IFAW lorry with them and while the MPs voted in an attempt to destroy a whole way of life we danced to the Barton Stacey Jazz Band, twirling round the embarrassed police to the tune of 'It's Raining Men'.

We were all there the day the police behaved like Nazi storm troopers in Parliament Square and Otis Ferry and his friends sent a message round the world when they broke into the chamber of the Commons during a hunting bill debate in September 2004. One day I shall write of these black days and of the heroes the countryside produced but for now I shall just plead the Fifth Amendment.

Some of my dear friends have died but most are still with me. Christine had a triumph in her new career; already a published poet who performs around the country and at the Edinburgh Festival, she has published her first book, *The Dangerous Sports Euthanasia Society*, a work as funny and pertinent as I would have expected, which we launched together at the Orange Studio in Birmingham with much success. She is currently working on a second novel. Carrots has the gift of healing and to my amazement has cured various parts of me despite my initial disbelief.

The writing of this book has proved a strange experience, at times quite toxic, at others a vale of tears. Looking back over the years I am amazed and grateful that I have survived to come out of the darkness and prosper.

I am sixty this year and all my friends will dance at my party. My friend Jan McCourt of Northfield Farm will be supplying the rare breed steaks from carefully selected Shorthorn and Hereford beasts. Peter Gott will bring down his sensational wild boar prosciutto (which once caused a vegetarian cameraman of seventeen years standing to relapse on the smell alone) from Sillfield Farm in Cumbria. Carin will come from Sweden to take the photographs, Isabel will drive down with the cake she has made and we shall all dance to the Barton Stacey Jazz Band. I regard myself as very lucky, in my friends, in the gifts I have been allocated this time round and in having reached the programme of

AA and the twelve steps, and of course my higher power. As I write this I am looking over the bay at Lyme Regis in the early morning and it is very peaceful. I am here for a week's reading holiday with April O'Leary, my Mistress of Studies from my schooldays, now a great friend.

Perhaps I may finish with the fact that this year, 2007, I was admitted to the York Butchers' Guild, a huge honour, and in welcoming me the Immediate Past Master said, 'loved by butchers and country people everywhere but none more so than in Yorkshire'! It doesn't get much better. What the future holds, who knows? To quote my mother: 'Leave it to God, Clarissa. He has a better imagination than you have.' Believe me on one thing: I have a splendidly enjoyable life.

Appendix: Twelve Steps

The twelve steps are the basic foundation of the programme of Alcoholics Anonymous and all other such fellowships. They form the basis of my personal recovery and that of millions of other recovering addicts, worldwide. They read as follows:

1 We admitted we were powerless over alcohol and that our lives had become unmanageable.
2 Came to believe that a power greater than ourselves could restore us to sanity.
3 Became willing to hand our will and our lives over to a God of our own understanding.
4 Made a full and fearless moral inventory of ourselves.
5 Shared such inventory with God, ourselves and another human being.
6 Became willing to have God remove all our defects of character.
7 Humbly asked Him to remove such shortcomings.
8 Made a list of all those we had harmed and were ready to make amends to them.
9 Made such amends wherever possible except when to do so would injure them or others.

10 Continued to take personal inventory and when we were wrong promptly admitted it.

11 Sought through prayer and meditation to improve our conscious contact with God, praying only for His will for us and the power to carry it out.

12 Having had a spiritual awakening as the result of these steps, we sought to help other alcoholics and to practise these principles in all our affairs.

Index

'C' indicates Clarissa Dickson Wright, and 'JP' indicates Jennifer Paterson.